THE WORD MADE CLEAR

A Guide to the Bible
for Contemporary Readers

To Chester Wozna
May the Word
be for you a
joy for ever

THE WORD MADE CLEAR

A Guide to the Bible
for Contemporary Readers

James P. McIlhone

THE THOMAS MORE PRESS
Chicago, Illinois

Much of the material in this book appeared in different form in the Newsletter of the same title published by the Thomas More Association.

ISBN 0-88347-268-6

CONTENTS

Chapter 1
Why is the Bible so important, and how do we read it?   9

Chapter 2
Why are Bibles different? Which is best for me?   19

Chapter 3
Is the Bible to be taken literally? What happens if it is?   29

Chapter 4
Did Moses write the early books of the Old Testament?   38

Chapter 5
What are they saying about Exodus?   47

Chapter 6
How did Israel view her King?   56

Chapter 7
What are they saying about the Prophets?   67

Chapter 8
What happened to the voice of the Prophet?   79

Chapter 9
Who is the Wise Man in the Old Testament?   91

Chapter 10
The Gospels: Who wrote them and why?   103

Chapter 11
Do Matthew and Mark tell us the truth about Jesus' birth?   115

Chapter 12
What was Paul really like?   126

Chapter 13
What did Paul have to say?   138

Chapter 14
The Johannine Community: Love that ended in hate   150

Chapter 15
The Book of Revelation: Should I read it or not?   160

Chapter 16
The Book of Revelation: The end of the story   169

Chapter 17
The Kingdom of God is like . . . the Parables of Jesus   178

Chapter 18
The Reign of God will come upon you. . . .   187

Chapter 19
Who do you say that I am?
What is Jesus called in the New Testament?   199

Chapter 20
How should I understand Jesus' Resurrection?   211

About the Author

JAMES P. McILHONE, a priest of the Archdiocese of Chicago, is Chairman of the Department of Sacred Scripture and Associate Professor of Biblical Languages, Old Testament and New Testament, at Mundelein Seminary of the University of St. Mary of the Lake, Mundelein, Illinois.

Chapter 1

Why Is the Bible So Important, and How Do We Read It?

"Words, Words, Words. I'm so sick of Words." This is how Eliza Dolittle (My Fair Lady, or Pygmalion) reacts to Professor Henry Higgins in a moment of extreme desperation after a lesson in "proper English." Yet, many times we feel the same way. We are bombarded by words on all sides and wish that we could just shut them out. We soon come to realize that we cannot survive for long without those very words.

Words have power to comfort, to harm, to cut, to shape. Words are effective. Yet, many times we are helpless to control their effect once they have left our mouth. A word, once spoken, cannot be recalled. It will inevitably produce its effect. Most of the time that effect is what we intend, yet, sometimes, it is not. I continually recall the sight of young teenagers slicing each other to ribbons with their words, yet freely making that ever heard reply, "Just kidding!" as if that would take the sting out of what they had just said.

As human words are effective, so is the Word of God. In the opening chapter of Genesis, we see the effectiveness of God's Word. The world is created through the Word of God. "And God said . . . and there was . . ." Isaiah tells us of the effectiveness of the Word. "For just as from the heavens the rain and snow come down and do not return there till they have watered the earth making it fertile and fruitful. . . . So shall my word be that goes forth from my mouth; it shall not return to me, but shall do my will." The prologue to the Gospel of John is a most significant text about the Word. It tells us that the Word was present in the beginning. The Word came unto its own to receive rejection, and the Word became flesh.

Here we see the uniqueness of the Word of God. It has a power, it is creative, it is challenging. God's Word calls us to realize our potential. In responding, we become our true selves. This is the mystery of the Word becoming flesh and dwelling among us. Many commentators understand this as God sending his Word to become one like us, to show us the way to become more like him.

9

JAMES P. McILHONE

If we look at the actions of Jesus in the fourth gospel, we realize that he always accepts the people he encounters. In those encounters, he challenges people to examine themselves, and decide whether they can accept themselves as he accepts them. For instance, the Samaritan woman, in the fourth chapter of the Gospel of John, is an outcast in her town. She has married five times and now lives with a man who is not her husband. Jesus encounters her and, much to her surprise, begins a discussion. During that discussion, he discloses her past life. Understandably, she wants to change the subject; yet Jesus persists. When she realizes that he accepts her as she is, a change occurs in her. She begins to have faith in Jesus and, in that act, begins to have faith in herself. Through this encounter, her life is changed.

This power to transform is what makes the Word of God different from all other words. This can be very frightening. As a result, many will handle the Word of God in the same manner as other words. Many prefer to read the Bible, the book of God's Word, as any other book. They seek information or meaning from biblical texts. The Bible does give us information about the origin of the world and the history of the people of Israel. It tells the origin and birth of Jesus, along with his life, death and resurrection. From the Bible, we can chronicle many events.

Those events are narrated from a specific viewpoint and are intended to present a distinct message. There is meaning which lies underneath the surface of biblical text, a meaning that will speak to us about the events which are being narrated. That meaning will also speak to us about our own lives today. For example, when a lawyer tries to trick Jesus by asking him the way to inherit eternal life. Jesus responds, "Love God and your neighbor." This is a message which is as valid in our day as in Jesus' day. The meaning of Jesus' answer has remained unchanged.

The scribe wants to be sure he understands, so he asks a further question concerning "neighbor." The lawyer, following the law, identifies "neighbor" with fellow Jews, and no one else. The lawyer wants to be sure that this is what Jesus means. In response to the second question, Jesus narrates the parable of the Good Samaritan. A man is left beaten, near death, on a roadside. Two good Jews pass by him. (They think he is dead. Lest they become ritually impure, they pass by.) A Samaritan (who is hated by the

10

Jews) sees this same man and has compassion for him. It makes no difference to the Samaritan whether he is Jewish or not; he is in need. The Samaritan dresses his wounds, brings him to an inn, and sees that he is cared for properly. Concluding the parable, Jesus questions the lawyer, "Who was neighbor of the three?" Although he had little love for Samaritans, he was forced to admit that the Samaritan was neighbor.

This admission caused a real difficulty for the lawyer. He had to rethink all of his original categories. Before, he saw neighbor as one who was a fellow countryman; yet now he realizes that fellow countrymen can pass by their neighbor. Yet, one who is despised can treat an injured person with care. To be neighbor means to treat all with compassion. There is a deeper level here than the story narrates. For both the lawyer and the reader today, this meaning elicits a challenge—a challenge to accept or reject. Many who read the Bible will see that meaning but will not let it affect their lives. They miss the real power of the Word of God.

Any text we read, we approach with certain pre-understandings. The text will either affirm or challenge these pre-understandings. The result is that we may have to alter our pre-understandings. This is all the more true of the Word of God. Properly read, the Bible will affirm and challenge our values. It is not enough to see the meaning in biblical texts, we must let that meaning speak to the way we live our lives. It must have a transforming effect in our lives. As encountering the Word changed the Samaritan woman or the lawyer, that encounter must also change us. God's word is spoken to bring about such changes and it will not return empty.

Inspiration and Inerrancy

What gives the Word of God such power? The texts that we find in the Bible are written by human authors under the "guidance" of the Holy Spirit. This is what is meant by "inspiration." This does not mean, as many have thought before, that God dictated the text through the Spirit and the human author merely wrote it down. There are two factors in inspiration—divine and human. How do these two factors work with each other? To answer this we must look at the process by which biblical texts have been produced. The authors of biblical texts did not sit down one day and say, "I am going to write a gospel, an epistle, or a prophetic book." The evangelists and prophets were part of a faith community. There were certain experiences which were foundational for those communities—the exodus, the exile, the death and resurrection of Jesus, Pentecost, etc. In these events, the community realized God acted decisively in their history. In the exodus and exile, Yahweh brought his people out of slavery or bondage into freedom. In the death and resurrection of Jesus, God definitively acted to free his people from sin. At Pentecost, God, through Jesus, sent the Spirit to enliven and encourage the community as it moved through history. The very events which were foundational to the believing community show the action of God in human history. They reveal a divine and human element.

After these foundational experiences, it became necessary to tell them to new members of the community and later generations. An oral tradition arose around those events. That tradition became very special. It not only narrated God's action in founding the community, but also his action in preserving the community in faith to the present. Again, we see the double element.

When those oral traditions were written down, we see the double element emerge again. Those written traditions were meant to recount the past and make it present for the community. The true meaning of the written document is the way it supports and encourages the faith life of the community which has preserved it.

The human author, when writing a gospel, for example, chooses those events which speak most clearly to the faith life of his community. Then, he narrates them in a way that is understandable to his community. Those events are actions of God in the history of the community. As God acted in the history of the community, he also acts in guiding the author who records that history through the Holy Spirit. The exact way in which this happens has never been explained. The mode of inspiration is something which we must grasp in faith. In the twentieth century, we are part of a believing community. We believe that God has been active in the formation of that community. We believe that God speaks to us through the religious traditions and sacred writings of that community. The sacred writings which the Bible contains, are written under the guidance of the Spirit. They have nurtured and continue to nurture the faith of the believing community we call church today.

THE WORD MADE CLEAR

We cannot overemphasize either of these elements in inspiration. Such overemphasis has been the source of many problems in the past. Some have placed too much emphasis on the role of the human author and downplayed the role of the Spirit. This results in scripture appearing as stories, fictional accounts composed at the whim of the author. Overemphasizing the role of the human author makes the Bible little less than a collection of good short stories. The truth and the historicity of the text is called into question.

On the other hand, there can be an overemphasis on the role of the Spirit which plays down the role of the human author. This is the position of those who take the scriptures literally. The human author is no more than an instrument through which the message is written down. As a result, every word of scriptures is to be understood as written. Every text must be true literally. There can be no error in the Bible. (In the third chapter of this book, we shall take a closer look at what happens when this view dominates biblical interpretation.)

The freedom of the Bible from error is known as "inerrancy." The meaning of "inerrancy" has been the subject of much debate. If the Bible is free from error, how can the Bible contain statements that would be considered erroneous in any other writing. For example, Genesis 1 states that light was created on the first day, while the sun, the source of light, was not created until the fourth. 1 Samuel narrates that Saul was presented to David for the *first* time on two separate occasions.

To answer this, we must turn the tables. If the Bible is free from error, then it must contain truth. We must look at what "truth" means. Is "truth" considered integrity, or is it precision and freedom from inconsistencies? In 1964, Pope Paul VI issued a declaration entitled, "On the Historical Truth of the Gospels," which will help answer this question. This document states that different communities preserved different aspects of the Jesus experience. Each community interpreted the Jesus-event according to the needs of the community. The authors of the gospels selected, chose and ordered their texts according to the needs of their readers. As a result, there are differences and inconsistencies in the gospel texts; but this does not mean they are not true. As we said above, the Bible is an account of God's activity in the history of his people, and the transformation that has taken place, and continues to take

13

place as a result of this divine activity. To the extent that the Bible continually witnesses to this activity of God, we must hold that it is true.

Method of Approaching Scripture

How can we approach biblical texts to uncover their meaning and allow them to challenge us? A very simple method has been developed by Father Eugene LaVerdiere for examining biblical texts. The method consists in asking six questions of the text: Where, When, Who, What, How, and Why? To illustrate this method, let us examine the unit, Mark 6:34-43, the multiplication of the loaves.

Where?

The first thing one does in examining a text is determine where the events take place, the spatial area. This includes any geographical locations, and any notes the unit may contain about the physical location of the action. In the Markan unit, there are no geographical elements mentioned. The only suggestion of location appears in a reply of the disciples that the locale is a deserted place. Since the passage begins with a reference to disembarking, we might suppose that the deserted place is near the sea.

When?

The next step is an examination of temporal elements. Here one looks for elements of time of day, seasons, etc. The Markan unit begins with a temporal clause, "When Jesus disembarked." There is also a reference to the time of day as being late, probably late afternoon.

Once the spatial and temporal elements have been established, one must examine whether the conjunction of time and place has any significance for the meaning of the unit. In this unit, the lateness of the day in a deserted place would pose the question of how the crowd would get food or even get home. In examining other units, the conjunction of spatial and temporal elements might have a greater significance, for example, on the third day during Passover in Jerusalem. In analyzing, readers must attune themselves to these conjunctions.

Who?

Having looked at the spatial and temporal information, we turn to the characters. Here the reader should carefully list *all* participants noting how they are described, and whether there are any special circumstances surrounding their introduction. In the Markan unit, there are three characters—Jesus, the crowd, and the disciples. I use the collective for crowd and disciples since no one in particular is singled out from either group. Jesus and the disciples have no particular descriptive notes attached to them in the unit. The crowd is described as vast. In fact, at the end, it is numbered at 5,000 men. The crowd is also characterized as "sheep without a shepherd." This ought to spark a question in the mind of the reader.

When the list of characters is complete, we must determine the main character in the unit. This will be the principal personage in the unit apart from Jesus. (Jesus is the main character of most passages.) The principal personage in the passage is the character who has the "problem." In the Markan unit, the disciples emerge as the principle personage. They present a problem to Jesus. When the principal personage has been determined, the reader should see how they are positioned with regard to Jesus and the other characters. In the Markan unit, the disciples are concerned about the crowd; yet they view the situation differently from Jesus. It is this difference that will provide one of the keys to the meaning of the unit.

What?

The fourth question concerns what happens in the story. Is an attitude or set of attitudes set forth, challenged, or altered? To see this more clearly, the fourth question asks, "What is the problem of the passage?" The immediate answer will be a statement of the problem for the principal personage. In the Markan passage, the problem would be the late hour, the distance of the locale from towns, and the lack of food. Given these, how can they feed the crowd? There can be a further statement of the problem from Jesus' point of view. Jesus' view of the problem will many times provide a further key to the meaning of the passage. In the Markan passage, the hour and the distance do not seem to be a problem for Jesus. He tells the disciples to feed the crowd. They respond that they do not have enough money to accomplish that. He then asks what they have, that is, five loaves and two fish. Jesus then takes that, blesses it, and gives it to them to feed the crowd. For Jesus, the disciples' problem is not a problem. The real problem is that they are unwilling to use what they have to nourish the flock.

How?

The fifth question concerns how the unit is related. Does narrative, dialogue or discourse play a role? In the Markan unit, we have a narrative which contains dialogue between the disciples and Jesus. The dialogue highlights the real problem. Another concern is whether names, titles, or special terms are used in the narrative. This is where the allusion "sheep without a shepherd" plays a role. Usually at the bottom of the text or along the side, there are references to Old Testament citations and allusions. If one looks there, they should find that the sheep without a shepherd is an allusion to Zechariah 13:7. Also, the command to sit down on green grass should summon some images from the Old Testament particularly Psalm 22 which portrays the Lord as a shepherd feeding his flock which is sitting on green pastures. These allusions confirm the shepherd theme in this unit.

Another point as one looks at the "how" of the unit is whether the narrator draws on language from well-known contexts, or uses biblical terms or expressions. Before Jesus gives the bread to the disciples, he looks to heaven, blesses the bread, and gives it to them. This series of actions is strikingly similar to the actions Jesus performs at the Last Supper. This language gives a clear eucharistic connotation to the narrative.

Why?

The final question is why does the author share this story with the readers? What in the life of the community does this story answer? The reader must spend a few moments reflecting on the original audience for whom this text was written. What do the answers to the five preceding questions tell us about them? In the Markan unit, we can infer that the original audience had a problem about the absence of the Lord. They were like sheep without a shepherd. The author using the shepherd imagery, particularly Psalm 22, emphasizes that the Lord is their shepherd. They probably had a problem answering needs within the community. Since Jesus was absent, they felt inadequate. The author narrates this story to tell them that they have all that is necessary to answer needs within the community. All they have to do is let Jesus multiply what they already have.

A second part of to this question is "Why use this unit today in our communities?" Here the reader must reflect on the contemporary audience and ask how the narrative relates to that audience as Christians in the modern world. In this unit, we might feel inadequate to answer the needs of those around us, and prefer to send them away to others. The unit tells us that we must have faith that we are adequate and let Jesus multiply what we have as we give of ourselves.

Study Questions

1) How have you experienced words in your life?
2) How have you experienced God's word?
3) What values do we bring to the biblical text?
4) What experiences are foundational in your faith life?
5) Do your foundational faith experiences resonate with the Scriptures?
6) Take your favorite Gospel passage and read it using the method of the six questions proposed in this chapter.

Bibliography

Collins, Raymond, *Introduction to the New Testament,* (Garden City: Doubleday and Co., 1983).

Fitzmyer, Joseph, "The Pontifical Biblical Commission's Instruction on the Historical Truth of the Gospels," *Theological Studies,* Vol 25. No. 3. September, 1964, pp. 386-408.

LaVerdiere, Eugene, *The New Testament in the Life of the Church,* (Notre Dame: Ave Maria Press, 1980).

McKnight, Edgar V. *What is Form Criticism?*, (Philadelphia: Fortress Press, 1969).

Patte, Daniel, *What is Structural Exegesis?*, (Philadelphia: Fortress Press, 1976).

Perrin, Norman, *What is Redaction Criticism?*, (Philadelphia: Fortress Press, 1969).

Powell, Mark Allan, *What is Narrative Criticism?*, (Philadelphia: Fortress Press, 1990).

Vatican II, *Constitution on Divine Revelation,* in *The Documents of Vatican II,* ed. by Walter M. Abbott, S.J., (New York: Guild Press, 1966), pp. 111-128.

Chapter 2

Why Are Bibles Different
Which is Best for Me?

In an earlier episode of *All in the Family,* Edith returns from the market quite disturbed. Understandably, Archie questions her about what has happened. She explains that she was walking along in the parking lot and tripped over something. A "can of cling peaches in heavy syrup" fell out of her grocery bag and landed on one of the cars parked in the lot, denting the hood. She continued telling him how she stopped, wrote down her name and address, and put it on the windshield. At this, Archie becomes rather upset. In the next moment, the doorbell rings. A Catholic priest is standing at the door. He informs them that it was his car in the parking lot.

Archie asks several questions to be sure that he is a real priest. Among the questions he asks is, "What is the Twenty-Third Psalm?" The priest begins "My God, My God, why have you forsaken me?" At this, Archie declares the "priest" a fraud. Everyone knows the Twenty-Third Psalm begins "The Lord is my Shepherd, I shall not want." The questioning could have continued with an inquiry into the number of books in the Bible. The priest would answer seventy-two, while Archie would probably say sixty-six. The priest, answering from his Catholic background, could not convince Archie that he was right, because Archie, arguing out of his Protestant background, was also right.

Different Versions of the Bible

The incident above centers around a major question about the Bible. Why are there differences in the numbering of Psalms, or in the number of books in the Bible? Where did these differences originate? The answer lies in the story of the formation of the Old Testament. That means we have to look at a little history. Around 500 B.C.E., after the exile, several Jews returned to Israel. Yet many decided to stay in Babylon. In the following centuries, Jews migrated to areas around the Mediterranean Sea—especially Egypt and Greece.

19

JAMES P. McILHONE

After the conquests of Alexander the Great, the dominant language of the regions surrounding the Mediterranean became Greek. Many Jews outside Israel became Greek speakers. Many of the sacred writings were translated from Hebrew into Greek—The Septuagint translation. By this time, certain books had achieved an "authoritative" status within Jewish communities. Yet, the authoritative books for every community were not the same. Several "canons" or lists of authoritative books existed during this period.

The answer to our question involves two of these "canons." The first list of books is the "canon" for the Jews in Israel, the Palestinian canon. This "canon" contained thirty-nine books written in Hebrew. The second list is the "canon" for the Jews in Alexandria, the Alexandrian canon. This "canon" contained the thirty-nine books of the Palestinian canon, yet added six more books (1 and 2 Maccabees, Wisdom of Solomon, Sirach, Tobit, and Judith). Also, there were additions to the text of Jeremiah, Esther, and Daniel.

We see that there were differences in the Jewish "scriptures" or "sacred texts." But this was not a major problem. There was no need to declare any of the "canons" official for all Jews until late in the first century of the Common Era. The advent of Christianity was the force which would bring this about. These Christians, followers of Jesus of Nazareth, were a source of much disturbance to Jewish leaders in Israel. As they moved to Syria, Asia Minor and Greece, many problems arose between the Christians and the Jews in these areas.

The Christians adapted to the Greek world around them. Their Jewish heritage also influenced them. They drew heavily upon the Septuagint as they set their traditions in writing. A split with Judaism was beginning late in the first century. The Jews initiated procedures which would end in a formal split with the Christians. The Jewish action culminated at a meeting of leading rabbis in the town of Jamnia, the Synod of Jamnia. The assembled rabbis declared that anyone who proclaimed Jesus of Nazareth as a Son of God was excommunicated from Judaism. They adopted the Palestinian canon as normative for all Jews. This answered clearly the Christian adoption of the Alexandrian canon. What was to become the Old Testament in the Christian Bible had six more books than the Hebrew scriptures.

THE WORD MADE CLEAR

By the end of the fourth century, the "canon" of the New Testament closed. This New Testament was joined to the Greek text of the Old Testament forming the Christian Bible. However, by this time, the major spoken language had become Latin because of the dominance of the Roman Empire. As a result, St. Jerome translated the Greek text of the Bible into Latin, the Vulgate.

As languages changed through history, the Bible was translated into several languages. Of interest to English-speaking Christians, the first English translation from the Vulgate was completed by Gregory Martin under the sponsorship of William (Cardinal) Allen. The text appeared in two French cities, Douay and Rheims, in the sixteenth and seventeenth centuries. All these translations used the Vulgate as their basis. Thus, they had the forty-five-book Old Testament of the Alexandrian canon. Early in the sixteenth century, a German monk, Martin Luther, began a German translation of the Bible. He realized that the Vulgate was a translation of a translation of the original Hebrew text of the Old Testament. Therefore, he used the original Hebrew as the basis for his translation. As a result, he discovered that some books of the Vulgate were not in the Hebrew. He placed them at the end of the Old testament as non-canonical books which were edifying.

A few years after he completed his translation, Luther was excommunicated. This began the Reformation, in which many groups split from the Roman Church. Luther and his followers accepted the thirty-nine book Old Testament as normative. At the Council of Trent, the Roman Church made the Latin Vulgate text the official normative text of scripture for the Catholic Church.

As further splits occurred during the Reformation, most reformers adopted the thirty-nine book Old Testament as Luther had done. The most significant English translation among the reformers was the *King James Version,* also known as the *Authorized* version since it was authorized by Church of England authorities for use in liturgical services. The translation was completed by a commission appointed by King James I.

From this information, one might say that the distinction in the number of books in the Bible was based on denominational differences. In fact, this is the impression given in the *All in the Family* episode. When we look at the whole story, this is not the reality. The real difference was never denominational; it was always linguistic. Although it seems that we have "Catholic" and a "Protestant'' Bible, we don't. Instead, we have a ''Hebrew'' and a ''Greek'' Bible.

Different English Translations

Most readers of the Bible are not interested in Greek or Hebrew Bibles. They are interested in English translations. If people go to their favorite bookstore to buy a Bible, they will find many English Bibles on the shelves. Which one is most appropriate? To answer this question, a prior question is necessary: ''Why does one want the Bible?'' Some translations are for the more scholarly reader. Others are produced for proclaiming the Word of God with ease. Others are intended for a meditative reader. The translation that a student of the New Testament might use will probably not be used by the lector on Sunday.

The leading English translations today are the *Revised Standard Version* (RSV), *The New English Bible* (NEB), *The New American Bible* (NAB), *The Jerusalem Bible* (JB), *The New International Version* (NIV), *The Good News Bible,* and *The Living Bible,* also known as *The Way.* Each of these translations is appropriate to the needs of different readers. We shall briefly examine their development and survey the positive and negative points of each.

The Revised Standard Version

The *Authorized,* or *King James Version,* was the standard Bible for English-speaking Protestants for nearly 250 years. Around 1870, several scholars undertook a revision of the *King James Version.* This revision was to reflect developments in biblical scholarship and changes in the English language since the Elizabethan period. The revision became known as the *Revised Version.* In 1901, the *Revised Version* was accommodated to American Protestant churches to produce the *American Standard Version.* The *Revised Version* met severe opposition in England, while the *American Standard Version* was adopted by many churches in the United States.

In 1937, the National Council of Churches commissioned a revision of the *American Standard Version.* The New Testament of the *Revised Standard Version* appeared in 1946, and the Old Testament in 1952. The scholars who worked on this revision were careful to reproduce the sense of the original Hebrew and Greek. They also wished to include contemporary biblical scholarship.

The result was a very scholarly translation of the Bible. The *Revised Standard Version* is the best English translation to reproduce the sense of the original Greek and Hebrew texts. To get a better understanding of these texts, one must learn those languages. The RSV is, therefore, excellent for serious students of the Bible. Yet, many who might use it for liturgical proclamation or reflective reading will discover it is somewhat complex. The *Oxford Annotated Bible,* a study version of the RSV, received endorsement by the Catholic Church from Cardinal Cushing of Boston in 1966. In short, if one is seeking a translation for scholarly endeavor or serious study, then the RSV is the choice.

In 1990, a revision of the Revised Standard Version appeared called the New Revised Standard Version (NRSV). The purpose of this revision was to provide a translation which takes into consideration the most recent discoveries in linguistics. The committee which guided this revision adopted the maxim, ''As literal as possible, as free as necessary.'' Paraphrase is used only when necessary. Also this revision attempts to take into consideration the question of inclusive language. In general, the revision has accomplished its goals. However, there are a few places where the guiding principles have skewed the translation.

The New English Bible

By the mid-40s, many churchmen in the British Isles also realized that the language of the *Authorized* or *King James Version* was somewhat archaic for the twentieth century. The General Assembly of the Church of Scotland recommended that scholars prepare a translation which would employ twentieth-century English. The Church of England, the Methodist, Baptist and Congregational Churches agreed. They recommended that this project not be a revision of the *King James.* It should be a completely new translation. As the project began, the Roman Catholic Church in England and Scotland sent observers to work with the committee of translators. The translation used the original Hebrew and Greek texts for its base. The New Testament was completed in 1961; the Old Testament in 1970. It became known as the *New English Bible.*

The commission of translators, under the leadership of C.H.

Dodd, wanted the new text to be faithful to biblical scholarship. At the same time, they wished to express the literary sense of twentieth-century English. The resulting translation contains a strong English idiom. It does not have any particular denominational bias. It is not as useful for scholarship as the RSV, though it is quite well-suited to liturgical proclamation, or private reading. In fact, Bishop Fulton J. Sheen strongly recommended this translation for private meditation and prayer. If one is searching for a Bible for prayer and meditation, they might want to examine the *New English Bible*.

The Revised English Bible

The *New English Bible* provided a good alternative to the traditional *King James Version* for a modern English audience. Nevertheless, according to some, it did not prove useful for the liturgical assembly. As a result, the same commission that prepared the NEB began a revised edition which is intended for use in liturgical assemblies. This revision, known as the *Revised English Bible,* has been completed. The basic difference between these two versions is that the emphasis on literary quality which marked the NEB has been superseded by an emphasis on clarity and ease of reading in the REB.

The REB has returned to the more classic translations in areas where literary flourish has previously been attempted. The REB also handles the question of inclusive language, trying to eliminate the word "man" whenever the reference is not specifically to the male. All in all, the *Revised English Bible* is a successful attempt to break with the traditional biblical translations and provide a readable, clear translation utilizing contemporary idiom.

The New American Bible

In the Catholic Church, biblical translations followed a path of revision like the *King James Version*. In the mid-eighteenth century, Bishop Richard Challoner revised the Douay-Rheims translation to produce a more modern version. The Challoner revision became the official Catholic text of the Bible for nearly two centuries.

In 1941, the Confraternity of Christian Doctrine Committee of the American Bishops commissioned a revision of the Rheims-Challoner New Testament. They wanted to adapt that version to a twentieth-century American idiom. This became the New Testament of the CCD edition. A similar revision of the Old Testament was commissioned, yet never reached completion. In 1943, Pope Pius XII, in his encyclical *Divino Afflante Spiritu,* encouraged translations from the original languages.

Following the encouragement of Pius XII, the American bishops commissioned a completely new translation of the whole Bible from the original languages. This translation, the *New American Bible,* appeared in stages—1952, 1955, and 1961 for the Old Testament, 1969 for the New Testament. The preface to this edition set forth a threefold purpose behind the translation. The committee in charge of the project wanted to provide a version of the Bible suitable for liturgical proclamation, private reading and purposes of study. The NAB translation provides a balance between scholarship and spirituality. It is one of the finest translations for the person who wants an understandable American idiom. This translation is used for liturgical proclamation in most parishes in the United States. It is also recommended for use by many teachers since it is clear, understandable, and very readable.

Due to the rapid cultural change in the twentieth century, the need for revision and updating of this translation became evident by 1978. A commission was established to begin revision. The completion of the project produced the revised edition of the New Testament of the *New American Bible* in 1986. This revision was to produce a translation which would be accurate and faithful to the meaning of the original Greek. It was also intended to reflect contemporary American usage. As a result, it would be understandable to people having had an ordinary education.

One problem that the revision addressed was discriminatory language. In our culture, there are expressions which show anti-Semitic attitudes, or appear offensive to other minorities. Also, women consider some expressions exclusive. The committee in charge of the revised NAB had the goal of producing a translation which would be sensitive to these questions while maintaining the sense of the original Greek text.

The revised New Testament of the NAB maintains the principles that were at the foundation of the original NAB while trying to be sensitive to many of the questions of our culture. The Old Testament of the New American Bible is currently under revision using the same guidelines that produced the Revised New Testament.

JAMES P. McILHONE

The Old Testament of the New American Bible is currently under revision using the same guidelines that produced the Revised New Testament. As a result, the NAB should remain the best version for Catholics who want to become more familiar with the scriptures.

Recently, a new edition of the *New American Bible* known as the *Catholic Study Bible* appeared. It incorporates the text of the *New American Bible* with a commentary written by noted Catholic Biblical scholars. This edition has an excellent cross reference system between the text and the commentary. It is an excellent tool for Bible study groups.

The Jerusalem Bible

While American scholars were working on the *New American Bible,* many in France saw the need for a new translation of the Bible into French. A dual purpose emerged for this project—(1) to keep abreast of the times, and (2) to deepen theological thought. The Dominicans at the French School in Jerusalem, L'Ecole Biblique, were commissioned to produce a translation of the Bible which would be useful for French Catholics. The result was *La Saint Bible*. It was a translation from the original languages, coupled with a most extensive cross-reference system. In addition, the notes were the most comprehensive in any Bible to date. As a result, it became the most significant achievement of Catholic Biblical Scholarship since *Divino Afflante Spiritu.*

The *La Saint Bible* was translated into English and appeared in the United States around 1966. Since the English was a translation of a translation many scholars cautioned its use. Many have noted that both the French and the English translations fail to use contemporary linguistic discoveries. In many places, a difficult Hebrew text will be emended in light of the Greek translation before it is translated into English.

About the same time that the revised NAB New Testament appeared, a revision of the *Jerusalem Bible* was completed. This does remedy many of the problems with the original version. The new translation, coupled with the notes and cross-references, make the *Jerusalem Bible* an invaluable tool for people who wish to do prayerful study of the Bible from a specifically Catholic perspective.

THE WORD MADE CLEAR

The New International Version

Unlike the preceding versions, the *New International Version* is not a revision, nor is it the product of a particular denomination. The concept of the NIV began at a meeting of scholars in Chicago in 1965. They saw the need for a new translation of the Bible from the original languages. This project was sponsored by the New York Bible Society International in 1967. This permitted scholars from around the world to participate in the project. The translators' concern was twofold. They wanted to preserve accuracy of the text and fidelity to its thought. They also wanted to produce a version that would be clear in style. Since this was an international collaboration, American or British idiom was avoided. They also wished to avoid archaisms (use of thee and thou).

The NIV is noted for its high quality. In some places the language incites the imagination. It is modern. Therefore, it is good for use with high school students, teen groups, and young people's Bible studies. The major disadvantage of the NIV is the translators' slight interpretations of key words. Instead of translating a word such as "flesh," consistently, they will translate it at one point, "flesh," at another "fleshy," at yet another "evil." This last translation shows signs of interpretation on the part of the translator.

The Good News Bible and *The Living Bible*

The *Good News Bible* is a translation sponsored by the American Bible Society. It is also known as *Today's English Version*. This is an attempt to produce for America a version of the Bible that would parallel the *New English Bible*. A further version, *The Living Bible* or *The Way,* is the result of the work of K.A. Taylor, who received his biblical background from the Inter-Varsity Fellowship. In the preface to his work, Taylor is perfectly candid about the fact that his work is a paraphrase, "a restatement of the author's thought, using different words than he did." It is an attempt to accomplish a similar goal as the author in less cumbersome language..

These versions do not claim to be faithful to the original text. They are "translations which interpret." Many times, the translation will show a doctrinal slant colored by the translator. When using these versions, one has to be careful of biases that are subtly contained in the text. These might not agree with the accepted understanding of the text in the Catholic Church.

27

JAMES P. McILHONE

We have examined several popular English versions of the Bible available today. There is a total of nearly seventy translations to choose from. I hope that from this short review of the more significant translations, it is clear that the particular Bible chosen depends on likes and interests. There is no one translation. The way to determine which is best is to sample several versions. Take a significant passage and see how various versions translate it. Choose ones you really like, then look at other passages and compare again. Then choose the one that sounds best to you.

Study Questions

1) What is meant by the term Canon?
2) Is the terminology 'Catholic' bible and 'Protestant' bible appropriate? Why or why not?
3) Which Bible do you like to use? (In other words, which is your favorite translation of the Bible?), Why?
4) Take your favorite biblical passage. Examine how it is translated in the various translations. Which do you like best. Why?

Bibliography

Bruce, F. F., *History of the Bible in English,* 3rd ed. (New York: 1978).

Greenslade, S. L. (ed), *The Cambridge History of the Bible,* Vol. III, The West from the Reformation to the Present Day, (Cambridge: At the University Press, 1963).

Hammond, G., *Making of the English Bible,* (Manchester: 1982).

Robertsen, E. H., *The New Translations of the Bible,* (London: 1959).

Chapter 3

Is the Bible To Be Taken Literally?
What Happens If It Is?

In the past few years, an increasing number of Catholic young people have expressed the view that "there is nothing to live for." They feel that they have no future. They are going through high school and college to get an education that they feel they may never be able to use. The reason given for this attitude is that the world as they know it soon may not exist. The advances in science which have contributed to the technological development of the twentieth-century world have become the means of its possible destruction. Nuclear power has made life easier; yet, it also has made possible instant total annihilation. Despite the wondrous advances in medicine, viruses such as AIDS spread, immune to attempts to halt them. Industry has provided jobs and eased many of the burdens of life. It has also left us with pollutants which slowly eat away at the ozone layer of the atmosphere destroying vital protection that our planet needs.

Many have sought to cope with this crisis through denial. They try to make their world as comfortable as possible so their feelings of hopelessness might vanish. Others have looked to religion to find an answer. Failing to find any consolation in organized religion, they have turned to television evangelists. In the past ten to fifteen years, such evangelists have used the power of the media to spread the "Word of God." They have mesmerized many into thinking that the Word of God provides the necessary answer. They preach with conviction a message based on the Bible interpreted literally. They are winning people from all walks of life to a view of the Word of God characterized as "fundamentalist."

What Is Fundamentalism?

Fundamentalism, as we shall describe it here, is a phenomenon which is peculiarly American. The phenomenon of sovereignty of the people has dominated America from pre-revolutionary days. When this phenomenon meets with the Protestant doctrine of "scripture alone," a theory of individual interpretation of scripture emerges. The individual has a "direct pipeline to God." There is no longer a need for church, or theology. The individual has his or her own interpretation, and it is authoritative because it is "from God directly."

Fundamentalism can be described as a sect. Robin Scroggs, in an article published several years ago, listed several characteristics of a sect. First, a sect is "egalitarian." This means that individuals are treated as equal. They are sustained by love and acceptance within the community. An attitude of love exists in fundamentalist communities. They make people feel at home. They make people feel accepted. Then they can present their views on scripture. Second, a sect demands total commitment from its members. Among fundamentalists, this is the notion of "giving oneself totally to Christ." It is the meaning of the question, "Have you been saved?" Some groups demand that members give up all that they have to be a part of the community. Finally, failure to live up to the sect's vision leads to expulsion. In fundamentalist groups, when one does not see the meaning of scripture the way that the group does, they are ostracized. It is this rigidity of interpretation that causes so much fragmentation among fundamentalist groups.

Fundamentalism is a vision or ideology. Scripture scholar Eugene LaVerdiere notes that an ideology is characterized by (1) adherence to a particular document which sets out the vision of the group, and (2) opposition to an enemy. For example, the ideology that our country was founded on is written in the Constitution, a document. Many groups in America feel themselves called to protect that vision from outside forces who might wish to corrupt it. The document which contains the fundamentalist vision is the Bible. It must be interpreted as it is written. The enemy would be anyone who sought to "misinterpret" biblical texts. Some of the enemies that fundamentalists oppose are Christian Scientists, Mormons, Cultists, and the Roman Catholic Church.

Fundamentalists see themselves as having a mission. They have committed their lives to Jesus and are called to bring as many people as possible into the same commitment. Characteristic of fundamentalists is their undying commitment to convince and convert. They are very evangelical. They present the gospel and try to bring people to a commitment of faith.

THE WORD MADE CLEAR

Where Did Fundamentalism Come From?

In the late nineteenth century, several movements appeared which helped the development of American fundamentalism. Primary among these is a reaction against modern tendencies in science, history and sociology.

The Theory of Evolution—In the late 1800s, Charles Darwin published his work, *The Origin of the Species.* This presented several theses which contradicted the traditional understanding of the origin of humanity in Genesis. Darwin's work denied the creative role of God in history. This upset people. To soothe this uneasiness, many turned to a literal interpretation of Genesis and reemphasized the role of God in creation.

Application of Scientific Methods to Biblical Study—After the scientific revolution of the sixteenth and seventeenth centuries, scholars began to look at the Bible using scientific methods of criticism. On the one hand, this produced a deeper understanding of the meaning of the Bible. On the other hand, many were afraid that meticulous scientific investigation would undermine the credibility of the biblical text. They refused to accept any critical methods which might undermine the ''truth'' or ''inerrancy'' of the text. As a result, they held to a literal interpretation of the scriptures.

The Social Gospel—The late nineteenth and early twentieth centuries saw significant population growth in the United States. This was the result of two factors—immigration and urbanization. Sociological studies have shown that between 1860 and 1920, the United States shifted from a rural country society to an urban society. As the country became more urban, the problems of poverty and social inequality that accompany an urban society became more significant. Ministers preached the social implications of the gospel. Despite much praise, some saw this ''social gospel'' as undermining a belief in the providential role of God. They felt that scripture tells us God will take care of the needs of his people.

Fundamentalism has its roots in the reactions to these movements. Darwin showed the development of the human species. Historical criticism concentrated on the development of the biblical word. The preaching of the social gospel concentrated on the problems of society as it developed. In each case, there is an increasing consciousness of historical development. This made fundamentalists uneasy. They believed that the Word of God as written in the Bible was complete, whole and unchanging. Any chance of developmental understanding was ruled out.

The Fundamentals''—In the early part of the twentieth century, a group formed to set down those truths which would be considered "fundamental." They published these in a pamphlet which was called *The Fundamentals*. The pamphlet was to provide a defense or apologetic for problems which arose concerning scriptural interpretation. They wanted to provide an offense, or polemic, that could be used for problems and attacks that might arise from outside groups, especially the Roman Catholic Church. *The Fundamentals* concentrated on two areas, biblical interpretation and evangelization.

A distillation of the principles contained in *The Fundamentals* was presented by Father LaVerdiere who has done extensive research on fundamentalism. He presents five principles:

1) *Divine inspiration and inerrancy of the scriptures.* The Bible is the divine Word of God. It contains no error. It is divinely inspired. God is the author of the biblical text. There is no room for a human author.

2) *Divinity of Christ and literal interpretation of the virgin birth.* Again, there is an insistence on literal interpretation. The divinity of Christ is accepted by most denominations, even though some have reservations about the virgin birth. The Catholic tradition differs in its insistence that Mary remained a virgin even after the birth of Jesus, that is, the perpetual virginity of Mary.

3) *Substitutionary atonement by Jesus for sins.* Jesus died for our sins. Jesus died to save us. This principle is accepted by all denominations. However, problems arise when this is interpreted that salvation is possible *only* through Jesus. Here, the Catholic Church differs from the fundamentals. This is clear from the *Constitution on the Church* of Vatican II.

4) *Literal view of the resurrection.* There is some debate among theologians concerning the resurrection, but most denominations teach that Jesus did actually rise from the dead.

5) *Literal view of the return of Christ.* Everyone agrees that Jesus will return. However, there is significant disagreement as to the

time, place and manner of that return. The fundamentalists hold to a literal view that he will return to the Mount of Olives as he left.

Fundamentalists use the scriptures to interpret these statements. For example, there are several fundamentalist sects who use the biblical evidence and dating to calculate the day on which the Lord will return. In the minds of many, this type of biblical interpretation is a bit extreme. Yet, fundamentalists feel that is the only way to view the text.

From this investigation, it would seem that the basic principles or *The Fundamentals* can be agreed on by all Christians. What then is the difference between those who hold these principles and Catholics?

To answer this question, we must look for a moment at what is fundamental for a Catholic. Let us look at the earliest formulations of the Christian community. These are known as creeds. The earliest New Testament creeds are found in the speeches of Peter in Acts, and in the traditions that underlie Paul's account of the resurrection in 1 Corinthians 15:3-7. Formal creedal statements are the Nicene or Apostles creeds. A distinction can be made between creeds, which contain what is fundamental for Catholics, and *The Fundamentals,* which are so significant to fundamentalists.

The early Christian creeds are the result of theological reflection on events. They relate events and the relationships they brought about. The creedal formulation, "Christ died for our sins," speaks of the event of Jesus' death. Implicit in this event is the motivation for that death, his love for humanity. This links the event to a love relationship. On the other hand, the fundamentals are propositions or concepts. They are absolute and unchanging. Creeds, involving relationships, are dynamic. They grow in depth of understanding.

The creeds show a sense of mystery. This mystery unfolds as we come to understand the underlying event and the relationships more clearly. The fundamentals are clear from the start. Both the creeds and the fundamentals contain revelation. The fundamentals use external evidence to verify their truth. If discrepancies are allowed concerning times or places—things which *are* visible— then that which is *not* as visible falls into question, e.g., the reality of Jesus as God. For the fundamentalist, every word, phrase and sentence must be shown to be true. The creeds, on the other hand, being based on experience, can be interpreted. There can be several interpretations of the same experience. The fact that the interpretations differ does not take away from the reality or truth of the original experience. Everything in the scriptures does not have to be literally true.

A Catholic Response

The American bishops published a "Pastoral Statement for Catholics on Fundamentalism" in 1987. Several principles can be drawn from that document which can guide the Catholic response to fundamentalism.

1) Fundamentalism indicates a person's general approach to life, which is typified by an unyielding adherence to a doctrinal and ideological position. In other words, the theology of the fundamentalist is based on assumptions rather than reflection. The biblical word is absolute; it can be understood by anyone at anytime. There is no cultural reflection. The reading of the fundamentalist becomes absolutized as *the* reading for all. This principle shows that the fundamentalist is usually not open to another point of view. Therefore, argumentation from the text does little good.

2) Biblical fundamentalists present the Bible, God's inspired word, as the only necessary source for teaching about Christ and Christian living. The fundamentalist holds that if it is not found in the Bible, it is not revealed by God. The Bible is the sole source of revelation. Therefore, the biblical word is the only point of departure for faith. This is not the position of the Catholic Church. For Catholics, Scripture and Tradition merge into a unity and tend toward the same end. Certainty regarding revelation does not come from Scripture alone. Consequently, there is a radical difference in presuppositions between Catholics and fundamentalists. It is important to know that the point of departure for Catholics is significantly different from that of fundamentalists. Much of what the fundamentalists decry in the Catholic Church is not found in the Bible, but is found in Tradition which is a legitimate vehicle of God's revelation.

3) Fundamentalists tend to interpret the Bible as being always without error, or as literally true, in a way quite different from the Catholic Church's teaching on the inerrancy of the Bible. The inerrancy of the Bible, for the fundamentalist, derives from the unchanging nature of God. He spoke his word in times past and it remains unchangeable even to this day. Catholics see the Bible as the result of a long process of formation. However, that process does not end with the written text. That text affects people in many times and many cultures. These determine how the Bible is interpreted. It is that time- and culture-based interpretation which is coupled with the biblical text to become the Word of God.

4) The Catholic Church does not look on the Bible as an authority for science or history. The truth of the Bible is derived from the fact that it is a chronicle of the ever-developing faith of the people of God. It is not intended to be absolutely correct with regard to scientific or historical facts. Many discoveries of science have come long after the biblical word was written down. Scientific discoveries will not deny the truth of the faith of the people of God. A fundamentalist insists that all discoveries of science or chronicles of history must be in agreement with the biblical text as it is written.

5) Biblical fundamentalism eliminates from Christianity the church as the Lord Jesus founded it. The church, for the fundamentalist, is a spiritual reality. The human church, which is in continuity with Peter and the apostles, is not satisfactory to the fundamentalist since it has no basis in the Bible as they understand it. As we saw above, many fundamentalists openly oppose the Catholic Church. The basis of such dissatisfaction is their belief that "commitment to Christ" is sufficient for salvation. However, commitment cannot last long unless it has a structure in which to grow. The sacraments, liturgical rituals, and other aspects of the church are necessary to nourish the commitment of faith through time.

6) The church produced the New Testament and not vice versa. The New Testament did not predate the church. Rather, the New Testament is the product of a process whereby certain sacred writings came to be regarded as inspired. These were collected by the church and finally declared to be sacred scripture. All the references in the New Testament to "scripture" are explicit references to the Old Testament. The New Testament did not as yet exist; yet, the early Christians were as much church as we are today. Fundamentalists would not agree. They see the scripture as sacred writings written under the guidance of the Holy Spirit.

That is what makes them sacred. For fundamentalists, the sanction of the church is not necessary.

7) In the past, the Catholic Church did not encourage Bible studies as much as it should have. This is most significant. The Bible became the rallying point of many Protestant sects after the Reformation. To counter this, the Catholic Church downplayed the scriptures in favor of the sacraments and ritual. As a result, most Catholics do not have an adequate knowledge of the scriptures. In the post-Vatican II years, the church has encouraged Catholics to read the Bible. Yet this encouragement also makes demands.

When the Bible is read, there will be questions. Therefore, those in teaching positions in the church from the hierarchy on down, must have answers. Seminaries must promote the careful study of the scriptures among their students. Parishes must see that their lectors are properly trained to proclaim the Word of God intelligently. Bible study groups need to be formed.

We cannot shy away from the challenge of fundamentalism. We cannot counter it with intellectual argumentation alone. Fundamentalism is an emotional response. Our response, then, must also involve our emotions. Fundamentalism challenges us to know and to love the scriptures. It will be our knowledge; but even more, it will be the deep love of the scriptures as a profound part of our being that will ultimately counter the challenge of fundamentalism.

Study Questions

1) What is a fundamentalist? How would you characterize one?
2) Do you believe the Bible is without error? Explain.
3) Has the consciousness of historical development affected the interpretation of the Bible?
4) Do you agree with the fundamentalists? Why or Why not?
5) How does your experience of God reflect in your interpretation of Scripture?
6) Describe your experience of fundamentalists. How did you react?
7) Do you think the Catholic Church emphasizes knowledge of Scripture enough?

Bibliography

Barr, James A., *Beyond Fundamentalism: Biblical Foundations for Evangelical Christianity,* (Philadelphia: Westminster Press, 1984).

Barr, James A., *Fundamentalism,* (Philadelphia: Westminster, 1978).

Keating, Karl, *Catholicism and Fundamentalism: The Attack on "Romanism" by "Bible Christians,"* (San Francisco: Ignatius Press, 1988).

Megivern, James, *Bible Interpretation,* (Wilmington: McGrath Pub. Co., 1978).

Nevins, Albret J., *Answering a Fundamentalist,* (Huntington: Our Sunday Visitor, 1990).

O'Meara, Thomas F., *Fundamentalism: A Catholic Perspective,* (New York: Paulist Press, 1990).

Chapter 4

Did Moses Write the Early Books of the Old Testament?

For centuries, when people asked who the author of the first books of the bible was, the answer was "Moses." During the first seventeen centuries, scholars had little difficult in accepting Moses as the author of those books. In fact, the last of those books, Deuteronomy, ends with the death of Moses.

However, as critical scholarship began to make its mark, many questioned Moses as author of the Pentateuch, that is, the first five books of the Old Testament. The clearest clue that the Pentateuch was not composed by a single author is the variation in style, vocabulary, and grammatical structure that is apparent when the text is read carefully.

There are two names for the mountain of God, Sinai and Horeb. Both names appear in Exodus. Sinai predominates in Leviticus and Numbers. But Horeb is used in Deuteronomy. Moses' father-in-law is given two different names, Jethro and Hobab. In Exodus, he is Jethro, while his name is Hobab in the book of Numbers. In the Hebrew text, two words appear for God, Yahweh and Elohim. The French scholar, Jean Astruc was the first to note that in Genesis 1, the Hebrew word for God is Elohim. But in Genesis 2 and 3, the expression changes to Yahweh Elohim. Sometimes translators have attempted to express this distinction in English.

Scholars also discovered that many narratives occurred twice in the text. Such double narritives are what scholars call "doublets." In Genesis, there are two narratives of creation. There are two versions of the Ten Commandments (Exodus 20:1-17; Deuteronomy 5:6-21). Abraham tries to convince foreign leaders that Sarah is his sister rather than his wife on three separate occasions (Genesis 12, Genesis 20 and Genesis 26). There are two versions of the call of Moses to lead the people out of Israel (Exodus 3 and Exodus 6). There are dual accounts of the covenant made with Abraham (Genesis 15 and Genesis 17). Jacob's dream is narrated twice (Genesis 32 and Genesis 35). And so on.

THE WORD MADE CLEAR

The Work of Julius Wellhausen

Biblical scholars such as Reus, Graf and Kuenen began to analyze these doublets along with the use of dual names. They wanted to see whether these duplications might be signs of multiple sources which were edited into a single work. However, it was not until the work of Julius Wellhausen that a clear theory of the sources of the Pentateuch emerged. Wellhausen presented this theory in his *Prolegomena to the History of Israel* (1878).

During the early history of Israel, most of the traditions were passed on orally. Songs, narratives and legends would be remembered during the temple liturgy. The sanctuaries of Israel became centers for retelling Israel's history. After the monarchy was established in Israel, culture flourished in the capital, Jerusalem. A new group, trained scribes, made it possible to preserve the traditions of the past in writing. The first such history became known as the "Yahwist" account since the name Yahweh is consistently used for God. This account was written from the point of view of David's tribe, Judah. Wellhausen chose the symbol "J" to identify the Yahwist history. (It is derived from the first letter of the German word, *Jahveh,* meaning Yahweh.)

After the death of David's son, Solomon, political pressures brought about a division of the kingdom. Ten of the northern tribes seceded and declared themselves a separate kingdom. This kingdom wanted to have nothing to do with the monarchy in the south, its royal family, nor its religious institutions. As a result, they sought to revise the Yahwist history. This revised history, is called the "Elohist" since God is called Elohim rather than Yahweh. It looked back to the days before the monarchy. Wellhausen refers to this history with the symbol "E," the first letter of Elohim. The Elohist stresses the time Israel spent wandering in the desert. It emphasizes the covenant between Moses and the Lord at Sinai. However, the Elohist wanted to avoid the familiarity between God and humans that characterized the Yahwist.

In 722 B.C.E., the northern kingdom fell to the armies of Assyria. Most of the inhabitants were deported to Assyria. Some northerners did escape to the south, bringing with them the Elohist history. There were many similarities between the northern Elohist (E) and southern Yahwist (J) histories. They were joined into a single document, JE, which is known as the "Old Epic History."

Some think that the JE document originated from an attempt by the south to win over northern refugees to worship at the Jerusalem sanctuary.

In the same period, several priests and prophets sought reform of the many evil practices that had infiltrated the monarchy and the temple. This movement grew in intensity when a scroll of laws was found hidden in the walls of the temple during a renovation about 622 B.C.E. That scroll stressed the need for obedience and faithfulness to the covenant by the people. The reward for this faithfulness would be blessings on their children and their children's children in the land. This theology stood in opposition to the earlier theology of blessing found in the J and E histories. Wellhausen referred to this document by the symbol "D" for Deuteronomy. This comes from two Greek words *deuteros* meaning "second," and *nomos* meaning "law." This name is appropriate, since the scroll of Deuteronomy did begin an extensive reform in the southern kingdom under the leadership of King Josiah. This led to the re-establishment of many ancient cultic practices. The D document was soon joined to the J and E traditions.

The reform initiated by the discovery of the Deuteronomy scroll did not last long. By the end of the century (605 B.C.E.), the southern kings were very weak. The southern kingdom soon fell to the armies of Babylon in 587 B.C.E. Larger portions of the population were deported to Babylon. Others fled to Egypt. Jerusalem, with its temple and palaces, was destroyed. All hope seemed lost.

In Babylon, a group of priests began to gather and codify many of the cultic and legal traditions of Israel, along with ancestral lists. The major portion of their work became the legal codes found in the present books of Leviticus and Numbers. Many traditions not contained in the JED history were also preserved by these priests. Since the school which produced the document is the priestly school, Wellhausen cited this document using the symbol "P." The purpose of compiling these laws was to provide for Israel the possibility of practicing her faith when she returned to the land."

Babylon soon fell to a new kingdom, Persia. In 539 B.C.E., the Persian king, Cyrus the Great, permitted the Israelites to return to their homeland, and rebuild the temple. The monarchy, however, was not reestablished. Ruling power passed to the priests. In this situation, Wellhausen sees the final edition of the Pentateuch developing under the guidance of the priestly school. The P document was joined to the JED traditions and edited to produce the Pentateuch as we know it today. I would now like to turn to an examination of the theology found in each tradition.

The Yahwist Tradition

The Yahwist tradition can be seen in the second creation story and the story of the fall of Adam and Eve (Genesis 2:4b-3:24). This tradition is characterized by distinctive vocabulary. God is portrayed as *fashioning* man in this narrative. The Hebrew verb, *yasar,* describes a potter fashioning his clay. There is a great involvement of Yahweh in creation for the Yahwist. In this tradition, "Adam" is a proper name for the first human male. The "dust" and the "ground" have a special significance for the Yahwist. They are the source and material of creation. Particular attention is also given to the "curse." The serpent is cursed because it has led Adam and Eve astray. The ground is cursed as a punishment for Adam and Eve's actions.

The Yahwist employs a colorful presentation of scenes. The narrative is artistically storylike. Descriptions are picturesque. One can almost see the animals parading past Adam as he searches for a helpmate in Genesis 2. The writing appeals to the imagination. As the writer sets the scene for the second creation account in Genesis 2, one can see the rivers flowing into the garden. The author incites the reader's imagination to see the Lord Yahweh forming Adam and breathing life into him.

The Yahwist depicts God as deeply involved with his creation. He is so immanently involved that he takes on human characteristics on several occasions. We see this anthropomorphism as Yahweh walks in the garden with Adam and Eve freely conversing with them. The mood is upbeat and positive. Even when Adam and Eve sin and force Yahweh to expel them from the garden, he provides them with all they will need for their survival.

This positive theology reflects the period in which the Yahwist history was written. The kingdom of David and Solomon was a prosperous period for Israel. The boundaries were the widest ever. Despite sinfulness among the people, there was a general sense of optimism. Yahweh is viewed as a forgiving God. After David's exploits with Bathsheeba and the murder of her husband, Uriah the Hittite, he repents and is forgiven, but also punished. This is the same God we see in the garden—forgiving, yet exacting punishment.

The covenant in the Yahwist is between God and his people (Abraham, in particular). Yet, that covenant does not make serious demands on Abraham nor the people. God promises to be their God, he will provide Abraham with progeny, and he will give Israel a land to call their own. No demands are made on them. This reflected the covenant between Yahweh and David (2 Samuel 7:14) which lies at the foundation of the monarchy. David and his descendants are not required to do anything. Yet Yahweh will strengthen David's throne, making it secure forever. We can understand this since the Yahwist tradition praises the Davidic monarchy.

The Elohist Tradition

We see the Elohist tradition in the call of Moses (Exodus 3:1-22). Here God is more distant than in the Yahwist. He does not speak directly to Moses; rather, he uses a medium, the bush that burns and is not consumed. There are several other places in the Elohist where God chooses to use a medium such as clouds, dreams, messengers, voices from the heavens, etc., to communicate with his people.

The theology of the Elohist tradition has its background in the reform initiated by prophet Elijah in the eighth century B.C. E. Elijah had campaigned strongly to rid the north of pagan practices. Perhaps the most significant example of this campaign is the encounter between Elijah and the four hundred prophets of Baal on the top of Mount Carmel (1 Kings 18:21-40). At the end, Elijah declares that all four hundred prophets be killed. Elijah began this reform because many of the northerners were being drawn away from worship of the God of Israel toward worship of local pagan deities. For more on Elijah, see Chapter 7.

The Elohist tradition shows a strong bias against foreign gods. In Genesis, Jacob is commanded to remove foreign gods (Genesis 35:2). God, in Exodus, commands the Israelites, "You shall have no other gods before me" (Exodus 20:3). Further, the Elohist tradition is interested in the experiences of Israel in the desert. Then Israel was totally dependent on Yahweh. There could be no chance of influence from foreign deities. Finally, the moral exhortations of the Elohist are much stricter than the Yahwist. In general the Elohist tradition is meant to teach. As a result, it is not as colorful or descriptive as the Yahwist.

For the Elohist, the covenant was made with Moses on Mt. Sinai. Yahweh promises to be Israel's God on the condition that Israel will be his people. There is an obligation incumbent upon Israel in the Elohist tradition. The Elohist sees the covenant and its stipulations as the logical follow-up to the saving acts of Yahweh in the Exodus. This is somewhat different from the Yahwist theology which sees the initiative of Yahweh as a gracious act which brings Israel through the Exodus and desert experiences making her who she is.

The Deuteronomic Tradition

Since the Deuteronomic tradition is based on a law code, it is natural that it would have a distinct prophetic vocabulary and hortatory style. Yahweh admonishes Israel to heed the "statutes and ordinances which I teach you, and do them; that you may live, and go in and take possession of the land which the Lord, the God of your fathers, gives you." Note that the emphasis on law is coupled with an emphasis on the land.

The tradition probably developed during the religious crisis that caused the reforms of Hezechiah in the seventh century B.C.E., during the ministry of Isaiah. However, it did not reach its final form until it was finally codified in the southern kingdom during the reforms of Josiah (See chapter 6). The Deuteronomic tradition teaches that salvation is possible only if there is obedience to the covenant stipulations. Primary among these is the command to worship Yahweh in Jerusalem. Much of the material contained in Deuteronomy is based on oral traditions which had been brought from the north after the fall of Samaria. We might, therefore, suspect that this tradition would also have the prohibitions against foreign gods similar to the Elohist. However, these traditions were put in writing in the south. Therefore, prohibitions against worship of foreign gods become secondary to a primary emphasis on true worship of Yahweh.

The central theological concept of the Deuteronomist is really a union of the covenantal theologies of the Yahwist and Elohist.

Given the history of the Deuteronomic tradition, this would make sense. Covenant in D is Yahweh's loving election. This is a central theme in Yahwist theology. Law, on the other hand, becomes Israel's response to Yahweh's election. This is a central theme in Elohist theology. The Deuteronomist sees this response as something which is incumbent on all (Deuteronomy 6:4-9). The way in which each responds to the election of Yahweh (by keeping the law) will determine Yahweh's action toward Israel.

The school which produced the Deuteronomist tradition of the Pentateuch also compiled the history of Israel from the death of Moses to the fall of the monarchy. This Deuteronomistic history is characterized by that same covenantal theology. If people follow the covenant, they will be rewarded by Yahweh. If they break the covenant, they will be punished down to the fourth or fifth generation. Many of the invasions, battles, and even the fall of Jerusalem itself in 587 B.C.E. are interpreted in this history as a failure of the people to follow the covenant. Deuteronomic theology, as it became known, continues to be found in many later Old Testament writings. It even makes its mark on the New Testament (John 9:2).

The Priestly Tradition

The concern with liturgical correctness and priesthood gives this tradition its designation as "Priestly." This is the latest of the traditions, and the easiest to spot. The opening chapter of Genesis (Genesis 1:1-2:4a) is a magnificent example of the work of the Priestly writer. To determine the characteristics of Priestly writing, we can compare this narrative of creation (Gen 1:1-2:4a) to that of the Yahwist (Gen 2:4b-25). Priestly writing is distinguished by repetition and balanced structure. The result is a narrative which appeals much more to the intellect than the imagination.

The Priestly narrative uses the Hebrew word, *barah,* for the act of creation. This word implies an act in which the creator is distant. This is quite different from the intimate "fashioning" by the Creator in the Yahwist. The Priestly writer uses special vocabulary, "the Deep," "the waters," "monsters." These are more "mythic" concepts than those of the Yahwist. In Priestly writing, *adam,* "Adam" is not a personal name; rather, it is a designation of the whole human race. "Adam," in the Priestly narrative, is "blessed" and commanded to fill the earth. The structure of the narrative (work on six days, rest on a seventh) reflects a Priestly concern—the sacredness of the sabbath. If it was good enough for Yahweh to rest on the sabbath, it is good enough for his creatures.

The impact of the Priestly narrative is order, majesty and sovereignty. Yahweh is transcendent, not involved in the process. Creation takes place by word. There is no need to attribute human characteristics to Yahweh. This view reflects the situation of Israel when this tradition was shaped during the exile. Israel was away from her homeland, her hopes seemed dashed. Yahweh seemed miles away. Faith demanded that the covenant that seemed shattered be maintained. Through obedience to the law, Israel will become holy. It is this holiness, like the holiness of Yahweh himself, that would help Israel continue (Leviticus 19:2).

Therefore, the Priestly tradition emphasizes those things which will make Israel holy—worship, prayer, temple and feasts. The history of Israel is told in a liturgical context. As we saw, creation emphasized the sabbath rest. The Exodus is presented as a great procession out of Egypt to offer worship to Yahweh on Mt. Sinai (Exodus 5:3). The history of Israel is a series of covenants (Adam, Noah, Abraham, Moses) which God has made with his people. Through these covenants, Israel will become his holy people. For Israel in exile, this history shows how she had achieved the ideal of holiness in the past, and how it becomes a goal for her to achieve in the present.

The Priestly writers also compiled the history of Israel after the death of Moses. Their history, known as the "Chronicler's History" looks at the period of the monarchy and the early post-exilic period emphasizing the priestly theology of "holiness of the people." Sometime during the post-exilic period, the Priestly school incorporated their writings into the existing traditions of Israel's early history. This produced the five books of the law, the Torah. It must have been completed sometime before the preaching of Ezra, the scribe, since we know that Ezra read the Torah to the people (Nehemiah 7:73-8:12).

Clearly, the Pentateuch is not the product of one person, Moses. Rather, it is the result of many traditions interwoven and tied together to reflect a past and present for the people of Israel. It is in that light, reflecting on the past in the present, that we must continue to view it today.

Study Questions

1) Examine Genesis 1:1-2:4a noting particularly what picture it presents of God, of Humanity, of Creation.
2) Do the same for Genesis 2:4b-24. What is similar and what is different?
3) Examine Exodus 20:1-20. What are the commands given and what motivates them?
4) Do the same for Deuteronomy 5:6-21.
5) What did the above exercises show you about the J(2), E(3), D(4), and P(1) sources?

Bibliography

Becker, Joachim, *The Formation of the Old Testament*, (Chicago: Franciscan Herald Press, 1972).

Brueggemann, Walter, and Wolff, Hans Walter, *The Vitality of Old Testament Traditions*, (Atlanta: John Knox Press, 1978).

Cassuto, U., "The Documentary Hypothesis" in *The Old Testament and Modern Study*, edited by H. H. Rowley, (Oxford: Clarendon Press, 1951).

Habel, Norman, *Literary Criticism for Old testament Critics*, (Philadelphia: Fortress Press, 1971).

LaVerdiere, **Introduction to the Pentateuch**, Old Testament Reading Guide, Vol. 1, (Collegeville: The Liturgical Press, 1971).

Noth, Martin, *A History of Pentateuchal Traditions*, trans. by Bernhard W. Anderson, (Englewood Cliffs: Prentice Hall, 1972).

Van Rad, Gerhard, *The Problem of the Hexateuch and other Essays*, trans. by E. W. T. Dicken, (New York: McGraw-Hill, 1966).

Chapter 5

What Are They Saying About Exodus?

I'm sure that many of us recall Cecil B. DeMille's famous movie, *The Ten Commandments,* either from the theater many years ago, or from watching it on TV around Easter or Christmas. We cannot help but be awestruck at some of the special effects, especially the parting of the Red Sea. Through masterful photographic effects for his day, DeMille portrayed Moses and the Israelites passing through parted waters that rivaled Niagara Falls. But I'm sure we asked, "Is that the way it really happened?"

Well, let's look at some ideas at the heart of Exodus, especially 1) the crossing of the sea, 2) the plagues, 3) the origin of Israel's belief in one God. We must also look at the events on Mt. Sinai, the covenant between God and his people.

The book of Exodus continues the narrative history of Genesis. At the end of Genesis, Jacob and his family migrate to Egypt to avoid famine in their own country. This migration became possible through Joseph, Jacob's favorite son. His brothers became jealous, sold him to a group of traders, and reported to their father that Joseph had been killed. The traders brought Joseph to Egypt and sold him as a slave.

Joseph proved a very masterful slave. He successfully predicted the need for conserving food while there was plenty, so the food could be used in time of famine. Because of this, Joseph rose to the second highest position in Egypt. During a famine, his father sent his brothers to Egypt to get food. Joseph identifies himself and invites his family to come to Egypt. A full narrative of these events is contained in Genesis 37:39-50.

The Book of Exodus begins some time after Joseph's death. The descendants of Jacob in Egypt have become numerous. A new king who is not favorable to the Hebrews has taken power in Egypt. He subjects them to slavery (Exodus 1:8-11).

Many have questioned whether these narratives are historically accurate. Would it be possible for a Hebrew to rise to such power in Egypt? The general opinion is that the Joseph story is probable. Toward the end of the period of Egyptian history known as the

Middle Kingdom, there was a period of decline. In the eighteenth century B.C.E., Egypt was overrun by a fierce group of invaders known as the Hyksos. The name means "foreign chieftains." They took advantage of the weakness of Egypt to establish themselves there. Archaeological evidence has shown that the Hyksos were a race related to the Hebrews who had migrated to Canaan.

The rise of Joseph probably coincided with the Hyksos' rule in Egypt. It is thus understandable that a man of Hebrew stock could rise to a position of power in Egypt. The king who subjected the Hebrew people to slavery was not from the Hyksos. Probably, he was a native Egyptian. Again history bears this out. In the late sixteenth century, the Hyksos were driven out of Egypt. Power was restored to native Egyptian rulers. This was the beginning of the New Kingdom.

One God: Israelite or Egyptian?

The Role of Akenaton and Monotheism—Early in the New Kingdom, Pharaoh Amenophis IV declared that the sun god (Aton) was the sole god. He changed his name to Akenaton ("Splendor of Aton") to demonstrate his belief in the divine status of the sun god. Pharaoh Akenaton saw himself as a worshipper of the sun god. The people of Egypt were worshippers of Pharaoh. In reality, Akenaton's cult was an attempt to raise himself to divine status.

Two factors are responsible for the short life of this cult. First, this new cult was more austere than the cults of many gods of the Egyptian pantheon. People did not care for such austerity. Second, Pharaoh Akenaton did not live long. When he died, the cult died with him. Nevertheless, Akenaton's religious movement left a legacy for future generations. It is very probable that the belief in one god was not as novel as one may think when it appears in the Hebrew religious sphere. Some have speculated that Akenaton's belief in one god influenced the Hebrew notion that their God was one. The Hebrews would have been in slavery in Egypt during and after the time of Akenaton. Nevertheless, such influence would be difficult to trace.

The Patriarchal Idea of God—God is described in many different ways in Genesis. He is the "God of Abraham," the "God of Isaac," the "God of Jacob." He is called the "God of the mountain top,'' among other titles. Whether Abraham, Isaac or Jacob acknowledged a single God is an open question. Rachel, Jacob's wife, steals her father's household gods when she comes to live with him (Genesis 31). The author implies there is nothing wrong in her action. Later, Joshua will speak of the patriarchs worshipping many gods beyond the river (Joshua 24) before they believed in one God. In the time of the patriarchs, there probably was no single God of the Hebrews.

Moses' Infancy—As the Hebrews grew in number, the Egyptians feared they might gain strength to rebel. Pharaoh commanded that the male children of the Hebrews be killed. One young Hebrew boy, Moses, was spared. His mother sent him down the river in a basket where he was discovered by the Pharaoh's daughter. He was raised in the court until he discovered his true identity. Realizing that he was a Hebrew, he gave up the splendor of the court to join his kinsmen as a slave. The murder of an Egyptian taskmaster forced him to flee into the desert near the mountain of God, Sinai. Sinai intrigued Moses. He ascended the mountain to discover a bush that burned, yet never was consumed.

Israel's One God—In that bush, Moses encountered God. From the bush, God identified himself as ''the God of Abraham, the God of Isaac, and the God of Jacob, the God of the Fathers.'' For the first time, one realizes that the gods of the patriarchs are actually titles for God. Moses questioned God concerning his name. God replied ''Yahweh,'' ''I am who am'' (Exodus 3:13-14). In this encounter, Israel's belief in one God, Yahweh, finds its roots.

Israel believes that Yahweh is their God. Their God is one God. That does not *eliminate* the existence of other gods. Rather, the believer in Yahweh will not *give allegiance* to other gods. This will become the first stipulation of the covenant Israel will make with Yahweh. Allegiance to Yahweh will also be the most difficult part of the covenant. The allure of the cults of the other gods will constantly draw Israel away from her allegiance to Yahweh.

The Plagues

Moses' First Encounter—When he has revealed his identity, Yahweh calls Moses to deliver his people from slavery in Egypt.

Yahweh also informs Moses that he will "harden Pharaoh's heart" in order to convince Pharaoh by signs and wonders. These signs will show the Egyptians that Yahweh is God.

Moses returns to Pharaoh with the request, "Let my people go!" Pharaoh responds by demanding a sign. Aaron, Moses' brother, throws his staff to the ground. It becomes a serpent. The Egyptian magicians counter by throwing their staffs down. They, too, become serpents. Aaron's staff swallows the Egyptians' staffs. Yahweh had promised that he would perform this sign to ease Moses' fears (Exodus 4:1-5). The power of Yahweh in Moses seems no more powerful than that of the Egyptian sorcerers. However, the swallowing of the staffs is a sign that Yahweh's power is stronger than that of the sorcerers. Although this sign seems to have proven nothing, it is a prelude to several wondrous signs that will not be matched by any Egyptian magicians.

Moses' Subsequent Encounters—These wondrous signs are a series of plagues inflicted on Egypt. The narrative is composed from material in the Jahweh Elohist, and Priestly sources. The narration of each plague follows a basic pattern. Moses requests that Pharaoh release the people. Pharaoh refuses. Moses calls down a plague on Egypt. Pharaoh begs Moses to stop the plague. Moses pleads with Yahweh. The plague stops. Pharaoh's heart remains hardened. He will not let the people go.

These plagues are not unusual phenomena for Egypt. Frogs, boils, flies, gnats, hail, etc. are all natural phenomena. There have probably been occurrences similar to the plagues many times in Egypt. The first plague, changing water to blood, is really a red silt that the Nile river picks up shortly after inundation. It remains a short time. Then the river returns to its natural color. The ninth plague, darkness, results from a wind that blows off the desert during March or April. It brings darkness and extreme heaviness in the air. How then can we say that these are miraculous? The skeptic might see nothing miraculous in these narratives. The eye of faith admits these are natural phenomena. Yet, there is also a supernatural element in them. Yahweh is in total control of these phenomena; Moses and Aaron are his instruments. Each plague begins at the word of Moses or Aaron, and each ceases at their word.

The full narrative shows the increasing power of God in the

plagues. The first plagues are simply a cause for aggravation. The next plagues affect the Egyptians and their property. The plague of darkness brings an awesome terror upon the Egyptians. The increasing intensity of the plagues heightens expectation and prepares for the final plague.

The Final Encounter—Moses announces the final plague. Every firstborn in the land of Egypt will die. The firstborn of the Hebrew slaves will be saved. Each Hebrew family is to get a lamb, slaughter it, and paint the door posts and lintel with its blood. This is a sign that the home is Hebrew. It will be passed over. Through the blood on the doorpost, the firstborn of the Hebrews will be saved. The lamb is to be roasted whole and eaten with unleavened bread in a prescribed ritual. This meal, the Passover, as it will be known, will become a memorial meal. Each year it will be eaten to remember this night.

The Exodus—Pharaoh remains unmoved until the final plague occurs. The first born of all Egyptians die while the first born of the Hebrews are spared. Pharaoh, at last, relents and permits the Israelites to leave. They travel out of Egypt toward Sinai in haste. Through the use of symbols such as cloud and fire, the narrators show that God is present with them. When the Hebrews reach the sea, they murmur against Moses wishing to return to Egypt. When Pharaoh realizes that he may have acted too quickly, he mounts his chariot and leads his army in pursuit. The Hebrews find themselves caught between the sea and the armies of Pharaoh.

The Crossing of the Sea—Scholars have debated which sea blocked the Hebrews' way. Tradition based on the Greek translation of Exodus 15:4, 21 identifies it as the Red Sea. The original Hebrew translates Exodus 15:4 as "reed sea" or "sea of reeds." This discrepancy has caused many to speculate that it was another body of water. We can be reasonably certain that some body of water was an obstacle to the Hebrews. Also, Exodus 14 tells us that some action of the wind dried up this body of water to allow the Hebrews to pass on dry land. Yet it changed rapidly, causing the Egyptians in pursuit to be caught in the mud. That would be highly improbable for a body of water as large as the Red Sea. There is a smaller body of water near the area in Egypt where the Hebrews dwelt. It is an arm of Lake Manzelah. Investigation has proven that wind conditions on that lake could cause the tide to be restrained to form what seemed a path. When the winds change, the tide is set free and the water returns to normal.

Again, a miracle seems to be reduced to natural occurrence. What is so miraculous about this? Yahweh's control is again evident. As the Hebrews need to get across the sea to avoid the armies of Pharaoh, the tide is restrained. It is set free as Pharaoh's armies are entering the sea. We must remember that historians of the Exodus did not have our interest in the precise locations for these events. They were interested in the religious meaning of the events. Today we see the religious meaning. And we search incessantly for exact locations. However, the chance that we will find with certainty the exact location of the RedŘeed Sea is very slim. Yet, we must also realize that our inability to determine precise locations for these events does not prove that they never happened.

The Covenant on Mount Sinai—After two months of travel, the Hebrew people reached Mt. Sinai where they entered into a covenant with their God, Yahweh. Many believe this covenant is central to the whole Old Testament. Yet, it is curious that the earliest formulations of the faith of Israel do not mention it. These creedal formulas (Deuteronomy 6:21-23; 26:5-9; Joshua 24: 2-13; 1 Samuel 12:8; Psalms 78; 105; 36) recall the slavery in Egypt, the plagues, the Exodus, the crossing of the sea, and the pursuit by Pharaoh's army, but contain no reference to the Sinai experience.

When scholars like Gerhard Van Rad subjected the creedal statements of Deuteronomy and Joshua to careful analysis, they concluded that the creeds contained only the gracious acts of Yahweh. In the earliest oral tradition, the Sinai traditions were separate from the traditions of the Exodus and the events surrounding it. Liturgical formulations such as the creeds drew heavily on the Exodus material. The creeds recalled the actions of Yahweh in the lives of his people. Later liturgical recollections of the events which form the foundation of Israel contained the covenant and Sinai material. Sinai became a response of the people to Yahweh's action in their lives. When all these oral traditions were written, the two strands were combined. Yahweh was seen acting on behalf of his people, and the people responded in the covenant.

The covenant made on Sinai is a bilateral covenant. There are demands made on both parties. Research has shown that the Sinai covenant is similar to covenants which have been recorded among other ancient civilizations, particularly the Hittites.

The Hittite covenant between an overlord and his vassals contained six parts:

1) A *preamble* which announces the titles of the overlord who is making the covenant.

2) A *prologue* which gives reasons from the history of both parties why the vassals should enter into covenant with this overlord.

3) The *demands or stipulations* of the covenant. These demands are made by the overlord and bind the vassals.

4) *Stipulations concerning preservation of the treaty document,* and public reading of the document. These are necessary so those who enter the covenant will know their obligations.

5) A *list of witnesses* to the covenant. Usually this list contains the gods of the two parties.

6) *Blessings and curses* which are the rewards for following the covenant and penalties for failure to follow.

Except for number 5, we can find these parts in the Sinai covenant. The God of the covenant is identified as "Yahweh, your God" (Exodus 20:2a). The reason for the Hebrews accepting the covenant is that Yahweh, their God, has brought them out of the land of Egypt, the house of slavery (Exodus 20:2b). The stipulations or commandments follow (Exodus 20:3-17). Later, in Exodus, there are commands concerning proclamation of the covenant, and blessings and curses which will come upon Israel for following or failing to follow the covenant.

It is important to view the narrative of the commandments through this structure. We may feel that the commandments are "rules" that must be followed in order to win God's love. Israel did not follow the commandments to win Yahweh's favor. Israel followed the commands in response to the loving acts of Yahweh in their midst. He has *already* brought them out of the land of Egypt, therefore they should acknowledge him as their God, speak his name with respect and keep holy a day in his honor. These are not means of winning God's love, they are responses to it.

How many times do we make demands on people, and then use their acceptance or rejection of those demands as a gauge of their love? That is not the message of Exodus. As Yahweh showed his love in his actions for his people, so also must we show our love to others before we make demands on their love. The central point is that Yahweh loved first. If Israel had chosen to reject the covenant, Yahweh's love for her would remain. When we choose to reject our covenant with God, his love for us remains.

The Ten Commandments—The stipulations of the Sinai covenant speak both to the people of Israel's relation to Yahweh, and to each other. Israel's first response to Yahweh must be acknowledgment of Yahweh as their God. Although other gods do exist, the God of Israel is Yahweh. Second, they are prohibited from making any image of Yahweh. They are to show respect for his name; that is, they cannot use his name in vain. This has become, among Jews, the practice of never speaking the name of God. When the divine name occurs in a reading, it is not pronounced; rather, the Hebrew "*Adonai*" meaning "my Lord" is substituted. Finally, they are to follow the example of Yahweh and rest on the sabbath day. As the Lord rested on the seventh day, so also should his people rest on the sabbath.

The next seven commandments concern relations to other members of the covenanted community. Although, through time, these have been generalized to include all human beings, Israel saw these stipulations binding them only in regard to their fellow countrymen. The first demands that parents be given proper honor, especially in their old age. Parents have given life to their children, and children have an obligation to care for their parents until the end of their lives. Next is a series of commands that protect the sanctity of life, marriage, and property. The final commands prohibit perjured testimony and illicit desires. These stipulations bind the Israelites only in regard to their neighbor. Leviticus 19:18 clearly shows that neighbor means fellow countryman, one who shares in the covenant.

The wondrous actions of Yahweh narrated in Exodus, and the response of the people of Israel in the covenant of Sinai is the basis for the remainder of the narrative sections of the Old Testament. The Deuteronomist will gauge the goodness of a person on his response to this covenant. The prophets will call Israel back to this covenant. The great moments of Israel's history, and the times of deepest depression, will be interpreted in terms of Israel's acceptance or rejection of this covenant. From what we have seen, we can say that an understanding of the Exodus and Sinai is crucial for an understanding of the Old Testament as a whole.

Study Questions

1) How does history support or contradict the narratives of Exodus? especially the Hyksos and Akenaton?
2) Describe the rise of Israel's belief in one God?
3) What is the truth concerning the plagues? Did or did they not happen?
4) What is the relation to the Sinai experience to the events of the exodus? How are these crucial for understanding the Old Testament?
5) What is meant by Covenant? What is the covenant operative today?
6) Reflect on God's gracious action in your life. How have you responded to this?

Bibliography

Bright, John, *A History of Israel,* 3rd ed. (Philadelphia: Westminster Press, 1981) expecially pp 107-182.

Burns, Rita, *Exodus, Leviticus, Numbers,* Vol. 3, The Old Testament Message, (Wilmington: Michael Glazier, 1983)

McCarthy, Dennis, *Treaty and Covenant, A Study in Form in the Ancient Oriental Documents and in the Old Testament,* (Rome: Biblical Institute Press, 1978).

McCurley, Foster R., *Genesis, Exodus, Leviticus, Numbers,* Proclamation Commentaries: The Old Testament Witnesses for Preaching, (Philadelphia: Fortress Press, 1979).

Noth, Martin, *Exodus,* The Old Testament Library, (Philadelphia: Westminster, 1962).

Chapter 6

How Did Israel View Her King?

There are many times when human nature exhibits feelings of jealousy. People are just not satisfied with who they are. They desire to be like friends, neighbors, or heroes they admire. This can be a good thing; but it can also be the source of much frustration. Shortly after settling in the land of Canaan after the Exodus and Sinai experiences, this was the problem that Israel faced. The governmental structures were weak and uncentralized. Enemies on all sides were attacking. Israel's most ardent wish was to be like the surrounding nations which had centralized governments. The people cried out for a king.

The Abimelech Incident—When the Hebrew people occupied the land of Canaan, they settled in every region. As Joshua, who had succeeded Moses as leader, began to grow old, there was no real successor appointed for him. Leadership in the tribes fell to local chieftains. Only in times of crisis did leaders arise who called the tribes together to fight. These leaders were known as judges (*shophetim*). When the crisis ended, the tribes went back to their own territories to care for their own needs. The first movement toward monarchy began in the time of Abimelech, son of Gideon, one of the judges.

When Gideon died, Abimelech assembled his tribesmen, suggesting it would be better for one person to rule over Israel. When he received approval for his suggestion, he hired assassins to murder his brothers. Afterward, the people gathered in Shechem to make Abimelech king. Jotham, the only surviving brother, spoke against it. He expresses his objection in a story. The trees searched for a ruler for all the trees. None of the strong trees wanted the position, only the bramble was willing to take the job (Judges 9:7-15).

Applying the story, Jotham concludes that Abimelech is not fit to serve as king because he has executed his brothers. If the people make him king, it will be very bad for them. Jotham's conclusion was soon established. The men of Shechem and Abimelech found themselves in disagreement. They began to distrust him because he murdered his brothers. Revolt soon followed. Shechem was burned to the ground, and ultimately Abimelech was killed. The first experiment in monarchy failed.

Israel Begs Samuel for a King

Later, the Philistines, a new and crueler enemy, attacked Israel. They came from the north armed with iron weapons and chariots. They settled along the eastern coast of the Mediterranean, west of the Israelite settlements. While Samson and Samuel judged Israel, Philistine attacks became more frequent. Many began to see the need for a more central and unified government.

As Samuel grew older, the people approached him at Ramah with the demand, "Behold, you are old and your sons do not walk in your ways; now appoint for us a king to govern us like all the nations" (1 Samuel 8:5). Scholars have isolated two sources which were used by the final editor of the narrative of the foundation of the monarchy. One source (1 Samuel 7:3-8:22; 10:17-27; 12) contains material which expresses opinions opposing the monarchy. The other source (1 Samuel 9:1-10:16, 11) favors a monarchy for Israel.

The anti-monarchy source reveals that Israel has begun to worship foreign gods. As a result, she has been overcome by the Philistines. Samuel, portrayed here as judge, *shophet,* urges the people to return to Yahweh. They will then crush the Philistines. The people repent, Samuel offers sacrifice, and the Philistines are routed.

As a result of this victory over the Philistines, the people demand a king as ruler. Samuel's response interprets their request as a rejection of Yahweh as king. In return for all the good Yahweh has done for Israel, they reject his sovereignty over them by demanding a human king. Samuel continues describing the rights of the king. He will conscript. He will tax. He will make them serve on building forces and in armies. They will no longer be free. (Samuel's description exactly depicts the situation at the time of Solomon.) Samuel's words cannot dissuade the people. They want a king to govern them and to lead them in battle.

Having no alternative, Samuel assembles the people to choose their king. They make their choice by drawing lots. The first lot fell for the tribe of Benjamin. The second lot fell to the Benjaminite family of the Matrites. The third and final lot fell on Saul, the son of Kish. Upon hearing this, Saul ran to hide. When found, he is brought before the people who proclaim, "Long live the king!"

In the pro-monarchy source, Samuel is portrayed as a seer (*ro'eh*) or prophet (*nabi'*). A Benjaminite, Saul, is sent by his father to search for his asses. When the journey proves unsuccessful, Saul remembers there is a man of God in the land of Zuph. So he sets out to enlist Samuel's help.

Samuel has received a vision from Yahweh telling him that Saul is coming to him. He will become prince (*nagid*) over Israel. He will "rule over Israel" and "save them from the hand of the Philistines" (1 Samuel 9:16). When Saul arrives, Samuel invites him to dine. During the meal, he informs Saul his father's asses have been found.

The next morning, as Saul is leaving, Samuel takes a vial of oil and pours it over Saul's head declaring that he shall reign over Israel. Further, Samuel announces signs that will occur to verify that the Lord has chosen Saul prince over Israel. As he travels homeward, Saul receives the Spirit of Yahweh.

There are differences in the two narratives of the institution of the monarchy. The pro-monarchy source shows that the monarchy is initiated by Samuel with the approval of the Lord. The anti-monarchy source stresses the displeasure of the Lord at the thought of a human king. Therefore, the king is selected by lot which allows the choice to fall to chance. Both stress a theology of kingship which realizes Yahweh is king of Israel. Therefore, any human king must represent Yahweh's will for the people.

The Reign of Saul

In the early years of Saul's reign, the Spirit leads him to serve faithfully as "prince" over Israel. He is faithful to Yahweh's commands. As Saul becomes more accustomed to his position, he begins to follow his own will. He interferes with the priests (1 Samuel 13:8-15) ordering a sacrifice to be offered, rather than waiting for Samuel as he had been commanded. During the war with the Amalekites, Saul explicitly violates the command of Yahweh. According to the *herem,* every living being must be put to the sword as a thank offering to Yahweh. (This is hard to understand since Yahweh has commanded, "Thou shalt not kill." In this period, the commandments of the decalogue apply only to those bound by the covenant. Enemy nations are outside the limits of the covenant.)

After conquering the Amalekites, Saul spared Agag, the Amalekite king, and the best sheep, oxen, fatlings, and lambs. He would not destroy them (1 Samuel 15:8-9). He kept the animals apart in order to offer sacrifice to Yahweh. Acting as prophet, Samuel speaks Yahweh's will to Saul. Samuel tells him "Yahweh wants obedience, not sacrifice." Because he has rejected the word of the Lord, the Lord now rejects him as king.

Yahweh now commands Samuel to go to the house of Jesse in Bethlehem to choose a successor to Saul. Samuel obediently fills his horn with oil and proceeds to Bethlehem. As Samuel is entertained by Jesse, his elder sons appear. None of them are the chosen of the Lord. Finally, Jesse's youngest, David, who was tending sheep, appears. Immediately, Samuel recognizes he is the one and pours the oil over his head. This anointing with oil marks the elevation to kingship. For this reason the kings in srael are called "the anointed of Yahweh," in Hebrew *(mashiah yahweh)*, the messiah of Yahweh.

Although David is anointed king, Saul remains. However, the Spirit of Yahweh has left Saul to rest on David. The remaining chapters of the First Book of Samuel tell of the struggle between David and Saul and the friendship that develops between David and Jonathan, Saul's son. That struggle reached its climax on the mountains of Gilboa where, in the face of certain defeat, Saul falls upon his sword and dies.

The Reign of David

After quelling several movements to name Saul's son, Ishboseth, king, David becomes king of all Israel at Hebron. In that act, the monarchy preserved the charismatic choice of Yahweh for king, over heredity.

David's reign begins with the final defeat of the Philistines. This inaugurates a period of peace and expansion. During the reign of David, Israel's borders encompassed more territory than it ever would again in history. David then captured the Jebusite fortress of Jerusalem to become his capital. He builds his palace, and settles his court in Jerusalem. The ark of the covenant, the central symbol of Yahweh's presence among his people, is brought to Jerusalem.

Having centralized the government and built his house (palace), David resolves to build a house for Yahweh (a temple). In a key passage of the Old Testament, Yahweh responds to David's resolve. Through the prophet Nathan, he announces the Davidic dynasty (2 Samuel 7:4-17). Through a play on the word "house," Nathan prophecies that David's plan to build a temple (house) for Yahweh will be completed by his offspring. Instead, Yahweh plans to build a house (dynasty) for David. He will establish the throne of David forever. David's house will be eternal. The monarchy will no longer be determined by charismatic choice. From now on, it will be hereditary. The king, the messiah, will always come from the Davidic line.

This promise is closely linked to the choice of Jerusalem and the temple. Because David's line is eternal, many will believe that Yahweh will not strike his holy city Jerusalem, nor the temple where his presence dwells.

David's Kingdom is Divided

David is succeeded by his son, Solomon, after a lengthy period of infighting. Many of the northern tribes had backed Adonijah, another of David's sons. Solomon was different from his father. He had no reservations against taxing and conscripting the people of Israel to sustain the many building projects that marked his reign. The prophetic voice of the anti-monarchy source had spoken the truth.

Solomon was succeeded by Rehoboam, his son. At the beginning of his reign, people were disillusioned with the monarchy. They resented the taxes, they disliked the conscription. They longed for more freedom. So they came to Rehoboam to ask him to relent. His reply was a pledge to be stricter than his father had ever been. The result was immediate division of his kingdom. The ten tribes of the north seceded in 922 B.C.E. to form the kingdom of Israel. They chose Jeroboam, a general of Solomon who had fled to Egypt, to be their leader. The two remaining tribes formed the kingdom of Judah ruled by the Davidic dynasty. The glory of David and Solomon was fading.

The Assyrian Crisis

For nearly two hundred years, each kingdom went its own way. There was trade between them, and occasional alliances, and even intermarriage between the royal families. During the reign of Uzziah in the south and Jeroboam II in the north, there was again prosperity. However, it was short-lived. After the death of Jeroboam II, political unrest gripped the north. Five monarchs reigned during the five years following his death. When stability was achieved under King Pekah, the threat of an Assyrian invasion loomed over Israel. The Assyrian empire began to exercise its strength over neighboring nations around 740 B.C.E. Pekah sought strength through an alliance with his northern neighbor Syria. This alliance was known as the Syro-Ephraimite Alliance. (The largest portion of land in the northern kingdom originally belonged to the tribe of Ephraim. So many referred to Israel as Ephraim. Hence the term Syro-Ephraimite.)

As the north lapsed into political unrest, the south continued strongly under the Davidic rulers. There was anxiety over the Assyrian threat. Yet the greater threat came from Israel and Syria. The members of the Syro-Ephraimite alliance saw value in bringing Judah into their alliance. When Judah's king Ahaz refused, they decided to force Judah into the alliance. This precipitated the Syro-Ephraimite War (2 Kings 16, Isaiah 7).

As the northern armies march south, King Ahaz inspects the fortifications of Jerusalem and the water supply. The prophet Isaiah meets him and informs him not to worry about an attack from the north. Those two countries will surrender to Assyria. He reminds Ahaz that Judah has Yahweh's protection which was promised to David. Isaiah exhorts Ahaz to remain strong in his faith, and he will be strong (Isaiah 7:9). He gives Ahaz a sign. A child will be born (most likely a reference to the birth of Ahaz's own son, Hezechiah). Before this child has the ability to distinguish right from wrong, those two countries will be no more. This child is a sign of Yahweh's abiding presence in Judah. So his name shall be called Emmanuel which is Hebrew for "God is with us."

The Syro-Ephraimite War does not succeed in forcing Judah to join the alliance. Shortly afterward, Syria falls to the Assyrian armies (732 B.C.E.). About ten years later, the northern kingdom of Israel falls (721 B.C.E.). Isaiah's prophecy has come true.

With the fall of Israel and Syria, Assyria prepares to march into Judah. Hezechiah assumes the throne after his father's death. Since an Assyrian attack may be imminent, he investigates the fortification of Jerusalem along with the water supply. He protects the water supply by enclosing all areas where water flows into the city. Also, he has a tunnel dug underground for water. It stretches from the Spring of Gihon outside the city walls to the Pool of Siloam inside.

Hezechiah's precautions seemed to be of little avail in the year 701. The armies of the Assyrian king, Sennacherib, swept down through the regions of Judea destroying every city before them. Finally, the army was encamped around Jerusalem ready to mount the final attack. Suddenly, in response to Hezechiah's prayer to Yahweh, a large portion of Sennacherib's army is slain. He retreats to his capital city, Nineveh. Jerusalem had been delivered through intercession to Yahweh.

Hezechiah, his court and the people thanked God for the mighty act of deliverance. The promises to David concerning the eternity of the dynasty, city and temple were true. If there had been any time in the history of the monarchy that it was close to extinction, it was certainly 701. People realized that Yahweh would protect his king, his temple, and his holy city, Jerusalem. A theological interpretation of the events of 701 known as "royal Davidic theology" began to emerge.

The unilateral nature of the covenantal promises to David was manifest here. The protection of the monarchy, the city, and the temple are not contingent on the people's conduct. Exemplary behavior did not characterize the people of Judah before the invasion of Sennacherib; yet the city was spared. This would have major consequences in the remaining years of the monarchy.

Jeremiah and the Deuteronomic Reform

When Hezechiah died, Manasseh, his son, succeeded him. He was probably the most evil king to reign in Judah. His son, Amon, was not much better. Bolstered by the belief that Jerusalem was impregnable, these kings allowed every possible infraction of the covenantal laws of Sinai that could be imagined. Altars to foreign gods were erected inside, outside and on the roof of the temple. Cults to foreign gods thrived throughout Judah. The cult of Yahweh fell to the background. Festivals such as the Passover were not celebrated.

No change seemed imminent until late in the sixth century. Amon's son Josiah took the throne in 640 B.C.E. He did not agree with his father's attitude toward the covenant. Josiah's policy found support when a scroll was discovered in 622 B.C.E. during the renovation of the temple (See Chapter 4).

This scroll contained legal commands and sanctions which had been codified centuries earlier, and brought to Jerusalem by refugees from the northern kingdom. The document became the basis for the Deuteronomic reform. (Recall Scholars call this Deuteronomic from two Greek words *deuteros* meaning "second" and *nomos* meaning "law.") When Josiah received this scroll, he rent his garments and said, "Great is the wrath of the Lord that is kindled against us, because our fathers have not obeyed the words of this book, to do according to all that is written concerning us" (2 Kings 22:13).

Immediately, Josiah began a far-reaching reform to return Judah to the original practice demanded by the Sinai covenant. The law in Deuteronomy originated with the Sinai experience, which was bilateral. The favor of God was contingent upon the people's acceptance of the commands and stipulations in the law. When prophets like Jeremiah began to preach the Deuteronomic code, they met opposition from the people.

While the reforms of Josiah were being carried out, another enemy appeared in the region north and east of Judah, the Babylonian empire. As Babylon steadily made its move westward, prophets spoke of imminent destruction to Judah. They employed symbols of cauldrons boiling over from the north, almond trees being cut down, and other similarly graphic images. The people would not listen, recalling accounts of the Assyrian invasion of 701. They could not be persuaded to give up their evil ways.

The prophets tried to enforce the stipulations of the bilateral covenant of Sinai discovered in Deuteronomy. They exhorted the people to reform and return to the practice of the law while there was still time. If the people continued to refuse, they would fall before the Babylonian armies. On the other hand, the people hearkened to the unilateral promises to David to protect the city, temple and monarchy. What Yahweh had done before, he would do again.

The Babylonian armies marched toward Judah. In 597 B.C.E., the city walls were breached. All the learned and wise men including Jehoiachin, the reigning king, and his family were deported. Zedechiah, his brother, was set up as puppet king to rule in Jerusalem. The temple was sacked for its gold and silver. Yet the city was spared, the temple remained standing, and the king was still alive. Even this action did not motivate the people to return to the covenantal law.

To show how obsessed the people were with royal Davidic theology, Zedechiah in 589 B.C.E. withheld the tribute money from Babylon and sought alliance with Egypt. These actions caused the Babylonians to destroy much of Judea. Finally, in 587 B.C.E., they marched on Jerusalem, and burned the city and the temple to the ground. All those who were able were deported to Babylon. Many others fled to Egypt. These actions devastated the populace. The city was destroyed. The temple was destroyed. Yet the monarchy still remained. Royal Davidic theology was seriously questioned among many.

The Monarchy in the Post-Exilic Period

The Babylonian empire began to decline after 587. In a matter of years, it fell to the Persians under Cyrus the Great. Cyrus immediately began to return those who had been deported by the Babylonians to their homelands. The Jews therefore began to return to Jerusalem. The leader of the first returning exiles was Sheshbazzar, son of Jehoiachin, a legitimate heir to the throne. Soon after his nephew, Zerubbabel led a large number of exiles to Judea. The initial tasks involved rebuilding the walls and the temple. Most of the building in the city and the temple was completed by 515 B.C.E.

With the restoration of the city and the temple, and the presence of a legitimate heir to the throne, many wondered when the monarchy would be restored. Prophets of the post-exilic period, particularly Haggai and Zechariah, saw the restoration of the monarchy as imminent (Zechariah 6:9-15; Haggai 1:12-15). However, the Persian government was not so optimistic. Cyrus and his successors were interested in allowing people to live on their own lands, exercise their own customs, and practice their own religion as long as they remained subject to the Persian empire. Establishing an independent monarchy was out of the question. To be certain that any messianic aspirations in Judah did not get too far out of hand, the Persian government quietly removed Zerubabbel and withdrew political power from the Davidic house. That action insured that there would be no rebellion in Judah, and no monarchy.

It was clear to all in Judah that the monarchy would not be restored. How did this action affect the promise of the eternity of the Davidic monarchy? The throne of David did not exist any longer. Local political authority fell into the hands of the priests, while the class of scribes arose as the chief interpreters of the law in Israel. The scribes saw the word of Yahweh as eternal and true. The promises to David still were valid. If there was no monarchy now, the promise must be reinterpreted to affirm that there would be a monarch at some time in the future. The expectation arose that some day at some time a descendant of the royal line of David would re-establish the throne. This royal messiah would secure freedom from domination for the Jewish people.

This expectation was strong when Jesus began his ministry. The Roman government of Palestine was strongly anti-Jewish. Rome's enemies felt that it would be a good time for the messiah to come. Several anti-Roman partisans claimed to be the messiah. They gathered groups of followers, but soon were dispelled by Rome (Acts 5:34-39).

Study Questions

1) What is the meaning of Jotham's story? Does it apply to any situation today?
2) Describe the development of the monarchy in Israel. How does it move from charismatic to dynastic?
3) What is the theology of kingship expressed in the narrative of the rise of the monarchy?
4) Saul fails as king because he sacrificed rather than obey. Does the phrase, "It is love I desire not sacrifice speak at all to today?"
5) Compare David and Saul. How did they act? How did they end?

6) Discuss the effects of God's promise to David on the developing history of Israel's monarchy?
7) What effect did the removal of Zerubbabel have on the promise made originally to David?

Bibliography

Bright, John, *Covenant and Promise: The Prophetic Understanding of the Future in Pre-Exilic Israel,* (Philadelphia: Westminster Press, 1976).

Campbell, Antony F., *Of Prophets and Kings: A Late Ninth Century Document (1 Samuel 1-2 Kings 10),* Catholic Biblical Quartelry Monograph Series, Vol. 17, (Washington: Catholic Biblical Association of America, 1986).

Jarvis, F. Washington, *Prophets, Poets, Priests and Kings,* (New York: Seabury Press, 1974)

Mowinckel, Sigmund, *He that Cometh,* trans. by G. W. Anderson, (Nashville: Abingdon Press, 1954).

Sternberg, Meir, *The Poetics of Biblical Narrative: Ideological Literature and the Drama of Reading,* (Bloomington, Ind.: Indiana University Press, 1985).

Chapter 7

What Are They Saying About the Prophets?

When Martin Luther King delivered his famous "I have a dream . . ." speech in Washington in August of 1963, he was hailed as a prophet. Founders of major religions such as Judaism, Islam, Zoroastrianism, and Christianity have been called prophets. Well-known writers have been acknowledged as prophets in their time. What makes people see these individuals as prophets?

A general answer would be that they were able to cut through the shallowness of life and call attention to the central questions and issues of their day. Dr. King, in that famous speech, spoke of his vision for the future. At the same time, he challenged the leaders of the present to make that vision a reality. Founders of major religions are called "prophets" because they are seen as having a special relationship with the divine. Through this relationship, they become messengers of God to people of their own day. Authors are prophets because their writing speaks to their readers and challenges them to look into their being and rethink attitudes and prejudices.

Prophecy in Ancient Israel

The role of the prophet throughout history has been twofold—to challenge and to mediate. This characterizes the prophets of Israel. As early as the patriarchal period, Abraham appeared as a prophet. Abraham convinced Abimelech, King of Gerar, that Sarah was his sister rather than his wife. The Lord appeared to Abimelech to urge him to return Sarah to Abraham who is called prophet, *nabi,* because he will intercede (Genesis 20:7). Later in Exodus, Moses protested that he was a man of poor speech. The Lord responded by appointing Aaron as prophet, *nabi,* for him (Exodus 7:1). In both cases, the prophet is mediator. One could easily translate the Hebrew *nabi* as "spokesman" since both Abraham and Aaron appear as "spokesmen" in those narratives.

During the desert wandering, the Spirit descended on the seventy elders at the tent of meeting. After they received the Spirit, they

67

prophesied. However, two of those who had been chosen to receive the Spirit were not present. They, too, received the Spirit and prophesied (Numbers 11:24-30). Here, prophecy is a gift or charism bestowed by the Spirit. As a result, prophesy was accompanied by unusual behavior. Prophets would fall into a trance, experience some sort of rapture, or find themselves caught up in a state of frenzy. These manifestations are "ecstatic prophecy."

A band of ecstatic prophets preceded by lyres, tambourines, flutes, and harps met Saul after he was anointed king (1 Samuel 10:5-7). The prophets of Baal whom Elijah encounters on Mt. Carmel are a more extreme group of ecstatic prophets (1 Kings 18:21-46). They "hop around the altar," "call loudly to their god," and "slashed themselves with swords and spears until blood gushed over them." Such is the frenzy that can accompany ecstatic prophecy.

The Book of Deuteronomy distinguishes the prophet who mediates and challenges from the fortune teller, soothsayer, diviner, charmer, or caster of spells (Deuteronomy 18:10-11). These must be removed from Israel. They are an abomination to the Lord. The prophet, on the other hand, holds a place of honor. The author continues applying the title "prophet" to Moses. "A prophet like me [Moses] will the Lord, your God, raise up for you from your own kinsmen" (Deuteronomy 18:15). This prophet will receive the words of the Lord in his mouth as Moses did. He will be mediator of Yahweh's commands to his people. If he chooses to speak his own word as the word of Yahweh, he shall die. The prophet's word is verified when it is fulfilled (Deuteronomy 18:22).

The Deuteronomic injunctions concerning prophets produced a double direction in Israel. The prophets of Israel were judged against these Deuteronomic ordinances. During the post-exilic period, a second tendency appeared, an expectation based on the promise of a prophet like Moses. When the voice of prophecy began to fall silent, people looked for the prophet whom Moses promised would mediate the Word of God.

Language Used to Designate Prophets

The primary word which the Hebrew Bible uses to designate prophets was *nabi*. Scholars agree that *nabi* is derived from an ancient Akkadian word meaning "one who is sent" or "one who

68

is a spokesman." The prophet as *nabi* is a person who is chosen and sent by another as their spokesman. The prophet in Israel is, therefore, one who is chosen and sent by Yahweh to communicate his will. The Septuagint, or Greek translation of the Old Testament, chose to translate *nabi* by the word *prophetes*. This word is a compound derived from the preposition *pro* which means "in place of" and the verb *phemi* which means "to speak." Thus, *prophetes* is one who speaks in place of another.

A second word, *ro'eh,* meaning "seer," is used in the Hebrew Bible to describe prophets. This term does not occur as frequently as the term *nabi*. Yet, some prophets were designated *ro'eh*. As a result, emphasis on the prophet as one who could foretell the future developed. It should be emphasized that foretelling the future is not the essential component of prophecy. The prophet, *nabi,* essentially communicated Yahweh's will to the people in the present. Even though the prophetic word might contain an announcement of future sanctions, the essential prophetic word is addressed to the present.

Origins of the Institution of Prophecy

During the early history of Israel, Moses typified the prophet as mediator and challenger. He heard the word of Yahweh on Mt. Sinai, and communicated it to the people. He challenged them to follow the ways of Yahweh through the covenant. He also was their leader through the Exodus, Sinai, and wilderness experiences.

Moses became a prophet through God's choice. He neither inherited it nor gained it by election or choice of the people. Moses was therefore a "charismatic leader." When he died, his role of leadership role fell to Joshua through the choice of Yahweh. Most of Israel's leaders before the monarchy were "charismatic leaders" chosen by Yahweh to guide, challenge, and direct his people by mediating his will.

When the monarchy was established, the leadership role was assumed by the king, but the prophet remained the challenger, mediator and spokesman of Yahweh's will. Prophecy existed side by side with monarchy. Samuel, the first prophet of the monarchy, is called both *nabi* and *ro'eh* in the pro-monarchical source. 1 Samuel 9:9 notes that he who was called a prophet *nabi* was formerly called a seer, *ro'eh*. Samuel thus assumes the role of advising Saul, Israel's first monarch, concerning the will of Yahweh. Yet, as we have seen in the history of the monarchy, Samuel's advice was at times heeded and at times ignored by Saul. Saul seemed to view Samuel more as advisor than as prophet, *nabi*.

Yet he continually realized his need for Samuel's counsel. After Samuel's death, Saul is in distress, ready to give up since he cannot get counsel. He goes to the witch of Endor begging her to conjure up the ghost of Samuel so he can consult with him. In this act, Saul recognized Samuel's role as advisor. However, he did not recognize Samuel's role as prophet *nabi* mediating the commands of Yahweh. In consulting a medium, Saul violated the will of Yahweh. Yet, even in death, Samuel's response to Saul mediates the will of Yahweh. He remains *nabi*. Through Samuel, Yahweh confirmed that Saul would lose the kingdom. It would be given to David. Saul will die on the next day. Saul is doomed by the ghost of Samuel.

When David becomes king, Nathan serves as prophet *nabi* for him. As we saw in the unit on the monarchy, the relationship between David and Nathan was good. David respected Nathan's role, mediator of Yahweh's will. Despite some shortcomings, David followed that will.

The prophecy of Nathan in 2 Samuel 7, which established the Davidic house as a dynasty, completed the separation between the leadership role of the prophet and the mediation role of the prophet. The monarchy, which had assumed the leadership role, became hereditary. The prophets, on the other hand, remained charismatic.

Cultic and Court Prophets

The rise of individual prophets such as Samuel and Nathan, who were closely associated with the king, did not diminish the role of ecstatic prophets. Many of these groups known as *bene' hanebi'im,* or "sons of the prophets," gathered around one of the more famous prophets. 1 Samuel 19:20 describes a group gathered around Samuel. Eventually these "guild prophets" or "professional prophets" as they also came to be known, settled at sanctuaries where they inspired religious fervor among the people. Others appeared at court where they sparked a nationalistic spirit among the people. Thus, the *bene' ha nebi'im* became diversified into "cultic prophets" and "court prophets." Among both groups a tendency toward personal gain became dominant. Many of these prophets would color their prophecy so people would hear what they wanted to hear.

The "cultic" and "court" prophets earned their living through prophecy. If the word the prophet spoke was not pleasing to the hearer, the prophet would not profit from his prophecy. For example, the prophet Amos prophesied the death of King Jeroboam. He was promptly ejected from the royal sanctuary at Bethel in the northern kingdom of Israel by the priest Amaziah. Amos was told to "earn his bread by prophesying elsewhere" not in the sanctuary of Bethel (Amos 7:12-13). Amos left. However, one who depends on earning his living at a sanctuary might easily be co-opted to shade the wording of his prophecy to make it more pleasing to the ears of the hearers.

The story of the prophet Hananiah in the book of Jeremiah (Jeremiah 28) provides another example of a "court prophet" who is willing to co-opt the Word of God for his own gain. The incident takes place during the reign of Zedekiah 597-587 B.C.E.). The first invasion of the Babylonians has taken place (598 B.C.E). The temple has been plundered and the first deportation to Babylon is finished. Yahweh commands Jeremiah to forge a wooden yoke for oxen and place it over his neck. This is to be a graphic demonstration of the situation the Babylonians are forging for Judah. If Judah submits to that yoke, she will live in peace. The "court prophet" Hananiah replies speaking a "prophecy of Yahweh":

"I will break the yoke of the king of Babylon. Within two years I will restore to this place all the vessels of the temple of the Lord which Nebuchadnezzar, king of Babylon, took away from this place to Babylon. And I will bring back to this place Jeconiah, son of Jehoiakim, king of Judah, and all the exiles of Judah who went to Babylon" (Jeremiah 28:2-4).

Jeremiah responds that in time past prophets have prophesied war, pestilence and famine. However, the prophet who prophesies peace is recognized as speaking the word of the Lord only when his prophecy is fulfilled (cf. Deuteronomy 18:22).

An infuriated Hananiah wrenches the yoke from Jeremiah's neck and breaks it, repeating the prophecy of deliverance for Judah. Later, the word of Yahweh comes to Jeremiah announcing that because Hananiah has broken the wooden yoke, an iron one will be forged. Jeremiah rebukes Hananiah for falsely raising the hopes of the people. He has not spoken the word of Yahweh; rather, his own word, which he knows the people want to hear. As a result, Jeremiah prophecies that, within the year, Hananiah the prophet will die for his rebellious preaching against the word of Yahweh. The text ends declaring that in that very year Hananiah the prophet died. He received the punishment prescribed in Deuteronomy 18:20 for one who prophecies falsely.

Elijah, Ahab and Jezebel

After David's reign, the prophetic voice in Israel appeared to fall silent. We do not hear of another charismatic spokesman for Yahweh of the stature of Nathan until Elijah (c. 860 B.C.E.). Elijah came from the town of Tishbe in Gilead in the Northern kingdom of Israel. He prophesied during the reign of King Ahab (874-853 B.C.E.).

Two themes dominate the cycle of narratives concerning his prophetic ministry—1) a drought, and 2) his reprimand of Ahab. The cycle begins with the prophet telling Ahab that for several years no rain will fall except at his word (1 Kings 17:1). The drought that follows provides the backdrop for the first narratives in the Elijah cycle.

The first story in the cycle shows Elijah entering the town of Zarephath where he meets a widow who lives with her only son (1 Kings 17:7-16). The drought has caused a famine. The widow has resigned herself to the fact that she and her son will die when the little oil and flour she has is used up. Elijah requests some food. The woman shares what she has. As a result, Elijah speaks the word of Yahweh that the flour will never run out, nor the jug of oil go dry until rain comes upon the earth. A second narrative (1 Kings 17:17-24) tells of the miraculous resuscitation of the widow's son by Elijah. This prompts the widow to recognize Elijah as a "man of God" from whose mouth the word of the Lord truly comes forth. Both of these narratives from the cycle are miracle stories. Many of the narratives in this cycle have influenced the way that the narratives of Jesus' ministry have been compiled.

The second theme in the cycle concerns Ahab, king of Israel, who was married to a Phoenician princess, Jezabel, daughter of the Phoenician King, Ethbaal. This marriage was part of a political alliance between Israel and Phoenicia arranged by Ahab's father, Omri. When Jezebel came to live with her new husband, she brought much of her religious heritage with her. Consequently, several shrines to the god Baal appeared in Israel. Jezebel was so strong about her religion that she ordered prophets of Yahweh executed. Ahab, weak as he was, cooperated with Jezebel. After these murders, Ahab meets Elijah. He addresses Elijah as a "disturber of Israel" (1 Kings 18:17). Elijah responds to this with a stern rebuke of Ahab's cooperation with his wife. He points out that Ahab's actions oppose the commands of Yahweh (1 Kings 18:18). This is a greater disturbance to Israel than any word or act of Elijah.

The narrative of Elijah's encounter with the prophets of Baal on Mt. Carmel (1 Kings 18:21-40) follows. This narrative combines the two themes of the cycle. Elijah graphically uses the drought to illustrate his rebuke of Ahab for setting aside the commands of Yahweh. The narrative depicts a contest between Elijah and Jezebel's prophets of Baal. The object is to prove whose god is really God. Each must pray to their god to send fire down to consume a sacrifice which has been prepared. The narrative is full of irony and sarcasm. Elijah taunts the prophets to shout louder when they receive no answer. Their god might be asleep or away on vacation. As they get to prophetic frenzy, they still receive no answer because, as the author ironically notes, "no one was listening" (1 Kings 18:29).

Before Elijah begins his prayer to Yahweh, he rebuilds the altar to Yahweh which had been desecrated. Then, he orders that the sacrifice be doused with water three times until the water flows from the sacrifice covering the ground below. He then prays to Yahweh to demonstrate that he truly is God. Yahweh answers sending fire down to devour the sacrifice. The people proclaim "Yahweh is God." Elijah orders that the prophets of Baal be seized and killed. (Since these prophets are not part of the covenantal people, Elijah is not bound by the covenant toward them.)

Elijah flees to Mount Sinai where he encounters Yahweh. At Sinai, he realizes that Yahweh must be found in the quiet and silence of one's own being rather than in the hustle that goes on outside one's being. Yahweh commands Elijah to anoint a new king in Syria, Israel's northern neighbor. He is also to anoint Jehu son of Nimshi, as king of Israel, and Elisha, son of Shaphat as prophet to succeed him. These commands prepare for the fall of the House of Omri (Ahab and his family) at the hands of Jehu.

The most serious violation of the covenant is Ahab's murder of Naboth (I Kings 21:1-29). Naboth owned a vineyard which Ahab wished to buy as a vegetable garden. The vineyard was located outside his palace. When Naboth protested because the vineyard was his ancestral inheritance, Ahab went to his room and sulked. Jezebel upbraided him for his childish behavior. She had Naboth killed and laid claim to the property. When Ahab took possession of the property he encountered Elijah. Elijah declares that because Ahab and Jezebel have spilled the blood of Naboth, their blood will also be spilled. That prophecy was fulfilled in the blood purge through which Jehu wrenched the kingdom from the house of Omri.

Elijah and his successor Elisha followed Nathan and Samuel using their calling as prophet to correct and rebuke the monarchs when they did not follow the covenant. The prophets who followed them continued that tradition, calling the king to follow the covenant. But, they also include the people in their exhortations.

The Social Prophets of the Northern Kingdom

After Elijah and Elisha, the voice of prophecy again fell silent for about one hundred years until the latter part of the reign of Jeroboam II (793-753 B.C.E.). Jeroboam II's reign was a period of prosperity in Israel. The rich lived a lifestyle that oppressed the poor. The prophets Amos and Hosea called Israel back to their original covenantal promises. These prophets were the first to write down their prophecies. Their message was social justice. Amos cites several examples of abuse of the poor. Businessmen want the sabbath to end so they can open their stores. They fix their weights and measures to give less while increasing the price. The result is that the poor customers suffer while the rich merchants gain (Amos 8:4-8). The court is also challenged by Amos. Their lifestyle oppresses the weak (Amos 4:1).

Both Amos and Hosea challenge the people's attitudes toward worship. There is too much emphasis on the externals of worship. It lacks internal intention. They bring their sacrifices and pay their tithes; but it means nothing. Famine, drought, winds and pestilence have been means Yahweh has used to show them their attitudes are wrong. The people have failed to hear. Therefore, through Amos, Yahweh declares he will treat them in his own way. The people are to prepare to meet their God (Amos 4:12) in the great day of the Lord when all will come to an end.

Hosea emphasizes the need for Israel to adhere to the covenant. Using his own experience of a wife who has forsaken him for another, Hosea shows that Israel's actions in forgetting the covenant parallels her to an adulterous woman who forsakes Yahweh for another. This image alludes to the law that a husband is not to take back an adulterous wife (Deuteronomy 24:4). Yet, in a beautiful poetic passage of the Old Testament, Yahweh declares that he will allure Israel until she realizes that he is better than foreign gods. Then he will take her back if she repents (Hosea 2:20-25).

Isaiah and the Court of Judah

Shortly after Amos and Hosea in the North, Isaiah of Jerusalem began his ministry during the reign of king Ahaz of Judah. Isaiah had a deep loyalty to the Davidic monarchy, and the temple. During the Syro-Ephraimite crisis, Isaiah, being a close confidant of Ahaz, had access to the royal palace. At the siege of 701, he provided counsel to Hezekiah. His loyalty to the Davidic line colors all his writing. Isaiah's message to both monarchs was to follow the covenant and remain firm in their faith. Yahweh's promises to David would be fulfilled. A major part of Isaiah's prophetic preaching to Ahaz and Hezekiah was covered in the section on the monarchy.

Isaiah also challenged the people to return to the covenant. During his ministry, the northern kingdom fell to the Assyrians. Isaiah used this to urge the people of Judah to remain faithful to the covenant, or a similar fate awaits them. Using a familiar drinking song, he shows that many in Judah, especially priest and prophet, spend too much time drinking and singing drinking songs (Isaiah 28:7-9). They counsel the people to enter into alliances which will be damaging to Judah. Unless they change, their drinking songs will become the rhythmic beat of the conqueror leading them off to slavery. Isaiah views this misguided counsel as a covenant with death.

Unless priests, prophets, and people remain loyal to the covenant, they will fall to the Assyrians who are coming toward Jerusalem.

Jeremiah, the Personal Prophet

About one hundred years after Isaiah, Jeremiah, son of Hilkiah, received the call to be prophet. Initially, Jeremiah is unwilling since he could not speak well. With the assurance of Yahweh's presence, he is able to speak. His message was a call to repent. The historical situation of Jeremiah's ministry was discussed in the chapter on the monarchy (Chapter 6). Therefore, we shall look at the person Jeremiah here. He spoke Yahweh's word to the people with deep feeling and conviction. Jeremiah suffered much both internally and externally for the Word of God.

Jeremiah is the only prophet in the Old Testament who reveals his struggles as a prophet. There are four personal reflections of Jeremiah which are known as the "Confessions of Jeremiah" (Jeremiah 15:10-21; 17:14-18; 18:18-23; 20:7-18). In these, he provides insight into his struggle with faith in Yahweh *vis-a-vis* his mission. The emotion Jeremiah shows toward Yahweh appears nowhere else in biblical literature.

The final confession (Jeremiah 20:7-18) sums up the themes of these writings. It opens with an outcry that Jeremiah has been tricked by Yahweh, and what's worse he has let it happen. He has accepted Yahweh's call to prophecy. It has gained him nothing but violence, outrage, derision, and reproach. He is so weary preaching the word of Yahweh that he decides to quit.

That decision leads to an internal struggle. The call to preach the word rises like a fire in his bones on one side. The weariness of people who refuse to listen counters on the other side. Jeremiah is in the middle. Those who claimed to be his friends have become his sworn enemies searching for the opportunity to bring him down.

Jeremiah is able to see a brighter side. He recalls his call to be a prophet. Yahweh had promised him that he would be with him. Realizing that those who are plotting against him may have momentary success, they will not be able to conquer him. He knows that Yahweh will take vengeance on those who seek to destroy him. For this he praises Yahweh.

The confession changes radically to a depressing tone. Jeremiah curses the day he was born, and the one who announced his birth

76

to his father. Jeremiah wishes that he had died in the womb. He questions "Why did I come forth from the womb?" We see the depths of depression which the experience of rejection has brought Jeremiah.

Through the confessions, Jeremiah reveals himself as one who is deeply committed to his mission. He shows he is a person of deep faith. Through that commitment, he is able to cope with the rejection that comes from those who hear his message.

Jeremiah lived to see his preaching fulfilled in the destruction of Jerusalem by the Babylonians in 587 B.C.E. Jeremiah's response to the destruction is found in the book of Lamentations. To sum up, Jeremiah lived during difficult and trying times in the history of Israel.

The destruction of the city of Jerusalem caused radical changes for Israel. The prophets no longer called for a return to the covenant. Their message changed from exhortation to encouragement. Developments in prophecy during the Exile and the period after the Exile will be the topic of our next unit.

Study Questions

1) What makes one a prophet? Do prophets exist today?
2) What is a charismatic leader? How is the prophet a charismatic leader?
3) Describe the relationship of prophecy to the Israelite monarchy?
4) Examine the Hananiah incident (Jer 28:1-16) in light of the deuteronomic principles concerning prophecy (Deut 18:15-22). What is the measure against which the truth of prophecy is measured?
5) Describe the prophetic vision of Elijah.
6) What is the message of the prophets of social justice. Does that message still speak today?
7) How do the careers of Isaiah and Jeremiah exemplify the prophetic mission?

Bibliography

Heschel, Abraham J., *The Prophets: An Introduction,* 2 vols. (New York: Harper and Row, 1962).

JAMES P. McILHONE

Mays, James Luther, and Achtemeier, Paul J., (eds), *Interpreting the Prophets,* (Philadelphia: Fortress Press, 1987).

Petersen, David L., (ed.), *Prophecy in Israel: Search for an Identity,* Issues in Religion and Theology, Vol. 10, (Philadelphia: Fortress Press, 1987).

Van Rad, Gerhard, *Old Testament Theology, Vol. II, The Theology of Israel's Prophetic Traditions,* trans. by D.M.G. Stalker, (New York; Sheed & Ward, 1961).

Chapter 8

What Happened
to the Voice of the Prophet?

With the destruction of Jerusalem, the end of the temple and the
monarchy, one might think the voice of prophecy would fall silent,
but in the years following these events, the prophets continued
to speak strongly. However, prophecy began a transformation.
Traditions from the sages or wise men of Israel entered the prophetic world. The prophets of this period were exposed to foreign
influences more than ever before. These influenced the manner
in which they communicated the Word of God. In this unit, we
shall examine how these influences transformed the pre-exilic institution of prophecy.

Prophecy During the Exile (587-539 B.C.E.)

The primary emphasis of exilic prophecy was encouragement
and consolation for the exiles who thought they had lost everything.
The prophet Ezekiel provided the basis for a new community. The
temple stood at the center, and power rested in the hands of the
priests. Deutero-Isaiah, on the other hand, pictured Yahweh coming
to ransom his people from exile, establishing them once again as
a nation among nations.

Ezekiel—Ezekiel, a member of the priestly line, was the first to
prophesy outside of the land of Israel. He was deported to Babylon
in the first deportation of 597 B.C.E. His ministry in Babylon spans
the years 594 B.C.E until sometime after the destruction of
Jerusalem.

Drawing on the images he finds around him in Babylon, Ezekiel
narrates several bizarre visions which relate the destruction of
Jerusalem. Most significant among these are his own call narrative
(Ezekiel 1:1-2:9), and the vision of the glory of Yahweh leaving
the temple (Ezekiel 8:1-4, 10:1-20).

After the destruction of Jerusalem, the tone of Ezekiel's writing
changes. In the parable of the sheep (Ezekiel 34:1-16), he blames
the leadership for the city's destruction. He also provides hope

for the exiles in the vision of the dry bones (Ezekiel 37:1-14). This vision is a particularly well-known section of the book. It depicts Judah as an army that has been slaughtered whose bones lie scattered on fields. As Yahweh takes those bones and molds them into a strong vibrant army, so will he mold Judah into a nation. He will again breathe his Spirit into her so she can live.

The hope this vision gives is strengthened in the visions of the final part of the book. In these chapters, Ezekiel presents a blueprint of the new Judah, a nation with God at its center (Ezekiel 40-48). For this reason, some have called him the father of Judaism.

Second Isaiah—This prophet has this unusual name because his writings are contained in the scroll of the prophet Isaiah. Scholars agree that the scroll of Isaiah as it exists today is not the work of a single author. The first 39 chapters are the work of the seventh-century prophet, Isaiah of Jerusalem. The next section, chapters 40-55, date from the period of the Exile. Since there is no clue to the identity of their author, they are attributed to "Second Isaiah." The remainder of the book, chapters 56-66, comes from the period after the Exile. They are attributed to "Third Isaiah."

Second Isaiah presents a vision of hope to the exiles in Babylon. He reaffirms the power of the "word" of Yahweh while emphasizing his mercy and forgiveness. He portrays Yahweh as an oriental potentate coming across the desert to rescue his people and bring them home. This signals the end of their time of slavery (Isaiah 40:1).

Second Isaiah sees Yahweh as the Redeemer of his people. His actions remind the prophet of creation and the Exodus (Isaiah 51:9-11). Employing several images from creation and the Exodus, he sees Yahweh's redeeming act as a new creation and a new Exodus.

Second Isaiah believes Yahweh is the universal God of history. He is not restricted to Israel. All powers in the world have a role to play in the execution of God's plan. He designates Cyrus, king of Persia, "messiah" or "anointed one" since Cyrus will be the human agent through whom Yahweh will accomplish the redemption of his people.

The most well-known section of his writings are the "Servant Songs." These four canticles (Isaiah 41:1-4; 49:1-6; 50:4-19; and

52:13-53:12) speak of the servant of Yahweh. This servant vicariously suffers for the people. There is much debate about the identity of this servant. In the first two songs, Second Isaiah identifies the servant with Israel. This would make sense since, during the Exile, Israel was suffering. However, in the last two songs the servant becomes an individual. Recently some scholars have noted that the difference extends to the thought and vocabulary within Chapters 40-55. Some are advancing a theory that Isaiah 40-49 are from one author, while 50-55 are the work of another. We would, therefore, end up with four different writers in the scroll which bears the name Isaiah.

Others hold that the servant is a "corporate personality" representing Israel in those songs. The exact identity of this servant will probably never be ascertained. Later generations would see in this servant, who innocently suffers, a model for Jesus. The servant songs would provide the early Christian community with arguments from the Jewish scriptures to justify the death of Jesus.

Prophecy in the Post-Exilic Period

When the Decree of Cyrus (539 B.C.E.) ended the Exile, the exiles began to return home. The prophets Haggai, Zechariah, Third Isaiah, and Malachi urged the people to rebuild the temple in Jerusalem. They also offered hope for the reestablishment of the monarchy.

Haggai and Zechariah—The message of Haggai and the first part of Zechariah was two-fold—complete the temple, and re-establish the monarchy. Haggai was straightforward in presenting this message. Zechariah presented it through visions—the four horsemen (Zechariah 1:7-11), the new Jerusalem (2:5-17), the lampstand (4:1-3; 11-13), the flying scroll (5:1-4), the flying bushel (5:5-11), and the four chariots (6:1-8). These visions, in the style of Ezekiel, often confused the reader. Zechariah is innovative in using visions in this manner. These innovations provide a basis for future apocalyptic literature.

The style of the second part of Zechariah changes radically. There are no visions, no temple, no mention of monarchy. Yahweh becomes the warrior who protects Israel against the foreign influences. Zechariah 9:9 depicts this warrior king coming to his people. With other nations, he may be a warrior; yet when he comes to his own people he is meek, bringing peace.

Malachi and Third Isaiah—The writings of Malachi and Third Isaiah date from a later period. They lack the stress on building the temple or re-establishing the monarchy in Haggai and Zechariah. These prophets stress social justice. Judah has been restored and prosperity has returned. The people have fallen back into the old ways. These prophets challenge them to recall their immediate past and change their ways. They were poor and slaves once. Now that they are rich and free, they must have compassion on those less fortunate.

These prophets also provide insight into some difficulties that have appeared in the governing structure. After the Exile, Judah was governed by the priests. As with any government, there was positive and negative opinion. Malachi represented a group which is against the temple and its priests. Most of his writing details abuses in the temple, giving warning to its priests. Third Isaiah concurs (Isaiah 66:1-2).

Prophecy is Transformed Into Apocalyptic—After Malachi and Third Isaiah, prophets seemed to disappear. However, the institution of prophecy did not die. The practical side of prophecy was assumed by the sages who counseled people on right living. This wisdom tradition will be the topic of the next chapter. The visionary side of prophecy continued in apocalyptic.

The Apocalyptic Literary Genre

Israel's literature before the prophets related the historical development of the people. Most of this literature would be the strands that eventually formed the Pentateuch. Prophetic literature acknowledged the importance of history. The prophets used the historical situation of the people to challenge them to evaluate their way of life in light of the covenant.

Prophetic literature also used visions to allow the people to see beyond the confines of this world. It also allowed people to see a future where unfulfilled hopes would find fulfillment. This visionary aspect was more noticeable in the later prophets. After

Third Isaiah and Malachi, a new form of writing emerged which depended on visions to communicate its message. This is the literary form of "apocalyptic." The name derives from the Greek verb, *apokalypto*, "to reveal."

Apocalyptic literature began to appear around the end of the second century B.C.E. The most important apocalypse in the Old Testament is the Book of Daniel. John Collins has defined an apocalypse as:

"A genre of revelatory literature with a narrative framework in which a revelation is mediated by an otherworldly being to a human recipient, disclosing a transcendent reality which is both temporal, insofar as it envisages eschatological salvation, and spatial insofar as it involves another supernatural world" (Collins, *Apocalyptic Imagination*, p. 4).

There are three elements which are necessary for an apocalypse: a person who reveals, a person who receives the revelation, and the content of the revelation. The person who reveals is usually a supernatural being such as an angel, or God himself, through the media of vision, dream, etc. The one who receives the revelation is a human being. In many cases, the recipient is the person whose name the apocalypse bears. The content of the revelation emphasizes the temporal or the spatial.

Depending on the emphasis, therefore, there are two major types of apocalypse. An apocalypse emphasizing the temporal provides a review of history up to the present. The Book of Daniel is an example of a temporal apocalypse. An apocalypse emphasizing the spatial narrates a journey which the recipient takes outside of this earth into the heavenly regions. There are spatial apocalypses in the Bible. An example of one would be the early part of the first book of Enoch.

Like its ancestor, prophecy, apocalyptic addresses a historical situation of crisis. However, apocalyptic literature addresses that crisis situation in a maner radically different from its ancestor.

Prophecy arose in conjunction with the monarchy and addressed the religious situation of the monarchy constantly calling people back to proper observance of the covenant. Failure to observe the covenant meant punishment from Yahweh in the form of invasion, destruction and exile. The historical situation from which apocalyptic emerges is much different. The Persian Empire was conquered by Alexander the Great of Macedonia. Alexander's aim was to bring the world under a common leadership with a common culture. His successors were successful in varying degrees in making his vision a reality.

During the second century B.C.E., the Jews were under the rule of Antiochus Ephipanes IV. He wanted to impose Greek customs, religion and political structure on all nations under his dominion. The Jews, therefore, were forced to forsake their traditions and embrace Greek culture and religion. This generated opposition from the Jews. The most vocal opponent of Antiochus' policy was the family of Hasmon later known as the Maccabees. On one occasion, Greek soldiers waited until the sabbath to ambush group of Jews who were hiding in caves. They knew that Jewish law prohibited fighting on the sabbath(1 Maccabees 2:32-38). The Maccabees vowed that this would never happen again.

This situation is opposite to the prophets. Vengeance comes upon those who follow the law and live according to the ways of Yahweh. How can this be possible? This is this basic question that apocalyptic literature attempts to answer. The deuteronomic understanding (follow the law and prosper, violate it and suffer punishment) does not hold up. A new understanding must emerge. There is a need for consolation and vindication. The situation makes the Jews seem so powerless that they cannot envision any solution in the current world situation.

The apocalyptic writers speak of a new situation in which the persecutor will be punished and those who endure the persecution will triumph. This punishment and triumph will not take place in the current world; the current aeon will be destroyed. Vindication will occur in another world. Therefore, the concepts of afterlife and resurrection dominate apocalyptic literature.

Since apocalyptic literature developed to bring consolation to those who suffer persecution, it is possible that it can fall into the hands of the persecutor. Therefore, it must be written in a style which will be understood by those it is intended to console. Yet its message must remain hidden from all others, especially the persecutors. Through bizarre imagery, numerology, and visions, the author of an apocalypse accomplishes this. To an unsuspecting eye, apocalyptic appears like a fairy tale; yet when one knows the true meaning of the images, it communicates a crucial message. Apocalyptic writers will mask their identity by making the recipient of the revelation a key person from the past, e.g., Enoch, Moses, Elijah or Daniel.

Interpretation of Apocalypses—As a result of this literary device, interpreters will argue concerning the time of composition for apocalypses. Some prefer to see these apocalypses as prophetic. They view the events contained in an apocalypse as actual revelations which occurred in the lifetime of the recipient. Enoch, Elijah or Daniel received a revelation which must be kept secret until the final days which are to come. The apocalypses are interpreted solely with a message for the present of the interpreter. This understanding is shared by many millennarianist and fundamentalist groups.

Others prefer to see the pseudonymous nature of the recipient as a means of hiding the identity of the author. It was common in the ancient world to attribute a work to another more famous person to gain authority for the writing. (It is curious to note that in the ancient world placing another's name on one's work was a compliment. Today that is considered slander or plagiarism.) In this view, the apocalypses do not speak primarily to the distant future; rather they address the present situation of the author. When an apocalypse contains a narrative of past history, that narrative is impeccably correct until it reaches the present situation of the author. When an apocalypse moves toward the future, that precision vanishes.

Reading Apocalyptic Literature

How should one approach an apocalyptic text? First, it is necessary to have a clear understanding of the historical situation of the apocalypse. For the Old Testament and most of the intertestamental apocalyptic writings, that situation will be the persecution of Antiochus Epiphanes IV. A historical survey of that period can be found in 1 and 2 Maccabees. When the historical situation is known, read the text paying close attention to the imagery, the numerology, and the cross-references since much of the imagery comes from other books of the Bible. Check the cross-references to see what the image meant in its original context. How does that shed light on its use in the apocalypse?

Since biblical apocalypses emphasize the temporal, the interpreter must attempt to develop a correspondence between the historical events and the literary images. Once this correspondence has been established, the reader can ask how the images communicate hope and consolation to the historical situation. This is the message which the apocalypse intends for the readers. When this process has been completed, it is possible to determine the meaning of the apocalypse for the current day. An example from the Book of Daniel will illustrate this process.

The Book of Daniel—The best example of the apocalyptic genre in the Old Testament is the second half of Daniel (Daniel 7-12). The first part of Daniel is a series of stories which were brought together to prove that Israel's religion would triumph over other pagan religions. They provide a picture of life in the Persian Empire and Hellenistic period. Many scholars feel that these tales date from the Persian period. However, they reached their current form during the Hellenistic period. A brief look at the dream in Daniel 2 will introduce us to the tales. This passage will provide necessary historical background for interpreting the apocalyptic vision of Daniel 7.

Nebuchadnezzar's Dream (Daniel 2:28-45)—This tale is set in the court of Nebuchadnezzar, king of Babylon during the Exile. Nebuchadnezzar had a dream which disturbed him. He commands those who interpret dreams to tell him the meaning of the dream. To be certain that the interpretation is true, the interpreter must tell the king his dream and then provide the interpretation. None of the Chaldeans can meet Nebuchadnezzar's conditions.

Daniel, a captive of Judah, is brought to the king. He is able both to tell the king his dream and to interpret it. In the dream, Nebuchadnezzar saw a statue composed of gold, silver, bronze, iron and a mixture of iron and clay. A stone hewn from a mountain struck the feet of the statue causing it to crumble into fine sand. The stone becomes a large mountain that fills the earth (Daniel 2:31-35).

The interpretation that Daniel provides shows that the statue represents four successive kingdoms. Nebuchadnezzar, the Babylonian, is the head of gold. After Babylon falls, another nation will take over. This would be the Medes who are the chest and arms of silver. The Medes will be conquered by another nation, Persia, who is represented by the belly and thighs of bronze. Finally, Persia will fall before a nation which is strong as iron. Since iron entered the Middle East at the hands of the Dorians, a Greek race, the iron feet represent the Greek empire of Alexander the Great. After Alexander's death, his empire soon split between his generals. The largest regions were given to Ptolemy (South and West, i.e., Egypt) and Seleucus (North and East, i.e., Syria). The feet are iron mixed with clay representing the Ptolemaic and Seleucid regions of Alexander's Empire. They are united by marriage, yet no more united than iron and clay can be mixed.

The stone that destroys the statue and becomes a large mountain represents a kingdom that Yahweh will set up. This shall be an eternal kingdom which will put an end to all other kingdoms. This will occur in the future. The history of the kingdoms is accurate until the time of the Ptolemies and the Seleucids. The focus then turns to the future. There is no solid evidence to verify it. This vision appeared in its present form sometime during the period of the Ptolemies and Seleucids.

The Vision of the Beasts Rising from the Sea (Daniel 7)

The apocalyptic vision of Daniel 7 relates the same historical sequence as the vision of Nebuchadnezzar in Daniel 2. The scene is set in the court of Belshazzar, king of Babylon. Daniel himself has a dream which terrifies him. The dream begins with the four winds of heaven stirring the sea—a reminder of creation (Genesis 1:1-3).

From this primordial sea emerge four immense beasts—a lion with eagle's wings, a bear raised on one side, a leopard, and a fourth different from all the others. This fourth beast had iron teeth and ten horns. Soon an eleventh horn breaks its way through three of the existing horns. The eleventh horn spoke with arrogance.

The scene then switches from the primordial sea to heaven where thrones are set up. The ancient one, an elder clothed in snow white garments seated on a throne of fire, convenes the court to pass judgment on the beast. This image comes from the inaugural vision of Isaiah (Isaiah 6:1-2) and the throne vision of Ezekiel (Ezekiel 1:26-28). The beast is slain and its body thrown into the fire to be burned. The other beasts lose their dominion but live for a short time.

One "like a son of man" (human being) appears riding the clouds of heaven to present himself before the ancient one. Again we see the influence of Ezekiel (Ezekiel 1:28). The ancient one bestows dominion, glory, honor and power upon the one like a son of man. He is made king of an everlasting kingdom (Daniel 7:1-15).

If the dream of Daniel 2 really does provide background for understanding this vision, the interpretation of Daniel 7 must be similar to the interpretation of Daniel 2. Daniel 7:17 gives a concise interpretation. The four beasts are four kingdoms. Daniel 2 showed four kingdoms. We can assume that the beasts represent Babylon, Media, Persia, and Greece. One of the major symbols of Babylon is a lion which has the wings of an eagle. Similarly the bear symbolizes Media, and the leopard symbolizes Persia.

The fourth beast makes war on the "Holy Ones of the Most High" until the ancient one pronounces in favor of the "Holy Ones of the Most High" who then possess the kingdom. These "Holy Ones" are represented by the "one like a son of man." The fourth beast is a kingdom which shall subdue the whole earth. This is the empire of Alexander the Great. The ten horns are ten kings who will be followed by an eleventh. This eleventh king will speak against the Most High and oppress the "Holy ones of the Most High" for a period of three and one half years.

Consulting a list of the Hellenistic kings who had influence over Judah, the eleventh king in succession from Alexander is Antiochus Epiphanes IV. A detailed history of these events can be found in the First Book of Maccabees 1:16-40. 1 Maccabees 1:41-63 shows how Antiochus instituted prohibitions against the Jewish religion. Since Antiochus has begun a persecution of the Jews which continues to the time of the author, Antiochus is the little horn.

The text continues promising consolation to those who endure. Yahweh, the Ancient of Days, will put an end to the power of this king. Kingship and power will be given to the "Holy Ones of the Most High." The "one like a son of man" is not an individual. He represents the people of Israel.

In this vision supernatural forces fight each other waiting for judgment from the heavenly throne to resolve the conflict. The final section of the Book of Daniel will present three more visions which speak to the situation of Antiochus' persecution.

Chapter 8 will use a vision of a ram and a he-goat. Chapter will be a reinterpretation of a prophecy of Jeremiah (Jeremiah 25:11-12), and Chapters 10-12 will employ a complex symbolic vision to detail the complexities of the Maccabean wars and the persecutions of Antiochus.

In the period after the Exile, the institution of prophecy found itself transformed into apocalyptic. The situation of the people of Israel changed radically. They became a subject people which produced several new problems that needed theological answers. The problem of innocent suffering became key in sparking the development of apocalyptic. That literary genre continued into the New Testament period in the Book of Revelation. In two later chapters, we shall look at that work as an example of Christian apocalyptic.

Study Questions

1) How do the visions of Ezekiel and Second Isaiah for the post-exilic community differ? Why?
2) Examine the servant songs of Second Isaiah. What can you conclude concerning their meaning? concerning the identity of the servant?
3) How do the post exilic prophets speak to the social and political situation of their day?
4) What is apocalyptic literature? How is it related to prophecy? How it is related to deuteronomic theology?
5) How should we read apocalyptic literature?

Bibliography

Collins, John J., *The Apocalyptic Imagination: An Introduction to the Jewish Matrix of Christianity,* (New York: Crossroads, 1984).

Collins, John J., *Daniel with an Introduction to Apocalyptic Literature,* The Forms of Old Testament Literature, Vol. 20, (Grand Rapids: Wm. B. Eerdmans, 1984).

Hanson, Paul D., *The Dawn of Apocalyptic: The Historical and Sociological Roots of Jewish Apocalyptic Eschatology,* revised edition, (Philadelphia: Fortress Press, 1979).

Hengel, Martin, *Judaism and Hellenism,* trans. by John Bowden, (Philadelphia: Fortress Press, 1974).

Morris, Leon, *Apocalyptic,* (Grand Rapids: Wm. B. Eerdmans, 1972).

Russell, D. S., *Apocalyptic: Ancient and Modern,* (Philadelphia: Fortress Press, 1978).

Russell, D. S., *The Method and Message of Jewish Apocalyptic,* (Philadelphia: Westminster Press, 1964).

Chapter 9

Who Is the Wise Man in the Old Testament?

For centuries, people have traveled miles, climbed steep mountains and faced many difficulties to encounter someone who lives very simply, yet exerts tremendous power over people. They seek this person to put to him the deepest questions of life. Such are shamans, or wise men. They give practical advice to those who seek to live their lives the "right" way.

Every culture has had such wise men. Wisdom sayings have been preserved by the Egyptian Pharaohs. The Chinese philosopher Lao-Tzu is credited with practical sayings such as "A wise man has no extensive knowledge; he who has extensive knowledge is not a wise man." Indian culture in the Pali Canon, Suttapitika, declares that wisdom is the art of correct living. "The wise and moral man shines like a fire on a hilltop, making honey like the bee, who does not hurt the flower." Israel was not without its sages and books of wisdom sayings. This chapter will examine the origin and development of the "wisdom tradition" in Israel.

The Origins of Wisdom in the Family

The earliest rules and codes of proper living developed in the family. For family life to prosper, rules were necessary. In these rules, the wisdom tradition originated. They emphasized the need for discipline, "The rod of correction imparts wisdom, but a child left to himself disgraces his mother" (Proverbs 29:15). They showed the importance of peace and harmony within the family, "Better a dry crust with peace and quiet than a house full of feasting, with strife" (Proverbs 17:1). Many of the wisdom sayings in the Old Testament point to family origin. The address, "My son . . ." is very common in this literature.

Influences on Israel's Wisdom

The development of Israel's history and culture has shown that it is essentially a mixture of the cultures of the nations surrounding Israel and the cultures that dominated Israel. Aspects of all these combined with the theological perspectives of Mosaic covenantal religion to produce a unique Israelite culture. Since the wisdom tradition is a part of that culture, we may suspect outside influence on the Israelite wisdom tradition, especially from Egypt and Babylon who were noted for their wisdom literature.

Egypt—Wisdom in Egypt was *sebayit*. This was the teaching of the Egyptian monarchs and ministers. It was usually utilitarian and pragmatic. The earliest forms of *sebayit* was given by a father to his son. Later the teacher addressed pupils to teach proper norms of conduct. Proper conduct demands that one live by the divine order preserved by God, *Maat*. When one infringes on *Maat,* it demands revenge. To live right, everyone must integrate themselves into *Maat*. When this does not happen, chaos reigns.

Family norms soon spread to the royal court. The monarch Khety III of the tenth dynasty admonished his son, Merikare on right living: "Be skillful in speech, that you may be strong; it is the strength of the tongue, and words are braver than all fighting . . . a wise man is a school for the magnates, and those who are aware of his knowledge do not attack him."

Egyptian wisdom also stressed the negative in life. This has been described among later scholars as *weltschmerz wisdom,* wisdom to address the "tiredness of life." These writings present a person who is questioning the life situation in which he finds himself. This wisdom provides consolation to those who are tired of living. For the Egyptians, afterlife was the purpose of existence. Therefore, when life seems overwhelming, the Egyptian sage would counsel, resign to the afterlife. The *Dispute over Suicide* is an example: "Death is in my sight today. Like the recovery of the sick man, like going out into the open after a confinement. Death is in my sight today. Like the odor of myrrh, like sitting under an awning on a breezy day.

Mesopotamia—Mesopotamian wisdom developed in a manner similar to Egypt. Beginning in the family, it also grew in the royal court. Mesopotamian wisdom literature took the form of proverb, fable, satirical dialogue and precept. Mesopotamian wisdom contains mandates for proper living. For example, the tales of Ahikar: "Let your mouth be controlled and your speech guarded; therein a man's wealth—let your lips be very precious. Let insolence and blasphemy be your abomination; speak nothing profane nor any untrue report. A tale-bearer is accursed.''

Exhortations concerning governance of the tongue are a major theme in wisdom writing of all ancient cultures. Mesopotamian wisdom also spoke to questions like the suffering of the righteous. The story of Shubshi-mashre- shakkan tells of a righteous man who endured calamities, sought consolation in three dreams, and finally received an answer from Marduk. Marduk's answer is that salvation is found in humble submission to Marduk. The story stresses the mystery surrounding how a god exercises justice. The route of humble submission is not the only one proposed by many sages. Some feel that there is no sufficient answer to the question. The only satisfactory solution is death.

The cultures influencing Israel had a double focus in their wisdom traditions. 1) They sought rules for correct living, proverbs which contained help for practical living. 2) They looked at the difficult questions of life, suffering and death, to provide various answers to these questions.

Wisdom in Israel

Wisdom During the Monarchy—When the monarchy developed, wisdom moved from the home to the royal court. The sages of the court drew upon the wisdom of the surrounding cultures. Israel's early wisdom tradition contained very little that is specifically Israelite. Since the monarchy was linked to the temple in Israel, there was exchange among the sages, priests and prophets. The priest preserved rituals, and the various codes of law prescribed for the temple. The prophets were charismatic messengers who were sent to communicate the will of God to his people. The sage used experience to explain how one was to live correctly. Sages freely chose experiences which people could readily understand and used them to explain the proper ways of living.

A prime experience they used was the order in the universe. When natural phenomena occur, people interpret them. For example, when it clouds up, rain is expected. When the sap is in the tree, spring is near. When this natural expectation is not met, people are thrown off. The sage will take those facts and show that when we act in a certain way, people interpret and respond accordingly. When we change our mode of action, people will be thrown off. The sages used the example of clouds appearing. When the clouds appear with no rain, that is unusual. Applying that to human experience, people have a tendency to speak of their many accomplishments. When a person speaks, yet has not accomplished everything he says, the sage compares it to the cloud without rain (Proverbs 25:14).

The sages are bound by neither law nor history. This eventually becomes a source of friction between the sages and the prophets and priests. The clash between the prophets and sages becomes bitter in Isaiah and Jeremiah. Isaiah says: "Therefore once more I will astound these people with wonder upon wonder; the wisdom of the wise will perish, the intelligence of the intelligent will vanish" (Isaiah 29:14).

Similar sentiments are expressed toward the sages in other parts of Isaiah (Isaiah 5:21; 19:12; and 44:15) and Jeremiah (Jeremiah 51:57; and 8:9). These prophets see a connection between history and faithfulness to the covenant. The sage does not see this connection. The sage counsels the people to a good life regardless of history. The message of the sage in times of crisis would be more pleasant to the people than the message of the prophet. Hence, the negativity of the prophets toward the sages.

Wisdom After the Monarchy—When the monarchy was not reestablished after the Exile, the sages did not disappear as did the prophets. Wisdom continued to exist outside the context of the royal court. Much of the wisdom tradition was compiled during this period. Since Solomon had emerged as the prototype of the wise man, many of these compilations were attributed to Solomon. The Book of Proverbs begins "The Proverbs of Solomon, son of David, king of Israel . . . ." The Book of Ecclesiastes opens with "The words of the preacher, son of David, in Jerusalem. . ." The Song of Songs begins, "The song of songs which is to Solomon . . . ." One wisdom book, the Book of Wisdom is specifically attributed to Solomon.

The post-exilic period brought many changes to the institutions of Israel. Wisdom was no exception. In this period, power was assumed by the priests. Emphasis on the law (Torah) became more and more important. During those years, the sages used experience to make sense out of the chaos of the time. The wisdom which had its roots in the family became more and more prominent. The sages equated wisdom with the virtue of fear of the Lord: "The fear of the lord is the beginning of Wisdom" (Job 28:28; Psalms 111:10; Proverbs 1:7; 9:10; 15:33).

Success or happiness becomes knowing one's place before God and before one's fellow human beings. This is the result of living according to practical common sense, i.e., avoiding bad companions, jealousy and pride. The priests and the Deuteronomic writers would say that success or happiness is the result of following the commands of the covenant found in Torah. There is a parallel path to happiness. The person who lives the practical life of wisdom will achieve the blessings promised in Deuteronomy. In later Judaism, this parallel becomes an equation. The Torah or the law becomes equated with wisdom (Sirach 24:23-24), the Book of Baruch 4:1 declares, "She is the book of the precepts of God, the law that endures forever. All who cling to her will live, but those who die will forsake her." (This excerpt is taken from a hymn to Wisdom, Baruch 3:9-4:4. In that hymn, Wisdom is explicitly identified at 3:12. Therefore, all the pronouns used thereafter must refer to Wisdom. Wisdom therefore becomes equated with the precepts of God and the enduring law.) The rewards of wisdom become the rewards of following the covenant: life, length of days, large family, success and prestige.

Israel's Wisdom Literature

The Books of Proverbs, Job, Ecclesiastes, Sirach, Wisdom and a few of the Psalms have been grouped together as the "wisdom literature." The basic literary form of these works is the proverb. A "proverb" is a sentence usually composed of two parts which exhibit parallel structure. For example, "The fear of the Lord is the beginning of wisdom; but fools despise wisdom and discipline" (Proverbs 1:7). The two parts of the proverb express a similar thought. The first part declares that wisdom is found in "fear of the Lord." The second reiterates that the fool, the one who refuses wisdom, despises the very things that fear of the Lord inculcates— wisdom and discipline.

This Israelite wisdom literature shows the same double focus as the wisdom writings of Egypt and Mesopotamia. The Book of Proverbs contains guidance and rules for practical living. The Book of Job examines the suffering of the righteous one. The Book of Ecclesiastes treats the problem of meaninglessness in the world.

The Book of Proverbs—Proverbs is the earliest of the Old Testament wisdom books. It is composed of short sayings meant to edify, in Hebrew, *mashal.* There are several collections of proverbs which make up the book. Two of these collections, Proverbs 10:1-22:16, and 25:1-29:27 trace their origin to the court of Solomon. Both begin with an explicit reference to Solomon. Other collections date from the time of Hezekiah, and the post-exilic period. The final edition of the book probably appeared toward the end of the 5th or the beginning of the 4th century B.C.E.

The Book of Proverbs was collected to enable the people of the post exilic period to adapt religion they had known so well to a new political situation without monarchy. The role of guiding the community which had belonged to the king, messiah, or anointed one was now transferred to wisdom. Proverbs 8:15-16 states, "By me (*wisdom*) kings reign and make laws that are just; by me princes govern and all the nobles who rule the earth." Without a king, wisdom can still rule. Through this, Wisdom acquires many of the characteristics that once had belonged to the Messiah. The author of Proverbs clearly sees the role that had previously been performed by the messiah falling to wisdom.

In Proverbs 1:20-33 and Proverbs 8, a development takes place. Wisdom speaks as a person. As scholars term it, wisdom is personified. In these hymns, especially Proverbs 8, Wisdom is transcendent, and closely related to Yahweh.

"The Lord created me at the beginning of his work, the first of his acts of old. Ages ago I was set up, at the first, before the beginning of the earth. When there were not depths I was brought forth, when there were no springs abounding with water" (Proverbs 8:23-24).

The translation "The Lord *created* me . . ." is problematic given the original Hebrew. The Hebrew verb *qanah* which is used here, primarily means to "acquire," or "buy." This text really says the Lord acquired wisdom. The next phrase "at the beginning of his work" is also difficult, since the Hebrew word, *derek,* has the primary meaning of "way," or "road." It can also be used to describe a way of behavior or "activity." Therefore, the best translation would be, "The Lord acquired me at the beginning of his activity.'' In any case, wisdom has a primary role in the creative activity of Yahweh.

The Book of Job—The Book of Job takes up the theme of the suffering of the righteous person and its consequences on one's attitude toward God. The book was compiled during the Exile and restoration. The Exile was viewed as a punishment of those who had forsaken the covenant. That punishment was meted out on everyone in Israel. In the aftermath of the devastation of the Exile, the question of why those who had tried to follow the covenant were punished with those who didn't must have been asked.

The purpose of Job is to show that there may be a wider concern in the mind of God than mere retribution when suffering enters into the world. The author draws on the story of a righteous man, Job, who was familiar to his readers from the prophecy of Ezekiel (Ezekiel 14:14-20). Ezekiel shows that if Job were in a land which was unrighteous, when God struck the land for its unrighteousness, *he* would be saved by his righteousness. Four punishments are listed which would ravage the land—famine, desolation by wild beasts, the sword and pestilence. In each of the four cases, Ezekiel reiterates that Job would be saved because of his righteousness.

The author of Job takes this frame and adds another trial, the death of Job's family. Job endures all those trials, yet he never loses his faith. This sets the scene for the entrance of three friends who come to console Job. Their consolation becomes an attempt to see what Job did wrong to incur such a terrible punishment. Each of the friends is applying the Deuteronomic theology of reward and punishment to Job's situation (Job 2:1-31:40).

Job points out that his friends have distorted the situation. *He* has not done any wrong to merit this lot. Thinking as they do, they do not address his feelings. Job is correct in this. However, when it comes to Job's attitude toward God, he is not correct. Job is searching for a meaning behind his suffering. The answer that God gives to Job is that the ways of God are many times incomprehensible to human beings. God has a view of reality that is much wider than any of us can see. Therefore, when we experience what we cannot understand, we must be willing to submit to God in faith (Job 31:1-41:34).

The prologue of the book shows clearly that Job is not a pawn in the hand of God. God is convinced of Job's faithfulness, and he trusts him to remain faithful. Job, for his part, must seize this opportunity and remain faithful to Yahweh. In the face of his lot, Job does not accuse Yahweh of injustice; rather, he submits providing a magnificent testimony of his love for God. Job illustrates the lesson that it is very easy to "love God" when things are going well, but how easy is it to "love God" when the chips are down?

Ecclesiastes—The Book of Ecclesiastes addresses the problem of meaninglessness in human life. Ecclesiastes gets its name from the opening lines of the book, "The words of the Preacher...." Preacher in Greek is *Ecclesiastes,* in Hebrew it is *Qoheleth,* both appear as names of the book. The first words of the Preacher sum up the tenor of the book: "Vanity of vanities," says the Preacher, "Vanity of vanities, all is vanity. What does man gain by all the toil at which he toils under the sun?"

The theme of the book is the transitoriness of human life. A note of skepticism pervades the book. That skepticism arises from the author's experience. Similar to Job, Ecclesiastes strikes out at the theory of divine retribution. Human dominion over creation extends even to a dominion over the creator. God has been placed in a box, as it were. He can act only in manners that are consistent with human understanding of God.

In treating wisdom, wealth, desire, folly, toil and obedience, Qoheleth finds everyone to be wanting. There is a set way of the world and nothing can be done to change it. "What is crooked cannot be made straight, what is lacking cannot be numbered" (Ecclesiastes 1:15). This is the author's experience. The answer Qoheleth gives views the situation from God's point of view. This allows God to break out of that box and have his freedom restored. God will act as he sees fit, and human beings do not have to understand the reasons behind his actions.

Wisdom in the Hellenistic Period

During the Hellenistic period, Greek philosophy exerted influence upon Israelite wisdom literature. The personified wisdom of Proverbs becomes an independent existence. As a result, transcendent wisdom becomes inaccessible. God alone knows wisdom. The Books of Sirach and the Wisdom of Solomon are two Old Testament texts which manifest the Hellenistic influence on the wisdom tradition.

The Book of Sirach—The earliest title for this book was the "Wisdom of Ben Sira." The book was probably written sometime between 200 and 175 B.C.E. Its author was Jesus ben Eleazar, ben Sirach (Sirach 50:27). The text that exists today is a translation of the original text of Ben Sirach into Greek. This translation was made around the year 132 B.C.E by Sirach's grandson who prefaced the translation with a foreword.

"Such a one was my grandfather, Jesus, who, having devoted himself for a long time to the diligent study of the law, the prophets, and the rest of the books of our ancestors. . . . I arrived in Egypt in the thirty-eighth year of the reign of King Euergetes, and while there, I found a reproduction of our valuable teaching. I therefore considered myself in duty bound to devote some diligence and industry to the translation of this book" (Prologue Sirach).

From the text of Sirach, we can determine that ben Sira was a conservative advocate of the aristocracy of Jerusalem in 200 B.C.E. The book is written to defend the religious practices and the cultural heritage of Judaism from the onslaught of Hellenism. To counter the Hellenistic claim that true wisdom can be found only in contemplating the good, or in philosophical inquiry, ben Sira seeks to show all, whether Jew or Greek, that true wisdom resides in Israel because the origin of true wisdom is none other than Yahweh himself.

A look at the twenty-fourth chapter of Sirach should provide a good introduction to the general theme and style of the entire work. The first thing that is noteworthy about Sirach 24 is its dependence on previous Old Testament passages. The hymn of wisdom in Proverbs 8 and the creation narratives of Genesis 1-2 provide the backdrop for this hymn in praise of wisdom. Yet Sirach adds a new twist to the text. Wisdom now comes from the mouth of the Most High, sings her own praises and, searches for a dwelling. The literary form of the hymn is aretology which is a hymn of self praise by a divine being. It is common in Hellenistic literature.

Following the introduction (Sirach 1:1-2), the hymn falls into two parts, Wisdom's speech (Sirach 1:3-22) and Sirach's commentary (Wisdom 23-34). The speech of Wisdom narrates how Wisdom came from the mouth of the Most High and dwelt on a pillar of cloud. She explores the universe seeking a place to dwell. Finally, she finds a dwelling in Jacob, ministering before the Creator in the holy tent. There are allusions to this hymn in the prologue to the Gospel of John where the *Logos* or Word which comes forth from the mouth of God takes a part in creation, and searches for a place to pitch its tent.

The commentary applies all that has been said concerning Wisdom in the hymn to the book of the Most High's covenant, the law or Torah, making explicit the equation of Torah and Wisdom to show that it is through the law that people achieve wisdom. And it is by practical living of the law that a person becomes truly wise. Thus, for the author of Sirach the greatest treasure of wisdom is the revelation granted by the Lord to his own special people.

The Wisdom of Solomon—The wisdom of Solomon is a late off-shoot of the Jewish wisdom tradition. Dated sometime in the late second century, it is the last of the Old Testament books to be written. The use of philosophical speculation and syllogistic argumentation points to an origin in Alexandria. Since the author of Wisdom attempts to link Platonic philosophy with the Jewish faith, some have thought that the great Jewish philosopher Philo was the author; yet that is probably not the ase. The author appears to be a Jew of the *diaspora* who lived in Alexandria. He wrote the work to defend his religion against the pagan ideas that were infiltrating from the Hellenistic philosophical milieu. In other words, he uses the philosophical training he has received to combat the pagan ideas that very philosophical training proposes.

The book of Wisdom can be divided into three parts—the book of eschatology (Wisdom 1:1 - 6:11), the book of wisdom (Wisdom 6:12-9:18), and the book of history (Wisdom 10-19). A look at the first part of the book will give a sense of the whole work. It begins and ends with an exhortation to judges and kings concerning wisdom, righteousness, sin, immortality and death. These are the major themes that the book addresses.

The wicked reject righteousness and immortality. They feel that death is the end. Therefore, the only course of action during life is to enjoy oneself even at the expense of others. The just man, on the other hand, preaches against the sins of the ungodly. He deserves to be called Son of God. The wicked plot against the just man and God does not rescue him. Therefore, there is no divine assistance. However, that argument is predicated on the fact that the just one must be rescued in this life.

The text continues (3:1) to show that the victory of the wicked in the death of the just one is merely illusionary. They have passed into immortality. The just are in the hands of God and no torment shall now touch them. What seems for the unjust their moment of victory becomes the moment of their defeat. The theme of victory being turned into defeat is taken up by early Christian authors when they wish to defend the death of Jesus against the Jews. Jesus will become the just one whose death in defeat will be turned to victory.

The Book of Wisdom, the last work of the Old Testament, has shown a continuation of the transformation of the Jewish wisdom tradition under the influence of Platonic philosophy. In the work of the great Jewish philosopher Philo of Alexandria that transformation will continue. Philo will identify wisdom with *logos* thus completing the triad—wisdom, law, *logos*. This triadic identification will become very significant as Christian wisdom will take shape in the New Testament.

Study Questions

1) What is wisdom in the biblical context? What is wisdom in the context of the ancient world?
2) How is wisdom the property of the common person?
3) What do we mean by the 'personification' of wisdom?
4) What is the relation of wisdom to creation?
5) How does Job challenge the deuteronomic history?
6) What is the influence of Greek philosophy of Israelite wisdom?
7) Where do we find wisdom in the world today?

Bibliography

Bergant, Dianne, *What are they saying about Wisdom Literature,* (New York: Paulist Press, 1984).

Crenshaw, James, *Old Testament Wisdom: An Introduction,* (Atlanta: John Knox Press, 1981).

JAMES P. McILHONE

Murphy, Roland E., *Wisdom Literature: Job, Proverbs, Ruth, Canticles, Ecclesiastes, and Esther,* The Forms of the Old Testament Literature, vol. 13, (Grand Rapids: Wm. B. Eerdmans, 1981).

Rankin, O. S., *Israel's Wisdom Literature,* (Edinburgh: T & T Clarke, 1964).

Skehan, Patrick, *Studies in Israelite Poetry and Wisdom,* Catholic Biblical Quarterly Monograph Series, Vol. 1, Washington: Catholic Biblical Association, 1971).

Van Rad, Gerhard, *Wisdom in Israel,* trans. by James D. Martin, (Nashville: Abingdon Press, 1972).

Chapter 10

The Gospels:
Who Wrote Them and Why?

The center of the Christian faith is the person Jesus Christ. People have, for centuries, wanted to discover as much as possible concerning his life. Unfortunately, there has been little material concerning him preserved outside the canonical gospels of the New Testament.

Since they form the major body of information concerning Jesus, they have been held in high esteem by Christians through the centuries. There have been positive and negative effects to this. The gospels are a means through which later generations share in the Jesus experience. They express the faith of those who walked the earth with him. This is good. However, as we move further and further away from this experience, these documents can cease being vehicles which lead to Jesus, the object of faith. They become the object of faith themselves. This is not good.

When the gospels become an object of faith, people view them as static. They see them as documents which describe *exactly* what happened in Jesus' time. The evangelists were eyewitnesses who wrote down exactly what they saw. There was no developing understanding of Jesus' identity by the early Christian community. This position is held by many conservative fundamentalists today.

When scholars say that John's portrait of Jesus is more developed than Mark's, these people become disturbed. When they are told that the miracles might not have happened exactly as they are narrated, their faith is shaken. The object of their faith, the gospel text, is becoming inexact. If some aspects of the gospel narratives do not conform to the actual situation of Jesus, then how can we know what is factual and what is not? More significantly, how can we know that anything in the gospels is factual and true?

Biblical scholarship in the past two hundred years has shown that the gospels are portraits of Jesus which express the developing understanding of the early Christian community. The varied portraits of Jesus that the gospels provide show that He was experienced differently by different groups. Putting all the portraits

103

together, one can develop a full picture of Jesus that can speak to the experience of later generations.

The key to understanding the gospels, therefore, is the realization that they are vehicles through which the early church expressed its experience of Jesus, the object of its faith. The gospels did not bring about faith, they built and enhanced it. Viewing the gospels in this manner, we allow them to reveal not only Jesus, but also the struggles and consolation that the early communities faced from faith in Jesus.

Given this background, it is possible to address some questions concerning the gospels. Who really wrote them? What are some characteristics of the communities which produced them?

Who wrote the Gospels?

When one reads the gospels carefully, it is clear that several facts the modern reader seeks to know were of no interest to the authors. Not one of the authors provides any information concerning their identity in the gospel texts. There is a tradition that Matthew was a tax collector called by Jesus. Yet when that event is narrated in Matthew, he provides no clue that he is speaking of himself. He gives the tax collector the name Levi.

Mark is identified in tradition as John Mark, cousin of Paul, and young son of the family who hosted Jesus and the apostles for the last supper. Many hold that he has left his autograph in the peculiar incident of the young man who runs away at the arrest of Jesus (Mark 14:51-52). If that were the case, it was a mighty peculiar way to identify oneself.

Luke plainly states his purpose for writing a gospel. He identifies the patron for whom he writes the gospel (Luke 1:1-4). Yet he never identifies himself. Tradition identifies him with Luke, the physician, who was a companion of Paul (Col 4:14). John also clearly states his purpose in writing (John 20:31). But he also gives no clues to his identity. Tradition has identified him with John, the son of Zebedee, a disciple of Jesus.

Based on evidence from the gospel texts, there are no clues concerning their authors. Then how did Matthew, Mark, Luke and John become identified as the authors of the gospels? The earliest text which lists the authors of the gospels is a fragment from the writings of Papias, a second-century bishop of Hieropolis. He lists Matthew, Mark, and John as authors of gospels. Irenaeus, bishop of Lyon in the late second century, states that Luke was the author of the third gospel. Papias and Irenaeus presumably express the tradition of the early church concerning the authors of the gospels. That evidence, however, does not make them the actual authors of the gospels.

The communities which produced the four gospels each grew up around eyewitnesses to the Lord. These eyewitnesses preached to their community and shared their experience of the Lord. Their preaching would build the faith of the community. As they grew older, their preaching was written down. These documents formed the basis for the gospel texts as we now have them. Whatever way that process might have taken place, it is clear that the traditions preserved in the gospels derive from eyewitness testimony. It is most likely to those eyewitnesses that the gospels are ascribed. [It is curious to note that the ascriptions say "according to . . ." not "by. . . ."]

What Did the Evangelists Want to Communicate?

Besides leaving no clue as to their identity, the authors of the gospels placed little importance on several facets of the Jesus experience which modern readers seek to know definitively. They saw themselves communicating faith experiences, not biographical data. For example, although the names of Jesus' parents are mentioned several times in the gospels, it is significant that the Gospel of John does not name Jesus' mother although she plays a significant role in the text. Nor does the Gospel of Mark name his father.

The Gospels of Matthew and Luke have narratives of Jesus' infancy, yet those narratives do not give the reader an exact time for Jesus' birth. All four gospels disagree concerning the length of Jesus' public ministry. Matthew, Mark and Luke appear to have a ministry of one to two years; while John would necessitate a ministry of two to three years. Matthew, Mark and Luke speak of only one journey to Jerusalem. While John has several trips during the public ministry. All the gospels state that Jesus died during Passover. Yet, they leave readers with no evidence which would pinpoint a specific year for his death. The modern reader cannot know exactly how old Jesus was when he began his public ministry, or when he died. These facts did not concern the authors of the gospels. Since we will consider the Johannine community in another chapter, we turn our focus now to the communities of Matthew, Mark and Luke in the remainder of this chapter.

The Gospel of Mark

Mark is accepted as the earliest of the gospels. Completed between 65 and 75 C.E., this gospel emerged from a mixed community. There were Jewish and Greek Christians. The discourse in Mark 13 shows that this community was experiencing trial from inside and from outside. The community was struggling to establish its identity as Christian over and against Judaism (Mark 13:9, 11).

Opposition from the Jews—The Markan community's experience of Jesus as divine (Mark 2:9; 10:18) became a source of friction between the community and the Jews. On the basis of Deuteronomy 6:4, the Jews claimed the community's understanding of Jesus was impossible. Jesus could not be divine since God is one. The Markan community also differed with the Jews concerning the kingdom of God. Judaism envisioned the kingdom of God as a universal dominion of God which would be inaugurated in the final days. The community experienced the kingdom already inaugurated in the action of Jesus. Through Jesus, God has acted definitively to establish his rule on earth.

The attitude of the Markan community toward the traditions and institutions of Judaism led to alienation from the Jews. Mark 7 shows the attitude of the Markan community to the legalism of the Jews. The interpretations of the Jewish law that have been promulgated by the Scribes and Pharisees have superseded the law itself. God's law has given way to human interpretation. This violates the very purpose of the law, bringing people to God. The weight of rabbinic law has made it a real burden to become close to God. The community, on the other hand, sees its relationship to God as an experience of intimacy and joy.

Opposition to the Temple—Analysis of Jesus' Jerusalem ministry in Mark (Mark 11-13) reveals an anti-temple stance in the community. When Jesus enters Jerusalem, he proceeds to the temple (Mark 11:11). His actions in the temple herald its end (11:15-16). The temple has not brought people closer to God. As in the days of Jeremiah, it has become a place where the people can perform empty rituals with no recognition of their relationship with God (Mark 11:17). The essence of their relationship with God is love. This must be the basis for worship. When one loves God and neighbor, it is more significant than the external temple ritual of burnt offerings and sacrifices (Mark 12:33).

Later, the support and upkeep of the temple takes the last coin from a poor widow (Mark 12:44). The end of the temple is predicted in Mark 13:1-2. At Jesus' arrest, the action of cutting off the ear of the high priest's servant illustrates the community's negativity toward the temple. Leviticus 21:21 prohibits anyone who has a blemish from coming near the sacrificial offerings—high priest or servant. Finally, the rending of the temple veil at Jesus' death marks the end of the temple economy. The temple has kept God separated from his people. In Jesus' death, that separation ceases. Through Jesus' Resurrection, the Markan community sees God as living and active in his people.

Trouble from within—The community is also warned concerning trouble from inside. False prophets and false messiahs will pretend to announce the return of the Lord. They will attempt to lead many astray. At the time the gospel was written, there was an expectation that Jesus would return soon. The community is warned about those who will usurp the position of Jesus and come to establish their own versions of the kingdom. Discernment is necessary lest the community be deceived.

Mark's Portrait of the Disciples

The Gospel of Mark presents a very negative picture of the disciples, Jesus' closest followers. As the narrative unfolds, the disciples become increasingly blind to the implications of the events they are experiencing. Represented by Peter, their spokesman, the disciples show their misunderstanding of Jesus' actions and words. They view Jesus' messiahship as fulfillment of the promises made long ago to David. He will re-establish the eternal monarchy of

David. When asked, "Who do people say that I am?" Peter answers, "You are the Messiah." (Mark 8:27-30). When Jesus counters announcing that he is going to Jerusalem to die, Peter is offended (Mark 8:32-33). Despite numerous attempts to correct these misconceptions (Mark 9:33-37; 10:35-45), the disciples never grasp the true nature of Jesus' mission. Jesus messiahship means giving his life in ransom for the many (Mark 10:45).

As he goes to his death, the disciples cannot remain awake with him in the garden. When the passion begins, they flee. They want no part of that mission. A group of women receive the good news of the Resurrection with the command to go and bring that news to the disciples in accord with Jesus' earlier promises (Mark 14:28). At the end of the gospel, those who seemed most to be on the inside with Jesus, the disciples, are really on the outside. Those who were outside, the women and those whom he healed, are on the inside understanding the significance of what had happened to them. The enigmatic words of Mark 4:11-12 have proven true.

It is possible that the negative view of the disciples in Mark must be interpreted in the context of the community's own experience. Such a view would come from a community which was having a problem in leadership. Just as the disciples are shown as weak and misunderstanding, it is possible that the leadership in the Markan community is weak and unclear as to their mission or even their understanding of Jesus' mission. That clarity of understanding must come from those outside the leadership positions.

The Gospel of Matthew

The Gospel of Matthew was written around 85 C.E. The Matthaean community was a mixture of Jewish Christians and Greek-speaking Gentiles. From the frequent use of Hebrew terms, and numerous citations of the Old Testament, the Jewish component of the community must have predominated. Matthew formally introduces the Old Testament citations with a formula, "All this happened to fulfill what the Lord had said through the prophet. . . ." These "formula citations" as they are known provide evidence from the Jewish scriptures for key doctrinal points in the gospel. The majority of these citations are in the infancy and passion narratives. The events narrated in those sections are the foundation of the community's faith. They are the points the community is being challenged on. Hence the necessity of evidence from the Jewish Scriptures.

The Structure of Matthew

Benjamin W. Bacon—A significant area of discussion in Matthean studies in recent years has been the structure of Matthew. For several decades in this century, Benjamin W. Bacon's structure for Matthew predominated in scholarship. In his work on Matthew, Bacon noted that the formula, "when Jesus had finished these sayings . . ." appeared five times in the gospel (7:28; 11:1; 13:53; 19:1; 26:1). Bacon used this formula to isolate five sayings-units; the Sermon on the Mount (5:1-7:27), the discipleship discourse (10:1-42), the parables discourse (13:1-52), the community life discourse (18:1- 35), and the eschatological discourse (24:1-25:46). Between these units, he found material which narrated miracles and other works of Jesus. Joining the narrative material to the discourses, he assumed that the author, Matthew, constructed his gospel around five books (3:1-7:27; 7:28-10:42; 11:1-13:52; 13:53-18:35; 19:1-25:46). The infancy narrative became a prologue to the five books, and the passion narrative an epilogue.

Through this structure, Bacon held that the Gospel of Matthew portrayed Jesus as the new Moses. The beginning of the first discourse, the Sermon on the Mount, confirmed this. When he saw the crowds, Jesus went "up on the mountainside" as Moses went up Mount Sinai. He "sat down." In the official teaching position of the rabbi, he taught the people. As Moses was the original teacher for Israel, Jesus now becomes the new Moses bringing the new Torah to the new Israel.

Reactions to Bacon's structure—For decades after Bacon first proposed this outline, scholars used it to justify many different portraits of Jesus. Recently, many began to find fault with Bacon's structure. Scholars became disturbed at relegating the passion and Resurrection narratives to the position of epilogue. They were the climax of the gospel. Further studies demonstrated that Bacon's neat division into five discourses was artificial. Evidence emerged to show chapter 11 was a discourse, and similarly chapter 23. Bacon had developed a structure and then divided the gospel to fit it.

Alternate Structures for Matthew

In Germany, Werner Georg Kümmel followed the same procedure as Bacon. He located a formula which was repeated through the gospel. Kümmel's formula was "from that time, Jesus began . . ." (Matt 4:17; 16:20). Using this formula, Kümmel arrived at an outline of Matthew which included four major sections:

1) Prologue (1:1-4:16),
2) the Proclamation of the Kingdom of God in Galilee (4:17-16:19),
3) Jesus on the Way to Jerusalem (16:20-25:46),
4) Conclusion: Passion and Resurrection (26:1-28:20).

This outline answered many of the objections to Bacon's structure. It did not depend on discourses, and it included the infancy narratives. However, it still separated the passion and Resurrection narratives from the rest of the gospel.

The first integral outline of Matthew was presented by Jack Dean Kingsbury. Using the formula "from that time on, Jesus began. . . ." as a basis for his outline, Kingsbury proposed a three-part structure for the gospel—the person of Jesus the Messiah (1:1-4:16); the proclamation of Jesus the Messiah (4:17-16:19); the suffering, death and Resurrection of Jesus the Messiah (16:20-28:20). In essence, Kingsbury's outline is the same as Kümmel's with the exception that he integrates the passion and Resurrection into the gospel narrative.

Kingsbury has analyzed the gospel as a whole, centered on Jesus the Messiah. The first section establishes for the reader who Jesus is. He is Messiah, son of God, who is manifest to the nations, and established in his home in Nazareth. Having received the Holy Spirit, he becomes the new Adam encountering the devil.

The second section builds on the first. Jesus' messianic mission is to build a kingdom. Jesus proclaims the kingdom of God and summons his hearers to enter it. The summons comes through Jesus' teaching, preaching, and healing. As he travels through Galilee, he gathers a group around him who will become the nucleus of the kingdom. Galilee is the place of preaching, the place where the kingdom breaks in. It is also the place where opposition and rejection are kindled.

Jesus' rejection provides the link to the third section of the gospel. Narrating the events concerning the Messiah's suffering, death and Resurrection, the third section focuses on Jerusalem as the locus of activity. Jesus travels toward Jerusalem where the public ministry comes to a close. In the final days, the relationship between Jesus and his disciples becomes paramount. In Jerusalem, Jesus' opponents will think they have conquered; yet in Jerusalem, Jesus himself will ultimately conquer. In that conquest, he will inaugurate the kingdom.

The Gospel of Luke

From the opening words of the text, one sees that the Gospel of Luke originated in a milieu significantly different from Matthew and Mark. The author intends to write a "narrative" or an "orderly account" of the events of Jesus' life. He models his work on the historian, Josephus, or the philosopher, Philo. This gospel more than the others is an example of Greek history. This would be expected since the community that produced this gospel was Greek-speaking Gentile. This community was located somewhere around the city of Antioch, and completed the gospel around 85 C.E.

At the beginning of Jesus' ministry, the community's vision of that ministry is stated. Jesus is "sent to bring glad tidings to the poor, proclaim liberty to captives, sight to the blind, release to prisoners, and a year of favor from the Lord" (Luke 4:18-19). As the mission is fleshed out in the gospel text, an emphasis on the poor, the prisoner, the captive, and the blind emerges. Luke stresses the message which Jesus proclaimed to the little people.

It is safe to speculate that the Lukan community was composed of such little people. Luke begins the Beatitudes, "Blessed are you poor . . ."; while in a parallel text, Matthew begins, "Blessed are the poor in spirit . . ." From the difference, it would seem that Matthew writes for a wealthier class while Luke is addressing the poor. When money is discussed in Luke, the monetary units used are usually smaller.

Luke has a special place for women. An adulteress is forgiven

(7:50). Several women follow Jesus and provide for him out of their means (8:1-3). Jesus takes time to visit and experience the hospitality of two women, Mary and Martha (10:38-42). Women are healed by Jesus (8:48; 13:12). A widow has her only son restored to her (7:14-15). And several women weep for Jesus as he carries his cross to Calvary (23:27-28).

Luke portrays Jesus dining with tax collectors and sinners, the downtrodden in society (7:29, 34; 15:1). He calls a tax collector, Levi, to be one of his followers (5:29). He chooses to stay at the house of Zacchaeus the tax collector (19:7). He tells a parable which shows the attitude of a tax collector is more sincere than the outward prayer of a Pharisee (18:11). In each of these cases, Jesus' ministry to the downtrodden results in conversion.

Jesus' miracles in Luke free those who had maladies so that they might become whole people. Miracles of sight show Jesus giving sight to the blind. Jesus' ministry as a whole shows him giving spiritual insight to those who are blind to the realities of the reign of God.

For some time, scholars have realized that the Gospel of Luke contained large sections which did not occur in the other synoptic gospels. Most of these are in the central section of the gospel, the journey. This journey which begins at 9:51 links the Galilean ministry of Jesus with the Jerusalem ministry, and the passion, death and Resurrection. When one closely reads the introduction to the journey in Luke 9:51, "As the time approached when he was to be taken from this world, he firmly resolved to proceed toward Jerusalem," the final destination of the journey is not Jerusalem, but Jesus' being taken from this world, the Ascension.

Luke narrates this journey to the Ascension as Jesus' journey. But it is also the journey of every believer. Interpreting the journey in this manner illustrates how Luke integrates the passion and Resurrection into the rest of the gospel. Jesus has moved from Galilee to Jerusalem where he embraces the cross and death, and passes through Resurrection to new life and through the Ascension to heaven. In Luke's theology, the cross is necessary for the Resurrection and Ascension (Luke 24:26). Unless Jesus embraces the cross in Jerusalem, he cannot complete his journey. Unless the believers embrace the cross as it manifests itself in their lives, they also cannot complete their journeys.

THE WORD MADE CLEAR

Concluding Remarks

We have seen that the early church's major interest was the presentation of a portrait of Jesus which would provide a foundation for faith. They preserved their experience of Jesus both as he lived and as he was present in the preaching of the apostles and other eyewitnesses. In these portraits, we have varied views of Jesus. Yet when we allow the experiences of each of these communities to touch our own experience, we come to a fuller understanding of who Jesus is.

Study Questions

1) What is your attitude toward the truth and historicity of the events in the Gospels?
2) What does it mean when we read the "Gospel according . . .?"
3) Describe the Markan community's experience of Jesus. How does it relate with yours?
4) How does the structure of Matthew describe the Matthaean community's experience of Jesus?
5) What is the significance of journey for the gospel of Luke? does the journey experience speak to today?

Bibliography

Achtmeier, Paul J., *Mark*, Proclamation Commentaries, 2nd ed., (Philadelphia: Fortress Press, 1986).

Danker, Frederick W., *Luke*, Proclamation Commentaries, (Philadelphia: Fortress Press, 1976).

Edwards, O. C., *Luke's Story of Jesus*, (Philadelphia: Fortress Press, 1981).

Edwards, Richard A., *Matthew's Story of Jesus*, (Philadelphia: Fortress Press, 1985).

Fenton, J. C., *Saint Matthew*, The Pelican Gospel Commentaries, (Baltimore: Penguin Books, 1963).

Flanagan, Neal M., *Mark, Matthew, Luke: A Guide to the Gospel Parallels*, (Collegeville: The Liturgical Press, 1978.

Harrington, Wilfrid, *Mark*, New Testament Message, Vol. 4, (Wilmington: Michael Glazier, 1979).

Kelber, Werner H., *Mark's Story of Jesus,* (Philadelphia: Fortress Press, 1979).

Kingsbury, Jack Dean, *Matthew,* Proclamation Commentaries, (Philadelphia: Fortress Press, 1977).

Kingsbury, Jack Dean, *Matthew: Structure, Christology and Kingdom,* (Philadelphia: Fortress Press, 1975).

LaVerdiere, Eugene, *Luke,* New Testament Message, Vol. 5, (Wilmington: Michael Glazier, 1980).

Meier, John P., *Matthew,* New Testament Message, Vol. 3, (Wilmington: Michael Glazier, 1980).

Nineham, Denis E., *Saint Mark,* The Pelican Gospel Commentaries, (Harmondsworth: Penguin Books, 1963).

Chapter 11

Do Matthew and Mark Tell us the Truth About Jesus' Birth?

Every year around Christmas, there are several television specials. Among them are *Amahl and the Night Visitors* or *The Fourth Wiseman*. These are fanciful stories based on biblical narratives. Their message is edifying, but they have no basis in history. When watching these productions, many ask, "What is so different about these stories and the accounts in the Bible?" There are some who would see every little difference. Others maintain that the biblical narratives tell the truth. How are we to interpret the narratives of Jesus' infancy which are found in the gospels of Matthew and Luke? To answer this question, we need a little background.

The Midrash Literary Genre

Toward the end of the Old Testament period, especially after the conquests of Alexander the Great, the sacred traditions of Judaism were written down. Once written, they lost the dynamism that characterizes oral traditions. Nevertheless, these scriptures had to be applied to the changing life situations of those who read them. In Rabbinic Judaism, this application took place in different ways. Biblical texts were reinterpreted to apply to the readers' needs. Commentaries on the Scriptures made them intelligible for contemporary readers. Philo, a Jewish philosopher of Alexandria (c. 25 B.C.E. - 40 C.E.), wrote a series of commentaries on the Torah in which he interpreted the Torah through Platonic philosophy. The Hebrew Scriptures were translated into the language of the people of the time, Aramaic. These translations explained foreign concepts, or added commentary to insure that the text would be understandable.

During the early years of the church, a rich tradition of interpretation of the Hebrew scriptures was available. This tradition introduced a method known as "midrash," derived from the Hebrew word *darash*, meaning to "interpret." Using this method the interpreter could explain unusual concepts in a passage. In developing a midrashic interpretation, one searched the scriptures for other occurrences of the concept. They were then used to explain the passage being interpreted. Thus, the midrashic method used scripture to interpret scripture. Rabbi Hillel's rule of interpretation from the synagogue provides an explanation. It states, "If two sections from different parts of the scripture contain the same word, they belong together and explain each other." Hillel's rule was based on the operative principle that scripture must be viewed as a whole. Each part, each unit, or book points to truth which is consistent with the truth of the whole.

Midrashic interpretation paid close attention to the use of words, etymology, wordplays, and analogy. These were the tools used to explain obscure texts, obscure concepts. Midrash became the means by which the Word of God spoken in the past remained living and active affecting the lives of people in the present. In the New Testament, the narratives of Jesus' birth illustrate the midrashic method of interpretation.

The Infancy Narratives

In biblical literature, there is a birth narrative for almost every major person, Ishmael (Genesis 16:7-12), Isaac (Genesis 17:1-21), Moses (Exodus 3:2-12), Gideon (Judges 6:12-22), Samson (Judges 13:3-22), and Samuel (1 Samuel 1:3-27). Since details of these births were not readily available, authors employed the methods of midrash to create those narratives. Similarly, the writers of the gospels did not have exact details concerning Jesus' birth or early years. Yet, Matthew and Luke begin their gospels with narratives of his infancy.

The early Christian community had experienced salvation in Jesus. He had given them a reason to hope in a world which seemed to be obsessed with sin and evil. When they began to write down the words and deeds of Jesus, they reflected on the events of Jesus' life and the events of their own situation. Then, they reread the Hebrew scriptures, using the midrashic method to reinterpret them in light of both the experience of Jesus and their own experience. The resulting narratives were not meant to present historical fact, rather they disclosed the community's understanding of Jesus' identity and his origin. These narratives were developed to show that the events surrounding the infancy of Jesus parallel the events that would dominate his life and the events which they were currently experiencing. This was the truth that the infancy narratives communicated. Therefore, in our analysis of these narratives, we shall look at how the authors have used the midrashic method to construct them, and we shall examine the truth they communicate to us about Christ.

Matthew's Infancy Narrative

In *The Birth of the Messiah,* a commentary on the infancy narratives, Raymond Brown adapts Krister Stendahl's outline of Matthew's infancy narrative. Matthew 1:1-17 is a genealogy which explains *who* Jesus is, the son of David and son of Abraham. Matthew 1:18-25 shows *how* Jesus becomes a son of David. Matthew 2:1-12 explains the significance of the place *where* Jesus was born. Matthew 2:13-23 shows *whence* Jesus will go. Through the hostility of Jewish authorities, he will become an exile in Egypt. later, he will return to dwell in Nazareth.

The Genealogy of Jesus (Matthew 1:1-17)—Matthew's Gospel opens with the words, ''The book of the origin of Jesus Christ, son of David, son of Abraham . . .'' They introduce a genealogy which traces the origin of Jesus from Abraham. Two crucial events in the history of Israel punctuate this genealogy—the reign of David and the Babylonian exile. During the first, God promised David that his throne would remain forever (2 Samuel 7). With the second, the monarchy in Israel came to an end, necessitating a reinterpretation of the promise to David. These events divide the genealogy into three sets of fourteen generations.

From a comparison with the genealogical information provided in the Book of Chronicles, one realizes that Matthew's structure is artificial. He is stressing Davidic origins. David is the key figure in the genealogy. The consonants of the Hebrew word for David add up to fourteen. So the three sets of fourteen generations may be a means of pointing to the perfect descendant of David. (Three in Hebraic understanding means perfection.)

Curiously, in a predominantly male genealogy, five women are mentioned. Why would the author include them? The four women from the Old Testament prepare for the introduction of the fifth,

Mary. Each of the women from the Old Testament had an unusual relationship with her partner. Yet each of them played an instrumental role in salvation history.

Perez, ancestor of David, is conceived through Tamar's disgraceful union in which she tricked Judah (Genesis 38:12-30). Rahab was a harlot who helped Israel enter the promised land by giving lodging to the spies whom Joshua sent to reconnoiter the area (Joshua 2). Ruth, a Moabite widow, entered into a somewhat unusual union with Boaz (Ruth 4:13-17). The wife of Uriah the Hittite, Bathsheba, entered into an adulterous relationship with David (2 Samuel 11:1-5).

Later reflection in Jewish writings portrayed these women's deeds as the work of the Holy Spirit. God uses the unusual to triumph over human obstacles. Against this background, the author introduces Mary who enters into an extraordinary union which will bring about the birth of the Messiah.

The genealogy is a compilation of Old Testament traditions which have been brought together to provide a backdrop for the introduction of the major characters of the infancy narrative. Through the genealogy, the author has shown that Joseph, the man to whom Mary is betrothed, is a member of the Davidic line.

The Origin of Jesus (Matthew 1:18-25)

Jack Dean Kingsbury has observed that the genealogy presents the "remote" origin of Jesus. The next unit of the narrative (Matthew 1:18-25) presents the "immediate" origin of Jesus. This unit shows how Jesus has his origin in the line of David and God.

The author highlights the unusual circumstances surrounding the conception of Jesus. As the unit opens, Joseph discovers that his betrothed, Mary, is with child. Knowing that he is not the father and being a just man, he does not want to subject her to the full consequences of the law concerning adultery in Numbers (Num 5:11-31). He decides to divorce her quietly in accordance with Deuteronomy (Deut 24:1-4). However, in a dream, an angel announces that Mary's pregnancy is acceptable. She has conceived through the Holy Spirit. Further, when the child is born, Joseph is to name him Jesus. This name in Hebrew translates "Yahweh saves." This name was chosen for the child since he will save his people from their sins. Joseph, as a result of his dream, takes

Mary into his house. When the child is born, Joseph names him Jesus as he was commanded.

Reading this narrative, one questions how Jesus can be part of the Davidic line. Jesus cannot be a descendant of David through Joseph. The answer is found in Jewish custom. When a father names his child, he accepts that child as a gift from God, and the child receives title to the inheritance of the father. Since Joseph is not the physical father of Jesus, when he names his child, he adopts him into his heritage, namely the Davidic line. Thus, Jesus becomes an adopted son of David.

This is a reinterpretation of several texts concerning the Davidic dynasty, particularly Psalm 2:7 and 2 Samuel 7:14. These texts proclaim the Davidic monarch as a son of God. In the discussion of the monarchy (Chapter 6), we saw that the king was a descendant of David by birth. At his coronation, he became an adopted son of God. In this unit, the author shows that has been reversed. Jesus has been adopted into the Davidic line. However, he is more than any other "anointed one" of the Old Testament since he is the natural born son of God through the Holy Spirit.

The flow of the narrative is interrupted by a citation of Isaiah 7:14. In its original context, Isaiah 7:14 stated that a child was to be born who would be a sign of Yahweh's presence with his people, a child Emmanuel. The name means "God is with us." Matthew's citation of that text in this unit shows that Jesus conceived through the Holy Spirit is a sign that God is once again with his people. This balances the final statement of Jesus in the Gospel of Matthew, "I will be with you always. . . ." (Matthew 28:20). Thus, through skillful exegetical technique in reinterpreting Old Testament texts, the author communicates to his readers that Jesus is the natural son of God who, by adoption, is also the fulfillment of Davidic messianic expectation.

Reactions to Jesus' Birth—The narrative continues in Chapter 2 with reactions to the birth of Jesus as Messiah and Son of God. The chapter is divided into two main parts—(a) 2:1-12, the visit of the Magi (a positive reaction), and (b) 2:13-23, the massacre of the innocents (a negative response).

The Visit of the Magi (Matthew 2:1-12)—Although many scholars argue for the unity of Matthew 2:12, Brown disagrees proposing that two sources have been joined for a specific purpose. The first concerns Magi who have seen a star that leads them to Jesus. This source is a midrash on Numbers 24:17, which tells of a star rising in Jacob. The second is built on the prophecy of Micah 5:2, which speaks of the Messiah coming from Bethlehem. Brown argues that if the star was leading the Magi to the newborn king, there would be no reason for a stop in Jerusalem. Conversely, if Herod had familiarity with Scriptures, he would have had no need of the eastern astrologers to inform him of Jesus' birth. Also Joseph, who had been so prominent in the first chapter, is completely absent from this unit. However, he will appear again in the second part of the chapter.

The author begins this chapter with a reference to Jesus' birth, "Now when Jesus was born in Bethlehem of Judea . . ." (Matthew 2:1). This introduces the first source which is a midrashic reinterpretation of Numbers 27:17, "a star shall come forth out of Jacob, and a scepter shall rise out of Israel." In later Targumim (Aramaic translations of the Hebrew scriptures), this text is interpreted as describing the coming of the Messiah.

Whether or not the star was historical, the author has used these interpretations of Numbers 24:17 to create a narrative about a journey of the Magi (Persian astrologers) to Judea. Isaiah 60:6 had described people from the east coming bearing gold and frankincense to proclaim the praise of the Lord. Similarly Psalm 72:10-11 describes the nations falling down in worship before the messianic king. Therefore, in constructing his narrative, the author has chosen gentiles from the east to bring gold and frankincense in order to pay homage to the new messianic king. Gold is a sign of royalty and kingship. Frankincense is a sign of divinity. To these a third gift has been added, myrrh, which is a burial spice. The gifts represent who this child is and what his future holds. This source highlights the acceptance of Jesus by the nations, the gentiles. The main lines of this narrative parallel the fate of Jesus' message in the early church.

The second source, Brown postulates, is built around a citation of Micah 5:2, "But you, O Bethlehem Ephrathah, who are little to be among the clans of Judah, from you shall come forth for me one who is to be ruler in Israel." The central character in this source is Herod the Great, king of the Jews. The news of the

Messiah's birth startles him and all Jerusalem with him. Upon inquiry of the scribes, he discovers that Bethlehem is the place of the child's birth. He (secretly) sends to Bethlehem with the command, "Search for the childı" Herod's intent in this command is to destroy the child. Thus, the second source portrays the negative attitude of the Jews toward Jesus, an attitude that will continue until his death.

These sources present two distinct reactions to the birth of Jesus—the homage of the Magi and the hostility of Herod. The author of Matthew has interwoven these two sources to produce the Magi narrative which we know today. The Magi (gentiles) are contrasted to Herod (a Jew). They are journeying to fall down and serve; Herod plots to destroy. The fate of Jesus, and the fate of those who preach his message in the early church, can certainly be seen in this narrative.

The Massacre of the Innocents

The Herod Source in the preceding unit provides the link to the following unit. The final unit of Matthew's infancy narrative is constructed on three citations from the Hebrew scriptures: Hosea 11:1, Jeremiah 31:15, and Judges 16:17. These citations provide the foundation upon which three narratives develop.

Hosea 11:1 provides the basis for a narrative that tells how Joseph is warned in a dream to take Mary and the child and flee to Egypt until Herod should die. Jeremiah 31:15 grounds a second narrative which describes Herod's massacre on all the boys two years old and under in the region around Bethlehem. The third narrative, based on Judges 16:17, relates another dream in which Joseph is told to return from Egypt to Nazareth in the land of Israel.

The unit which results from combining these three narratives presents the consequences of Herod's negative reaction to Jesus, and Jesus' deliverance from Herod. Despite Herod's attempt to destroy Jesus on the cross; yet, through the resurrection, he will be saved. Because of that connection, this unit has been interpreted as a gospel in miniature.

We can see that the intent of Matthew's infancy narrative is not factual history. Rather, the author wants to present a christological reflection on the origin of Jesus, the fate of Jesus and the fate of his message in the early church.

JAMES P. McILHONE

Luke's Infancy Narrative

The infancy narrative in the Gospel of Luke highlights the parallel between John the Baptist and Jesus. In the earliest stages, these traditions were joined to produce a narrative which resembled a diptych (a series of pictures which are carved opposite each other on a hinged tablet). The first set of narrative pictures concerns the annunciation. The announcement of John's birth to Zechariah (Luke 1:5-23) followed by Elizabeth's pregnancy (Luke 1:24-25) is set opposite the announcement of Jesus' birth to Mary (Luke 1:26-38). Elizabeth's praise of Mary's pregnancy in the Visitation narrative (Luke 1:39-45, 56) forms a conclusion.

The second set of narrative pictures concerns birth. The narrative of John the Baptist's birth (Luke 1:57-66) followed by a statement on John's growth (Luke 1:80) parallels the narrative of Jesus' birth (Luke 2:1-29, 34-39) followed by a statement on Jesus' growth (Luke 2:40).

At a later stage of composition, the Canticles [*Magnificat* (Luke 1:46-55), *Benedictus* (Luke 1:67-79), and *Nunc Dimittis* (Luke 2:28-34)] were added. The final unit concerning the finding in the temple was also added to close the narrative. Since many themes in these narratives parallel themes in the Matthaean infancy narrative, we shall restrict our attention to the unit describing the birth of Jesus (Luke 2:1-20), and the unit known as the finding in the temple (Luke 2:41-52).

The Lukan Account of Jesus' Birth

Luke's narrative of the birth of Jesus contains three major sections, the Setting (Luke 2:1-7), the Annunciation (Luke 2:8-14), and the Reactions (Luke 2:15-20). The narrative setting of this unit is a census which provides the occasion for Joseph and his wife to journey to Bethlehem. However, this census poses several problems. There is no other evidence that Augustus took a census of the entire empire. And, even if he did, there were no requirements that people had to register in native towns. There was a census of the province of Syria, which included Judea, while Quirinius was Governor of Syria, but the date of that census is 6-7 C.E., nearly ten years after the death of Herod the Great.

Luke agrees with Matthew in placing Jesus' birth toward the

end of the reign of Herod the Great. When Herod died, there was political upheaval in Judea protesting his son, Archelaus, as ruler. About ten years later, Rome agreed that Archelaus was an inept ruler. He was replaced by a Roman procurator. That would coincide with revolts by Jews in Judea over the census imposed by Quirinius. A solution to the end of the problem of the census may be a confusion of details of those two times of political unrest.

Despite the difficulties concerning the date of the census, the author uses the census to assure Jesus' birth in Bethlehem, the city of David. After a somewhat lengthy explanation of the census and the journey of Joseph and Mary, it is curious that the author chooses to describe the birth in a rather curt manner. From the description, it would seem that the author intended to highlight the poverty of Jesus' birth. After his birth, he is laid in a manger, a feeding trough for animals.

In the second section, the scene shifts to shepherds who were tending flock. Because of their proximity to Jerusalem, these shepherds may have been tending animals used for the temple. Mention of shepherds in the regions near Bethlehem recalls David, who was called from shepherding near Bethlehem to become king. These shepherds receive the good news that the savior, the Messiah, has been born in Bethlehem. They are given a sign. The child will be wrapped in swaddling clothes and lying in a manger. A great hymn of praise follows.

For Luke, the shepherds, who represent the poor and the downtrodden, are the first witnesses of the birth of the Messiah. This foreshadows Luke's portrayal of Jesus bringing the good news to the poor and the downtrodden. The third section narrates the shepherds' journey to the manger to see the sign. When they arrive, they find the parents and the child who is lying in a manger.

The manger and the child appear in all three scenes (2:7; 2:12; 2:16) providing a link between them. What does the author wish to accomplish in making the manger so significant? In the opening chapter of Isaiah, Yahweh says, "The ox knows its own and the ass its master's manger; but Israel does not know, and my people do not understand" (Isaiah 1:3). The shepherds, being Jewish, represent Israel, Yahweh's people. Their movement toward the manger and their response of praise shows the misunderstanding of the people of Israel has come to an end. Yahweh's people have found the manger of their God. The negativity of the manger in Isaiah is reinterpreted to show God's people coming to the manger of his son to feed. Throughout the Gospel of Luke, the poor and downtrodden of Israel will flock to Jesus to feed on the words of comfort and hope that he will speak.

Luke's narrative of Jesus' birth is a recognition of God's action by the poor. In typical Lukan style, this recognition is set against the backdrop of world history. Again we see a parallel between the events narrated in Jesus' infancy and the events of his life.

The Temple Incident

The final unit of Luke's infancy narrative, the finding in the temple, was added at a later stage of development. The parallel between Luke 2:52 and Luke 2:40 confirms this. The unit is set at Passover. Jesus and his parents go up to Jerusalem as was their custom. However, the main action of the unit does not involve Passover, but rather the return journey. As Jesus' parents are on their way from Jerusalem, they realize he is not with them. Not finding him with relatives after a day's journey, they return to Jerusalem.

On the third day, they find him in the temple. He is discussing with the teachers of the law who are amazed at his understanding. His parents' initial response is also astonishment. Yet that soon becomes a sense of being let down (2:48). Jesus responds announcing he has a higher calling. He "must be about his Father's business." Joseph is his adopted father. Joseph's concerns must take second place to the concerns of his heavenly Father. The answer is a statement about his identity which is misunderstood by his parents.

Again, we find a parallel with the later events of the gospel. When Jesus reveals his identity to the disciples, they will misunderstand. When he speaks of his mission, they will misunderstand. The loss of Jesus and his reappearance on the third day parallels another loss at Passover when Jesus will also be about his Father's business. Luke, in a manner similar to Matthew, has chosen to construct the narrative of the events of Jesus' birth and early life in order to communicate the truth of who Jesus is and what his mission is. For this reason, these narratives can be called "gospels in miniature."

THE WORD MADE CLEAR

Conclusions

From this discussion, it is clear that the infancy narratives do not provide verifiable historical evidence concerning the birth of Jesus. However, that does not mean we should discount them. There is truth in these narratives. the authors of Matthew and Luke have attempted to construct a narrative of Jesus' infancy which describes his origin, his identity and his mission. These narratives are reflections of communities who are struggling to articulate their experience of Jesus, and their experience of preaching his message. The message that they communicate in these narratives should challenge us in the twentieth century to articulate more clearly our experience of Jesus and our experience of hearing and preaching his message.

Study Questions

1) Try to write a narrative of your birth and infancy. Why are some things included and some left out?
2) What truths concerning Jesus emerge from the infancy narratives?
3) What experiences of the early community are enlightened by the infancy narratives?
4) What experiences of our lives are explained by the infancy narratives?
5) How are the infancy narratives 'gospels in miniature?'

Bibliography

Brown, Raymond E., *The Birth of the Messiah: A Commentary on the Infancy Narratives in Matthew and Luke,* (Garden City: Doubleday & Co., 1977).

Brown, Raymond E., *A Coming Christ in Advent: Essays on the Gospel Narratives Preparing for the Birth of Jesus (Matthew 1 and Luke 1),* Collegeville: The Liturgical Press, 1988).

Danielou, Jean, *The Infancy Narratives* (New York: Herder & Herder, 1968).

Neusner, Jacob, *What is Midrash?,* Guides to Biblical Scholarship, (Philadelphia: Fortress Press, 1987).

Chapter 12

What Was Paul Really Like?

When Paul, the apostle, is mentioned, he is immediately associated with a preacher of the early church noted for his negative attitude toward women. A look at Paul's life and background shows that, although there are statements in Paul's writing that can be understood as anti-feminine, usually these are expressions of the cultural milieu of the day more than Paul himself.

To see what Paul was really like, it is necessary to look at the New Testament testimony concerning him, along with what he tells us of his life and background in his letters. This will give insight into Paul's person and the faith that motivated him.

Sources for the Life of Paul

The primary source for Paul's life are the letters he wrote. Jerome Murphy-O'Connor, among others, has developed a chronology of Paul's life based on the letters. The second source is the Acts of the Apostles. However, one must be cautious when drawing material on Paul's life from Acts. We must realize that Acts was written 20-30 years after Paul's death. The material concerning Paul in Acts is adapted according to Luke's theological plan, the movement of the gospel from Jerusalem to the ends of the earth. Generally, these sources agree concerning the major events of Paul's life. However, there are places where they differ significantly. It is necessary to assess the validity of the source before accepting its evidence.

Paul's Early Life

Saul, also known as Paul, was born in Tarsus, the capital of the Roman Province of Cilicia. Xenophon's *Anabasis* describes Tarsus as a "large and prosperous city." According to the Greek geographer Strabo, the schools of Tarsus surpassed Athens and Alexandria. The people of Tarsus were dedicated to education.

There is no evidence for the date of Paul's birth. Fitzmyer notes

126

that Paul refers to himself as an "old man" in the letter to Philemon (1:9). For the time, that would mean a man in his fifties. If that was the case, he would have been born in the early part of the first century, within ten to fifteen years of the birth of Christ. This agrees with the evidence in Acts 7:58 where Paul is called a "young man" at the time of Stephen's martyrdom.

Paul was the son of Jewish parents. In his letters, he states that he was descended from the tribe of Benjamin (Romans 11:1; Philippians 3:5). Both sources agree that Paul was a Pharisee (Acts 23:6; 26:5; Philippians 3:5). Acts 23:6 continues stating he was a "son of a Pharisee." The Pharisees originated at the time of the Maccabean revolt as a group who separated themselves from the power hungry Hasmonean family in order to preserve the traditions of Judaism and the Jewish law in its pure form. After the Maccabean period, the Pharisees became champions of the law. They devoted themselves to the study and transmission of the law.

During the second Triumvirate, Marc Antony granted freedom and the rights of immunity and citizenship to the City of Tarsus. After the Battle of Actium, these were approved by Augustus. Thus, Paul was born a Roman citizen. That would prove significant in Paul's later life. Paul's birth in Tarsus gave him a double background. By descent he was a Jew who adhered to the Pharisee party, yet by nationality he was a Greek from Cilicia who held Roman citizenship. This explains his double name. As many of his day, Paul had both a Jewish name, Saul, and a Gentile name, Paul.

Little is known of Paul's early life. His early education was probably in Tarsus, evidenced by his knowledge of the Greek language and Stoic philosophy. However, later he would tell the Corinthians that he was not trained in speaking (2 Corinthians 11:6). At a young age, Paul became a rabbinical student in Jerusalem. He studied under the great Rabbi Gamaliel I who taught in Jerusalem between the years 25 and 50 C.E. As a rabbinical student, Paul excelled beyond his peers (Acts 22:3; Galatians 1:14).

Paul entered rabbinical school after the period of the Amoraim or the "five pairs." During that period, there were two teachers who held the highest authority in Judaism. The final pair, Shammai and Hillel, headed the two rabbinical schools that flourished at the time of Christ when Paul was a youngster.

The School of Rabbi Shammai taught strict observance and rigorous interpretation of the law. The smallest part of the law could not be changed. The School of Hillel, on the other hand, taught a more lenient interpretation of the law. Many discussions and debates took place between rabbis from these schools.

A story is told in the tractate Shabbat (31b) of the Talmud which will illustrate the differences between the schools. One day a prospective convert to Judaism approached Rabbi Shammai and declared he would convert on the condition that, "you teach me the whole Law while I stand on one foot." Rabbi Shammai, taking the strict view of the law, knew that would be impossible. So he drives away the prospective convert with the builder's cubit he is holding.

The same person later approached Rabbi Hillel with the same challenge. Rabbi Hillel, taking the more lenient view of the law, responded, "What is hateful to you do not do to your neighbor: that is the whole Torah, while the rest is the commentary thereof; go and learn it." Hillel chose to present a single overarching principle that governed the rest of the law.

The purpose of this short rabbinic digression is to provide some background to Paul's place in that tradition. The Talmud in tractate Aboth tells us that Paul's teacher, Gamaliel I, was a descendant of Rabbi Hillel. In fact, he succeeded Hillel as teacher in the first generation of the Tannaim. Paul received his training in the school which taught lenient interpretation.

Upon completing his rabbinical education, Saul become an active member of the Pharisee party. Paul, the zealous Pharisee, followed the party in their opposition to Jesus of Nazareth and the movement that was founded by him. His first appearance in the New Testament is Stephen's martyrdom (Acts 7:58). He is introduced as a young man at whose feet Stephen's accusers placed their cloaks. After Stephen's death, Acts reports a persecution that broke out against Greek-speaking Christians. During this persecution, "Saul was ravaging the church . . . dragging off men and women to prison" (Acts 8:3).

Paul's Conversion

Paul relates his persecution of the church of God in his letter to the Galatians (Galatians 1:13). On one occasion, when he had received authorization to bring followers of Jesus of Nazareth in

Damascus back to Jerusalem, Paul set out on the road to Damascus. The events that occurred on the road are described in three separate places in Acts (9:1-31; 22:3-21; 26:2-23) and in the letter to the Galatians (1:15-23). In his own account, Paul describes the events on the Damascus road as God "revealing his son to me in order that I might preach him among the Gentiles" (Galatians 1:16).

The accounts in Acts are more detailed. As Paul is traveling, he is knocked to the ground and a bright light surrounds him blinding him. A voice says, "Saul, Saul, why are you persecuting me?" (Acts 9:4; 22:7; 26:14). When he asks who is speaking to him, he is told "I am Jesus who you are persecuting"(Acts 9:5; 22:8; 26:15). Two of the accounts in Acts describe Paul being led into Damascus where his sight is restored by a devout Jew named Ananias. Afterward, he is baptized.

In the Galatians account, Paul disclosed this experience to no one. Rather, he went to Arabia (Galatians 1:17) for an undetermined period. Then he returned to Damascus where he preached. Acts agrees that Paul preached in Damascus (Acts 9:27; 26:20), but there is no mention of a trip to Arabia. Paul's preaching incites the Jews in Damascus to plot his death. Paul describes this incident in his second letter to the Corinthians. He recalls that the governor of Damascus had the city guarded. To escape arrest, he had to be lowered from a window in the wall in a basket (2 Corinthians 11:32-33).

After his escape, Paul returns to Jerusalem where he wishes to join the apostles. The apostles' response to Paul was fear (Acts 9:26). Through the intercession of Barnabas, Paul is introduced to the apostles (Acts 9:27). In Galatians (1:18) Paul writes that he visited Jerusalem about three years after his conversion. He does not mention Barnabas's role in that visit. The visit with Peter (Cephas) and James, the leader of the Jerusalem community, lasted a few weeks (Galatians 1:18-19). After this visit, Paul returns to his native Tarsus (Acts 9:30; Galatians 1:20).

The First Journey

Paul's account in Galatians continues with another visit to Jerusalem fourteen years later (Galatians 2:1). There is no information on the events of those fourteen years in the Pauline letters. Acts attempts to fill the gap. Most Greek-speaking Christians in Jerusalem fled northward because of the persecution which began after Stephen's death. They preached the message of Jesus as they traveled through Samaria and Galilee. Eventually, they settled in Antioch in Syria (Acts 11:19). Within a few years, Antioch became the center for Greek-speaking Christians. This Antiochene community experienced new growth when several Christians from Cyprus and Cyrene appeared. They fostered a missionary movement to the pagan Greeks of Antioch (Acts 11:20).

As the number of Gentile Christians increased, the leaders of the Jewish Christian community in Jerusalem became more and more uncomfortable. They sent Barnabas to Antioch to investigate. Barnabas realized that the hand of God was on the work of all in Antioch and so he gave it his blessing (Acts 11:23).

Shortly after his visit to Antioch, Barnabas went to Tarsus to look for Paul (Acts 11:25). Barnabas brought Paul to Antioch. Shortly afterward the Holy Spirit prompted the community to commission Barnabas and Paul. They sent them with Barnabas's cousin John Mark to evangelize the regions of Asia Minor (Acts 13:1-3).

Their journey took them first to Cyprus, home of Barnabas and John Mark. They crossed the island preaching the message of Jesus at Salamis and Paphos. When they cross to Perga in Pamphylia, John Mark leaves the mission and returns to Jerusalem. His departure would have an effect on the way Paul and Barnabas would collaborate in future missions.

At each stop on the journey, they preached in the local Jewish synagogue (Acts 13:14; 14:1). The Jews did not accept their message. Jews, in most towns, drove them out of the synagogue (Acts 13:45; 14:2; 14:19). Rejected by the Jews, Paul and Barnabas discovered that the Gentiles in the area were curious about the message that they preached. Consequently, they turned their attention from the Jews to the Gentiles who were embracing the faith in large numbers (Acts 13:46; 14:21).

What the community had experienced in Antioch was repeating itself in the mission. Gentiles were flocking to hear the message of Jesus preached by Paul and Barnabas. Traveling and making converts as far inland as Derbe in southern Galatia, they retraced their steps and returned to Antioch.

The experience that Paul and Barnabas had on the mission and the experience of the Antiochene community posed what was to become the most significant question for Christianity—its relationship to its mother religion, Judaism. Was it necessary for a Gentile convert to Christianity to accept circumcision and become a Jew?

The Jerusalem Meeting

While Paul and Barnabas were still in Antioch upon completion of the missionary journey, some envoys came from Jerusalem. They taught the necessity of circumcision according to the law of Moses for salvation (Acts 15:1). Paul and Barnabas did not agree with them. Therefore, they led a delegation to Jerusalem to discuss the question. This journey to Jerusalem is most likely the same journey that Paul describes in Galatians 2:1.

According to Galatians, Paul, Barnabas and Titus privately speak to the leaders of the Jerusalem community, presumably James, Cephas (Peter), and John. In this conference, Paul presents the gospel he preached to the Gentiles (Galatians 2:2). The result of the conference, as Galatians narrates it, was an approval of the mission of Paul and Barnabas. Circumcision was not necessary for Gentile converts. The only stipulation that was placed on Paul and Barnabas was that they "remember the poor" (Galatians 2:9-10).

The account of this meeting in Acts agrees with Galatians that circumcision is not necessary for Gentile Christians (Acts 15:19). However, there is no mention of a collection for the poor. Acts, however adds a series of further stipulations. These appear in a letter to the Gentiles delivered by a delegation consisting of Judas Barsabbas, Silas, Paul, and Barnabas. Among these stipulations are: (1) abstain from the pollutions of idols, (2) abstain from unchastity, (3) abstain from what is strangled, and (4) abstain from blood (Acts 15:20).

During a later visit to Jerusalem (Acts 21:17-26), Paul is informed of a letter that was sent to the Gentiles making the same four demands. Paul's reaction is as though he was hearing this for the first time. There is no mention of the stipulations in the letter in any of Paul's writings. If Paul was present when the letter was originally sent, as Acts 15 implies, this is most curious. On the basis of this evidence, many scholars follow Paul Achtemeier arguing that Paul and Barnabas had left the meeting in Jerusalem when the material in the letter was formulated.

Both sources agree that Paul and Barnabas returned to Antioch after the meeting in Jerusalem. Shortly after Paul arrived in Antioch, Peter followed. Peter was in the habit of eating with Gentiles. However, when some emissaries from James appeared, Peter was quick to leave the Gentiles and eat only with Jews for "fear of the circumcision party." Many other Jews, even Barnabas, were influenced by Peter's action. Seeing this, Paul strongly reprimands Peter for his two-facedness. How can Peter demand that a Gentile live like a Jew when he himself freely lives like a Gentile (Galatians 2:14)? Paul continues, formally proclaiming the gospel that he has preached, "one is not justified by works of the law, but through faith in Jesus Christ" (Galatians 2:16).

This incident highlights the question of table companionship and dietary laws. It is possible that the letter which was mentioned in Acts 15:20 is related to this incident. In Acts, Luke may have telescoped the two into a single narrative.

The Second Journey

After the decision of the council, Paul suggests that Barnabas accompany him on a second journey to visit the converts they had made during their earlier journey. Barnabas is most eager on the condition that John Mark accompany them. Paul prefers that he stay home since he had left them in Pamphylia. A bitter argument between Paul and Barnabas eventually leads to their separation. Barnabas takes John Mark and goes to Cyprus. Paul selects Silas to accompany him. They travel through Syria and Cilicia.

Arriving at Derbe in Asia Minor, Timothy, son of a Jewish mother and a Greek father, joins them. Paul commands that Timothy be circumcised "because of the Jews" (Acts 16:3). Many commentators feel this amazing reversal on the part of Paul is a faulty report or perhaps a misconception of the account concerning Titus (Galatians 2:3).

The journey continues through the Galatian country. They are prevented from entering the province of Asia, so they travel northward to the province of Mysia arriving in Troas, the site of the ancient city of Troy. Paul has a vision inviting him to cross into Europe to the province of Macedonia in northern Greece. The first community they establish is Philippi, a leading town of the province. Philippi, being a Roman city in Macedonia, counted some

Jews in its population; yet it had no synagogue. Paul, nevertheless, preaches by a "place of prayer."

One of the first converts in Philippi, is Lydia from Thyatira. She provided a dwelling for Paul and his companions. The letter to the Philippians also mentions Euodoxia and Syntyche who have labored with Paul for the gospel (Philippians 4:2-3). It would seem that women played a significant role in the Philippian community.

Because Paul cured a possessed girl who was being used for profit, he and his companions are imprisoned, tortured, and mistreated (1 Thessalonians 2:2). During the night an earthquake opens the prison doors. The next day the magistrates propose that Paul and his companions be set free. Because he is a Roman citizen, Paul demands an apology for the imprisonment and mistreatment (Acts 16:37). The magistrates apologize and request that they leave the city.

From Philippi, they travel to Thessalonica, a port city of Macedonia. From there they proceed to Beroea. Paul leaves Silas and Timothy in Beroea with instructions to join him as soon as possible (Acts 17:15). Paul continues journeying south toward Athens, the cultural center of Achaia. Paul's preaching to the Athenian philosophers proved somewhat unsuccessful. Therefore, he continues west toward Corinth, the capital of the senatorial province of Achaia. Corinth was a prosperous city that had a reputation for licentious living.

In Corinth, Paul meets Aquila and his wife Priscilla who shared his trade, tent making (Acts 18:3). They had recently arrived in Corinth after their expulsion from Rome by an edict of the Emperor Claudius. Accepting lodging from them, Paul preaches in the synagogue where his message is rejected. Therefore, he turns to the Gentiles and establishes a vibrant community. Soon he is joined by Silas and Timothy. During this stay in Corinth, Paul wrote his first letter to the community at Thessalonica (1 Thessalonians).

Paul and his companions remain in Corinth for a year and a half (Acts 18:11) until they were brought before the proconsul of Achaia, Lucius Junius Gallio by the Jews. He refuses to hear the case because there was no hard evidence of wrongdoing. It was only "a matter of questions about words and names and Jewish law" (Acts 18:15).

This is the key event in determining the chronology of Paul's life. Lucius Junius Gallio was appointed to a single term as proconsul of Achaia from June 52 C.E. to May 53 C.E. However, he developed a fever and left in October 52 C.E. The incident narrated here must have taken place in late summer or early fall of 52 C.E. That would mean Paul arrived in Corinth in early 51 C.E.

After the unsuccessful trial before Gallio, Paul and his companions, accompanied by Priscilla and Aquila, cross the Aegean Sea to Ephesus. Paul and his company then sail for Syria and Caesarea. From there he visits the church in Jerusalem and returns to Antioch (Acts 18:22).

The Third Journey

After some time, Paul journeys a third time to Asia Minor and settles in the city of Ephesus, the capital of the Roman province of Asia, for nearly three years. During this time he preaches in the lecture hall of Tyrannus.

Paul writes a short letter to the community at Philippi. He also writes to Philemon, a wealthy respected Christian requesting, that he grant freedom to his slave Onesimus who was now with Paul. He writes to the Galatian churches opposing the influence of the Judaizers who, contrary to the decisions of the Council in Jerusalem, were still advocating circumcision. He also sends a short letter to the community in Corinth. (This letter has not survived in the canon of the New Testament. It is known as the pre-canonical letter.)

Problems had been developing in the Corinthian community. They were breaking into factions. Peter had arrived making some converts in Corinth. An eloquent Alexandrian Jewish Christian convert, Apollos, had a considerable following in Corinth. Paul was informed of this through messengers of Chloe, a wealthy businesswoman who had branches in Ephesus and Corinth (1 Corinthians 1:11).

A letter was also brought to Paul by a delegation led by Fortunatus, Stephanus, and Achaicus which contained a number of questions. To answer these questions and address the problem of factions, Paul wrote the canonical letter 1 Corinthians.

This letter was not received well in Corinth. Paul made a hasty visit which accomplished little but furthered his anxiety over the Corinthian situation. He speaks of it as a "painful visit" (2 Corinthians 2:1). Returning to Ephesus, Paul sends Timothy and

Erastus to Macedonia (Acts 19:22). Timothy then was to go on to Corinth (1 Corinthians 4:17). His missions unsuccessful, Timothy probably returned to Macedonia. Paul writes a hasty letter to the Corinthians which was strong in tone. This was the "letter in tears" (2 Corinthians 2:4). It was delivered personally to the Corinthians by Titus.

After Titus's departure, a riot broke out in Ephesus among the silversmiths who had crafted images of the goddess Artemis. Paul's preaching caused large numbers to forsake worship of Artemis in favor of Jesus. The market for images of Artemis dropped (Acts 19:23-40). Paul barely escaped the anger of the silversmiths. Leaving Ephesus, he journeyed to Troas to rendezvous with Titus. Upon arrival in Troas, he was exceedingly troubled because Titus was not there (2 Corinthians 2:13). He crossed to Macedonia where he met Titus who told him the "letter in tears" had convinced the Corinthians. Paul then writes a fourth letter to Corinth, the canonical 2 Corinthians. Titus returns to Corinth with this letter which prepares for Paul himself to follow. Arriving in Corinth, Paul spends the winter there.

After winter, Paul plans his return to Jerusalem to deliver the collection which he had taken up in Galatia, Macedonia, and Achaia. In preparation for a future visit to Rome and possibly Spain, Paul writes a letter to the Roman community. After Passover, Paul returns to Jerusalem.

Journey to Rome

Arriving in Jerusalem, Paul meets with James to report his missionary achievements. He then preaches in Jerusalem and incites a riot in the temple. He is arrested and brought before the Sanhedrin. In his defense, he says he is on trial over the question of the resurrection of the dead. This was a point of contention between the parties of the Sanhedrin. An argument erupted among the parties of the Sanhedrin and Paul demanded to be returned to his cell (Acts 23:6-10).

Jews in Jerusalem plotted to kill Paul (Acts 23:12-13) so he was transferred during the night for a hearing before Antonius Felix, the governor at Caesarea. Waiting for the accusers to arrive, Felix postpones the hearing. After five days, the delegation arrives and Felix hears their charges and Paul's defense (Acts 24:1-23). He is unwilling to decide the case alone. His hesitancy was a hope that Paul might bribe him with some money (Acts 24:26). Paul was not interested in bribery so Felix would question him on occasion over a period of two years when he was succeeded as governor by Porcius Festus.

Shortly after his appointment, the Jews requested Festus to return Paul to Jerusalem for trial. Their intent was to kill him on the way. Festus replied he would handle the matter in Caesarea and ordered Paul brought before him. When Festus suggests that Paul go to Jerusalem for trial, Paul invokes his privilege as a Roman citizen to appeal to the emperor (Acts 25:11). By Roman law, Festus is forced to grant Paul's request.

Guarded by a centurion of the Augustan cohort, Paul begins his journey to Rome. The journey lasted nearly six months due to storms and a shipwreck near Malta (Acts 28:1). They finally arrive in Rome where Paul is kept under house arrest for two years (Acts 28:30). During that time, he preaches the kingdom of God.

Neither Acts nor Paul's own writings give any information concerning Paul's final days. When Paul arrives and preaches in Rome, Luke's theological program is complete. Since Paul's letters are not biographical, they do not contain any information about this time.

Some conclusions can be drawn from the data we possess. In Rome, Paul either was given a hearing before Caesar or it was denied. If it was denied, it is likely that he died in Rome while under house arrest. If it was granted, he was found either guilty or innocent. If he was found guilty, he would have been executed in Rome. If he was found innocent, he would have been set free presumably to continue the journey to Spain where he might have died.

From this survey of Paul's life, some points surface that will be significant in understanding Paul's theology. First, he was educated both in Greek and Jewish ways. Thus he was able to blend the Judaism and Hellenism of his day. Second, he was profoundly influenced by his conversion experience. He realized that in persecuting individual Christians he was actually persecuting Christ. Third, his experience of mission, namely rejection by the Jews and acceptance by the Gentiles, helped him form his gospel, the message of salvation by faith. Finally, he received substantial aid and assistance from women during his ministry. He must not have been as anti-feminine as he is pictured.

Study Questions

1) What are the main sources for information on Paul's life?
2) Why is it significant Paul was born with the name Saul in Tarsus of Cilicia?
3) Describe Paul's Jewish background and education?
4) What is the significance of Paul's conversion experience for his later theology and preaching?
5) How is Paul's preaching accepted in the missionary journeys?
6) What is the significance of the Jerusalem meeting for developing Christianity?

Bibliography

Achtemeier, Paul J., *The Quest for Unity in the New Testament Church,* (Philadelphia: Fortress Press, 1987).

Bornkamm, Gunther, *Paul,* trans. by D. M. G. Stalker, (New York: Harper and Row, 1971).

Fitzmyer, Joseph, "Paul" in the *New Jerome Biblical Commentary,* edited by Raymond E. Brown, Joseph Fitzmyer, and Roland Murphy (Englewood Cliffs: Prentice Hall, 1990) pp 1329-1337.

Chapter 13

What Did Paul Have to Say?

Paul's thought has been the object of significant study, especially since the Reformation. Both the Catholic Church and the Reformers sought justification for their positions in the writings of Paul. Having looked at Paul's life in Acts and Paul's own writings, we now turn to the content of Paul's letters to discover key aspects of his thought. After a few preliminary comments on the question of authorship of the Pauline letters, we shall examine Paul's understanding of the human being (anthropology), his understanding of Christ and his saving work (Christology and soteriology) and finally his understanding of the relation between Christ's saving work and humanity (justification).

Authenticity of Paul's Letters

Thirteen letters of the New Testament are attributed to Paul (Romans, 1 & 2 Corinthians, Galatians, Philippians, 1 & 2 Thessalonians, Colossians, Ephesians, Philemon, 1 & 2 Timothy, and Titus). Scholars are in almost unanimous agreement that 1 Thessalonians, Galatians, Philippians, 1 & 2 Corinthians, Romans and Philemon are authentic letters of Paul. Due to differences in writing style and thought patterns, doubt has been raised concerning Paul's authorship of 2 Thessalonians, Colossians and Ephesians. Therefore these letters are referred to as "Deutero-Pauline" letters because they probably arose in the Pauline churches, were written by a disciple of Paul, and ascribed to him. Such literary ascription was popular in the ancient world. (This was discussed in relation to Apocalyptic literature Chapter 8.)

The remaining letters, 1 & 2 Timothy and Titus, are accepted by most scholars as not from the hand of Paul. Since they claim to be written by Paul, scholars have referred to them as "pseudo-Pauline" letters. They present a picture of church which is vastly different from the picture presented in the authentic Pauline letters. They seem to come from a period toward the end of the first century. Also, the understanding of Christ contained in these letters confirms the fact that they date from a period significantly later than Paul. Due to the constraints of space, we will concentrate on the theology of Paul contained in the authentic letters.

The Major Thrust of Pauline Theology

A major debate among scholars has concerned the central core of Paul's theology. Many have found it in the doctrine of "justification by faith." Some claimed it was in the "redemptive work" of Christ, while others sought to discover it in the dichotomy between "flesh" and "Spirit" which is so prominent in the writings of Paul. In the twentieth century, two major views have surfaced.

In his monumental work, *The Theology of the New Testament,* Rudolf Bultmann presents the theology of Paul in two major sections, "Man Prior to the Revelation of Faith" and "Man Under Faith." This division has a number of major Bultmannian themes lurking under it. In his theology, Bultmann sees the proclamation of the saving message of Jesus as primary, the proclamation of *kerygma.* Faith becomes a response to this proclamation. Influenced by the philosophy of Martin Heidegger, Bultmann defines this response of faith as an "existential decision" by which inauthentic human existence is radically changed into authentic existence (using the terminology of Heidegger). The inauthenticity brought about by "The Fall" is corrected when one accepts the proclamation of salvation achieved in Jesus. Inauthentic existence Bultmann sees as life in the "flesh," while authentic existence is life in the "Spirit." In essence, Bultmann has used the flesh/Spirit distinction of earlier scholars to show that the essence of Paul's theology is his understanding of humanity. This is known in theological terms as "Anthropology."

This reduction of Paul's theology is not accepted by many contemporary Catholic theologians. Most prominent among its opponents is Joseph Fitzmyer. He feels that Bultmann's view is too heavily dependent on the letter to the Romans. As he says, "The reduction of Pauline theology to an anthropology has, in effect, minimized Christ's role" (*New Jerome Bible Commentary* 82:26). Fitzmyer states that the center of Pauline theology must be found in Paul's own words, ". . . we proclaim a Christ who has been crucified" (1 Corinthians 1:23). For Fitzmyer, Christ stands at the center of Paul's teaching and, as he says, "all else in Paul's teaching must be oriented to this christocentric soteriology.'' Fitzmyer feels the key to Paul's theology is found in his Christology.

To understand the theology of Paul properly, it is necessary to look at both his understanding of humanity (anthropology) and his understanding of Christ (Christology). This will be our task in the next two sections.

Pauline Anthropology

Vocabulary—Since Paul was trained in the Jewish rabbinical school, one should expect that his understanding of humanity should closely resemble Hebraic notions. Hebraic understanding sees human beings composed of *basar,* ''body and flesh.'' When God breathes *nephesh,* ''the breath of life'' into *basar,* it is enlivened. In this understanding, a human being is a unity. There is no combination of different principles. The *basar,* ''flesh/body'' of itself is not living. When enlivened by *nephesh,* ''the breath of life,'' a living person emerges. In the Hebrew mentality, a human being is a ''living person.''

This is radically different to the Hellenistic (later Greek) understanding of the human being. From the time of Plato and Aristotle, the Greeks understood that a human being was a composite of two basic principles: *soma,* ''body,'' and *psyche,* ''soul.'' The body was corruptible, while the soul was immortal. Since Paul wrote in Greek, it was easy for many to interpret Paul's understanding of humanity in Hellenistic philosophical terms rather than through the Hebraic background Paul intended.

For Paul, a human being was a unity of two elements. The first he called body using the Greek word, *soma.* This was visible and tangible. On occasion, he used a second term for this element, *sarx,* flesh. This designation usually appears when Paul wants to emphasize the sinful nature of humanity (Romans 7:5,18,25). The second element was the life-giving force which makes the body alive. For this he chose the Greek word *psyche. Psyche,* for Paul, was not only a life-giving force; it also denoted the intelligent consciousness of a human being. For Paul, *soma* and *psyche* denote the whole human being.

Paul employs another term, *pneuma,* ''spirit'' which is used in a manner similar to *psyche.* There has been debate concerning the relationship between *psyche* and *pneuma*. All three terms appear in 1 Thessalonians 5:23. In that verse the three terms, "spirit, soul, and body" are parallel to the phrase, "may the God of peace sanctify you wholly." It is thus generally accepted that the three terms as they appear in that verse are an expression for the whole human being. In attempting to distinguish *pneuma* from *psyche,* most accept the view that *pneuma* is that aspect of the self which is most open to the reception of the Holy Spirit.

Paul uses one more term to designate the human being as a knowing and judging subject. This is the term *nous,* which is translated "mind." But again it is necessary to recall that Paul's use of this term must be seen against his Hebraic background. In the Hebrew view, the seat of intellectual activity was the heart, *leb.* Therefore Paul's use of the term *nous* is very close to his use of the term *kardia,* heart.

Paul's View of History

When looking at Paul's writings, one can clearly see that he envisions three distinct periods of history. The first spans the time from creation to Moses. This is the period when humans lived without the law. The second is the period from Moses to the coming of the Messiah. This is the period when humans lived under the law. The third and final period is the period of the Messiah. This final period would mark the perfection and fulfillment of the law. Such a division of history is typical of the rabbis of Paul's time. It therefore stems from his rabbinic training. The rabbis taught that they were in the second period expecting the arrival of the Messiah who would inaugurate the third period.

A major shift in Paul's understanding resulted from his experience on the road to Damascus. There, he realized that the third period had been inaugurated in the person and action of Jesus Christ. Yet, that third period was not fully established in the actions of Christ. Jesus was expected to return in full glory very soon. Therefore, Paul and his followers lived in a tension between the inauguration of the final days of the Messiah in the decisive *actions* of Jesus, and the final culmination of the messianic era in the glorious *return* of Jesus. A deeper look at each of these periods will show how Paul understood the human situation in each of them.

Humanity Before the Law—The human situation before the law can be described by the phrase, "in sin." Humanity was sinful and on the way to death (Romans 6:22). Human beings were unable to achieve the purpose for which God created them. They consistently failed, they "missed the mark" as the Greek word, *hamartia,* implies. (This word had its origin in archery where it meant, "failure to hit the bull's eye.") No matter how hard human beings tried to do what God intended for them, they failed. What was the origin of this sinful situation? The answer is to be found in the narratives of Genesis 3.

The Origin of Sin—Genesis 3 presents a narrative containing an early reflection of Jewish writers on the origin of the sinful human situation. The major characters in the narrative are Adam, from the Hebrew *Adam,* meaning "human being," and Eve, from the Hebrew *Hawwah,* meaning "the living person." Even in their names the first human beings are representative of all humanity. God and the tempter, who appears as a cunning serpent, also play important roles. Without presenting a detailed analysis of the Genesis passage, I shall highlight several points that it presents concerning the origin of sin. First, the tempter presents Eve with an offer she can't refuse (Genesis 3:5-6). He tells her that if she violates the command God has given (Genesis 2:16-17), she would be like God, *knowing good from evil.* This plays into Eve's desire to be more than she is. She hears the first part of the tempter's offer. (She would be like God.) However, from the narrative it is clear that she failed to hear the second part which qualified it (knowing good from evil). She violates the command and partakes of the forbidden fruit.

Eve then presents the tempter's proposition to Adam who is also taken in by the desire to be more than he is. He also partakes of the fruit. Immediately both become aware of their transgression of God's command. They have experienced evil and in that experience, they are now able to distinguish good from evil. Thus, they are like God knowing good from evil. Genesis 3 plainly shows that the sinful condition of humanity originated with human beings, *not* with God. It is the result of a natural human tendency to become "like God." Paul follows this understanding of Genesis 3 when he recalls in Romans 5:12: "Therefore, as sin came into the world through one man and death through sin. . . ."

142

THE WORD MADE CLEAR

From Adam to Moses—Immediately following the sin of Adam and Eve, the promise of a redeemer is made (Genesis 3:15). Later, Noah is promised that the wrath of God will never manifest itself in a flood again (Genesis 9:11). Hence, this is called the time of "promise." Paul sees the Covenant made with Abraham as the primary manifestation of the "time of promise." In Galatians 3, he notes that God gave the inheritance to Abraham by a promise (Galatians 3:18). The content of that promise was (1) God would make Abraham a great nation; (2) he would make Abraham's name great (Genesis 12:2); and (3) he would make Abraham's descendants as numerous as the stars of heaven (Genesis 15:5).

In the letter to the Romans, Paul develops the picture of Abraham and the promise made to him. Abraham received the promise from God through "the righteousness of faith" (Romans 4:13). Genesis tells us that "Abraham believed God, and it was reckoned to him as righteousness"(Genesis 15:6). The promise was not something which was owed to Abraham, rather it was something which he received through the graciousness of God on account of Abraham's faith. Paul wishes to stress that the promise made to Abraham not only rests on the graciousness of God, but also was made to Abraham and his descendants by blood and by faith (Romans 4:16). The promise made to Abraham was then passed on from generation to generation.

Humanity Under the Law—In the period of Moses, a new concept is introduced into the history of humanity, *nomos*, "law." This heralds the beginning of the second period of history. The term appears in the Pauline writings referring to (1) general laws, (2) various principles, (3) the Old Testament, and (4) the law of Moses. This final designation is most prominent in Pauline usage. The key to Paul's understanding of the relationship between *nomos*, "law," and *anthropos*, "humanity," can be found in Galatians 3:12. The man who follows the statutes of the law shall live by them. This is a paraphrased citation of Leviticus 18:5: "You shall therefore keep my statutes and my ordinances, by doing which a man shall live." The law has been provided by God in order to aid humanity in attaining "life."

However, the actual situation is quite different. Romans 2:24 states that the name of God is blasphemed among those without the law (the Gentiles) because of the actions of those who have the law (the Jews). The Jews have boasted in their possession of the law, while all the time violating it (Romans 2:23). Galatians 3:13 speaks of the "curse of the law." Therefore, Paul can make the astounding statement that "no human being will be justified in his (God's) sight by works of the law" (Romans 3:20; Galatians 2:16). He cites Psalms 143:2, "no living man is righteous before thee (God)," adding the prepositional phrase "by works of the law." Law, *nomos*, which was to lead to life and proper relationship with God for humanity, *anthropos*, has failed. Paul now must probe the reasons for this.

In looking at the authentic Pauline writings, two explanations emerge, one in Galatians 3 and one in Romans 7. In Galatians 3, Paul portrays the role of law, *nomos*, as a custodian. The Greek word used is *paidagogos* which referred to a slave who was hired to supervise the conduct and study of school age young men. The *paidagogos* would be responsible for instructing, guiding and disciplining the young man so that when he came of age, he would know how to act. The period of the law becomes the teen age years of humanity. In Galatians, Paul is careful to note this role of the law dows not invalidate the promise made to Abraham.

Romans 7 provides a different explanation. Paul turns to an analysis of the situation of humanity. Law, *nomos* according to Paul, is good and holy (Romans 7:12). How can what is good and holy bring death? Paul answers that sin is able to use the law to bring about death. Of its nature humanity, *anthropos*, is carnal (of the flesh). Inheriting the effects of Adam's sin, *anthropos* is kept in bondage by sin. Humanity finds itself in a situation where its actions (what it does) do not match its will (what it wants). The will of *anthropos* wants to follow the law, yet the actions of *anthropos* are dominated by another force, sin, *hamartia*. Paul notes that despite a human being's delight in the law, another law is at war with God's law in human flesh. The human being becomes captive to this other law which abides in the flesh, the law of sin (Romans 7:22-23).

Humanity in Christ—The answer to this situation comes in the third period of history. Galatians 3 continues the analogy of the *paidagogos* showing that through faith in Christ Jesus, humanity has reached adulthood. A custodian, *paidagogos*, is no longer necessary. Adapting the image slightly, Paul continues to speak of an heir under the care of guardians and trustees until he comes of age. When God sent Christ to redeem humanity from the law and grant it full rights as adopted children (Galatians 4:4), humanity achieved its true state. Therefore, it can call God by his proper title, *"Abba,* Father." In the preceding age, humanity was merely an heir under the custody of the law. In the present age, humanity has achieved adoption as sons.

Romans 7 presents another solution. Paul exclaims: "Wretched man that I am! Who will deliver me from this body of death?" He continues, answering the question: "Thanks be to God through Jesus Christ our Lord!" (Romans 7:24-25). In Chapter 8, Paul declares that the spirit of life in Christ Jesus frees humanity from the law of sin and death (Romans 8:2). Through this spirit of life, humanity can walk according to the spirit, *pneuma* rather than according to the flesh, *sarx.* Paul observes that in sending Christ, God has done what the law was unable to do, achieve a state of right relationship with God for humanity. Another way of saying this is that humanity is now able to stand before God "justified." This brings us to a discussion of Paul's understanding of Christ and the doctrine of Justification by faith.

Pauline Christology—Titles for Jesus

Christ—A look at the way Paul refers to Jesus gives an initial idea of how he understands him. On occasion he uses the name Jesus alone. It is almost always used in conjunction with the title "Christ." In Greek the title *Christos* was used to translate the Hebrew term *mashiah,* which meant "anointed one." The title was used in the Old Testament to designate the king. This title was given to Jesus at an early stage of the church's preaching. It signified the early Church's understanding that Jesus was the expected one and in him the new age had begun. Paul, in his conversion experience, came to the same realization. Paul's frequent use of this term shows that his understanding of the messiah was radically changed in that experience.

Son of God—Angelic beings in Genesis were known as "sons of God." Also the person who follows the way of wisdom is known as "son of God." Another title that Paul applies to Jesus is "Son" or "Son of God." This title also referred to the Davidic monarch.

On the day of his coronation, he became adopted "son of God." In the Old Testament world, a son was obedient to his father in all tasks that the father entrusted him to perform. This is the understanding that grounds Jesus being called "son of God" in the New Testament. He is obedient to the Father in all things.

Lord—The word Lord, or *kurios* as it appears in Greek, is the word used to address another man. It means simply "Sir" or "Mister." However, it is also the word used by slaves to address and speak of their master. Hence, it also has the meaning "Master." Later Jewish writings begin to address God as "Lord." "Lord" was used in the Septuagint to translate the divine name. Recall that when the divine name occurred in a text it could not be spoken, the term *Adonai,* My Lord, was used instead.

The word became common in the early church for the risen Lord. Many suppose influence of Hellenistic mystery religions where *Kurios* was a title given to several dying and rising gods such as Osiris or Serapis. Paul's use of this term to designate Jesus as risen, coupled with the contemporary use of the term for God, implies that Paul understood Jesus as having a status beyond the human.

The Role of Jesus

Paul sees Jesus' central role played out in the events of the Paschal Mystery. For Paul, these events form a continuous unity. The hymn which Paul adapts in the second chapter of the letter to the Philippians best sums up his understanding. In this hymn, Paul presents Jesus as a new Adam. Jesus has what Adam desired. Jesus was in the form of God, yet he did not seek equality with God as Adam did. Rather, he does just the opposite. In humility he empties himself to become less than God, a human being. Yet that was not enough, he accepted the greatest humiliation a human could endure, death on a cross. All this was done in obedience (again contrary to Adam who disobeyed). Nevertheless, God exalted him and raised him on high (resurrectionàscension) with the result that all proclaim him as Lord. It is clear here that the exaltation cannot take place without the humiliation, and the humiliation gains meaning only through the exaltation. Therefore both form one continuous whole.

THE WORD MADE CLEAR

Through Jesus' humiliationèxaltation, God inaugurated the new age. He regains for humanity what Adam lost, life in the spirit. Paul puts it clearly in 1 Corinthians 15: "The first man, Adam, became a living being; the last Adam became a life-giving spirit" (1 Corinthians 15:45). As life-giving spirit, Jesus brings about the possibility of justification and salvation.

Effects of Christ's Work

Justification—When describing the effects of Christ's work, the term Paul most frequently uses is "justification." This is expressed by the Greek verb *dikaioun* which is a legal term meaning to "declare someone righteous" or to "acquit someone." Paul speaks of Christ "justifying" human beings (Romans 3:23). This means that one effect of the work of Christ is that humanity now can stand "acquitted" before the throne of God. This acquittal is the gracious act of God. It is God who is "just" and it is God who makes humanity just. Through the act of salvation in Christ, sinful humanity is "set right" with God.

A person understands justification through the experience of faith. Faith is a reaction to hearing the gospel. When one hears the gospel, they acknowledge in their mind that Jesus is Lord. This leads to a commitment of the whole person to God. The commitment of faith that justifies is therefore not merely an intellectual assent. It is a radical reorientation of the whole human being toward God. The model of such faith is Abraham. In his discussion of Abraham, Paul distinguishes the physical descendants of Abraham (the Jews) from the descendants of Abraham through faith. This distinction explains Paul's ready acceptance of the Gentiles who accept Jesus in faith. Through the proclamation of the gospel, they are led to a commitment of faith through which they are justified.

Salvation—A second effect of the work of Christ is "salvation." This is linked with justification in Romans 10:10; "For man believes with his heart, and so is justified, and he confesses with his lips and so is saved." In the Old Testament, the savior was one who rescued Israel from evil or harm. This role was most commonly ascribed to God. Paul's use of the term recognizes that in Christ, humanity is saved, i.e. rescued from evil, the evil of not living in right relation with God. In the central passage of Romans 1:16, Paul clearly states that the power of God for salvation to the believer is found in the gospel. Thus, salvation is related to justification by faith.

Conclusion—From this short survey, we can see that Paul's theology turns on two poles, his understanding of humanity, and his understanding of Christ. These two are intricately intertwined. One cannot fully understand Paul's view of humanity unless one takes into consideration his understanding of Christ. Conversely, one cannot grasp Paul's understanding of Christ unless one sees Christ's work in relation to Paul's understanding of humanity. When this relationship is grasped, Paul's understanding of church (his ecclesiology) and his ethical principles flow naturally.

Study Questions

1) Why are the letters which are said to have been written by Paul divided into 'authentic' and 'deutero-Pauline' letters?
2) What, in your opinion, is the central focus of Paul's theology?
3) How does Paul understand the human being? Is this understanding viable today?
4) What is the function of law in Paul's view of history? Is Paul's view valid?
5) How does Genesis 3 present a psychology of temptation?
6) What is meant by justification? How is justification operative in faith today?

Bibliography

Banks, Robert, *Paul's Idea of Community: The Earliest House Churches in Their Historical Setting*, (Grand Rapids: Wm. B. Eerdmans, 1980).

Bristow, John T., *What Paul Really Said About Women*, (San Francisco: Harper and Row, 1988).

Fitzmyer, Joseph, "The Theology of Paul" in the *New Jerome Biblical Commentary*, edited by Raymond E. Brown, Joseph Fitzmyer, and Roland Murphy (Englewood Cliffs: Prentice Hall, 1990) pp 1382-1416.

THE WORD MADE CLEAR

Meeks, Wayne, *The First Urban Christians: Social World of the Apostle Paul,* (New Haven: Yale University Press, 1983).

Murphy O'Connor, Jerome, *Becoming Human Together: The Pastoral Anthropology of St. Paul,* Good New Studies. Vol 2, (Wilmington: Michael Glazier, 1982).

Perkins, Pheme, *Ministering in the Pauline Churches,* (New York: Paulist Press, 1982).

Chapter 14

The Johannine Community: Love that Ended in Hate

Many times I am sure, we have heard people lamenting the state of the church in the present time. Often implicit in that lament is a secret desire for the peace and harmony of the church of the apostles, and the late first century. They had heard Jesus and had received the Holy Spirit. If there was any ideal time for the church, it had to have been then.

In the past decades many studies have appeared on the communities of the first century. Scholars have determined their origin, composition, theological leanings and, in some cases, the reasons for their downfall. The work of Raymond E. Brown and J. Louis Martyn has produced a most fascinating glimpse into one community of the late first century, the Johannine community.

The Beloved Disciple

From the evidence contained in the gospel, the Johannine community originated around the "beloved disciple." This disciple is introduced in the second half of the gospel as one who is very close to Jesus. He sits next to Jesus as the Last Supper. He is present at the foot of the cross during the crucifixion. He is given custody of Jesus' mother. He is present with Peter at the tomb after the resurrection. Through the beloved disciple, the community has a direct link to Jesus.

Although this disciple is given a very prominent place in the gospel, his identity is never established with certainty. Tradition has identified this disciple with John, the son of Zebedee. However, this may be a case of reverse identification. As we saw in an earlier segment, the names of the evangelists are derived from a fragment of Papias which ascribes the four canonical gospels to Matthew, Mark, Luke, and John. If this ascription is at the basis of the traditional identification of John, son of Zebedee, with the beloved disciple, then we are reading Papias' understanding back into the gospel. It is certain that the final editors of the gospel did not see the identity of the beloved disciple as a major concern.

150

Otherwise, they would have made it clear which of the followers of Jesus he was. As it is, all they are clear about is who he is not. Scholars continue to search for the identity of the "beloved disciple."

The Origins and Early Development of the Community

Brown and Martyn in their research have shown that the community founded by the beloved disciple had a short but complex history. The group which originated the community lived in Palestine during the sixties and seventies. It was composed of Jews who believed Jesus was the expected messiah. They did not see themselves separate from Judaism; rather they participated in the synagogue. At the same time, they actively sought converts.

Under the direction of the "beloved disciple" the community began to collect and compile traditions concerning Jesus. Particularly, they were interested in the miracles of Jesus which were preserved as evidence for Jesus' messianic claims. The resulting traditions formed the "signs source" for the Gospel of John cited by many scholars today.

A second group of Samaritan origin soon joined the originating group. These Samaritan believers did not share the expectation of a messiah from the line of David. They saw Jesus as a new Moses, the prophet promised in Deuteronomy 18:15. They also showed strong hostility toward the temple in Jerusalem. This is understandable when we look at the history of relations between Jews and Samaritans. The Samaritans had much hostility toward the Jews and their temple from the time of John Hyrcanus (c. 106 B.C.E.). The Jews under Hyrcanus' orders destroyed the temple which the Samaritans had build on Mt. Gerezim. The basis for this action was the command of Deuteronomy that there be only one temple, the temple of Jerusalem. Since they accepted only the Pentateuch, the first five books of the Bible, Samaritan expectations centered on a prophet like Moses. The expectation of a Davidic messiah dates from a later period.

A Community Crisis

The entrance of this Samaritan group into the community provided the needed spark which "catalyzed," to use Brown's term, the formation of the Johannine pre-existence Christology. Armed with this deeper understanding of Jesus, members of the community openly entered into debate with Jews in the synagogue. Many of the synagogue Jews felt that the community was setting aside the traditional understanding of Jewish monotheism. In their debates, the community presented Jesus as a divine being alongside Yahweh. Synagogue leaders saw this as a direct violation of Deuteronomy 6:4 and Isaiah 45:21.

The tension in these debates soon caused members of the synagogue to take sides. Hostility reached such a pitch that synagogue leaders felt that something had to be done. A plan was formulated to systematically identify and expel adherents of this "heretical" view from the synagogue.

After the fall of Jerusalem in 70 C.E., leading Pharisees fled to the seacoast town of Jabneh (Jamnia) to reorganize. Their leaders were Rabbi Johanan ben Zakkai, and Rabbi Gamaliel II. Part of this reorganization was elimination of all groups who did not support the Pharisaic position. Because of the debates in the synagogues, Christian Jewish debaters became a prime target of the Pharisees. Under the direction of Rabbi Johanan ben Zakkai, Samuel the Small was directed to reword the twelfth benediction of the eighteen benedictions contained in the *Shemoneh Eshreh.* The *Shemoneh Eshreh* was a series of blessings led by a member of the synagogue toward the end of the service.

The twelfth benediction, also known as the *Birkat ha-minim,* the blessing of heretics, was specifically reworded to include those who proclaimed Jesus as Messiah among the heretics, the *minim.* As one might suppose, this "blessing" was not a positive blessing; rather, it was a curse. When the benediction was reworded, members of the synagogue who were suspected of being believers were invited to lead the congregation in the *Shemoneh Eshreh.* The leaders and congregation would then pray quietly until the leader reached the twelfth benediction. At that point, he would face a choice. Either he could call the curse upon himself by reading the benediction, or admit his belief in Jesus by refusing to say the benediction. If he chose the latter course, the leaders would immediately excommunicate him from the synagogue. A serious split resulted among Christians who were part of the synagogue. Many now shied away from public expression of their faith to remain safely within the synagogue. These were the "crypto-Christians." Those who publicly expressed their faith suffered excommunication and banded together to form an ever stronger community, the Johannine Christians.

Martyn and Brown have shown that the gospel alludes to these excommunications. In the ninth chapter of the gospel, a blind man has received his sight. An investigation of the healing by the Pharisees begin. Two witnesses called in this investigation are the man's parents (John 9:18-23). The parents are willing to cooperate to a point. However, when faced with the question of how their son sees, they refuse to answer. An editorial comment follows to explain their refusal. "They feared the Jews, for the Jews had already agreed that if any one should confess him to be the Christ, he was to be put out of the synagogue" (John 9:22). There is no evidence to verify the existence of such an agreement during the time of Christ. The agreement referred to here originated at the time of the rabbis in Jamnia. Now it is read back into the gospel. A further allusion to expulsion from the synagogue can be found in John 16:2.

It is easy to see how the attitude of the fourth gospel toward the Jewish leaders and the Jews developed. No one will look kindly upon a group which has expelled them. Yet this was not the end. A second crisis quickly followed. Many of the Jews in the synagogue who had been impressed with the arguments of the Jewish Christians chose to follow the Christians out of the synagogue. This became a grave concern to synagogue leaders who, in turn, began to put members of the Johannine community on trial. Eventually some members of the community were executed. Evidence of this is found in the gospel text (John 16:2). Jesus is telling the disciples that a "time will come when anyone who puts you to death will claim to be serving God!"

These persecutions heightened the rift between the community and the Jews. This increasing division brings an almost dualistic world view into the gospel. Jesus becomes one from above who is sent to the world below. He is rejected by "his own," but accepts as followers all those who are willing to put faith in him. Such dualism appears in other ways in the gospel—light/darkness, life/death and world/community.

It was probably during these persecutions that major parts of the gospel were put in writing. Against this background, we can easily understand many of the ideas in the gospel which at first sight may seem difficult—most especially the attitude of Jesus toward the Jews. They are so separated, at points, that the author has Jesus himself saying, "As it says in your law . . ." (John 8:17). This is a most unusual statement for Jesus. He was a Jew and the law of Moses was his law. However, by the end of the century when the gospel was being written, readers would have experienced expulsion and, in some cases, persecution at the hands of the Jews. They were no longer Jews, and wanted no part of the Jewish law.

Brown notes that the gospel also recounts the entry of Gentiles into the community (12:20-36). This accompanies the climactic announcement that the time has come for Jesus' glorification. The Gentiles see the reality of Jesus; yet the Jews, completely blinded, seek his destruction. This is the historical situation. As the other churches of the first century have sought converts from the Gentiles rather than from the Jews; so now the Johannine community makes the turn to the Gentiles.

Brown supposes that the community leaves its roots in Palestine and moves to the Greek world. The split caused by the Johannine understanding of Jesus has become so wide there could be no reconciliation with Judaism.

Developing Community Identity

Martyn sees the years following the completion of the early gospel text as a time when the community sought to establish its identity against the various other groups. Two groups stand out. First, those Christians who refused to leave the synagogue at the time of expulsion, the "crypto-Christians." The community had little use for this group. In the dualistic tone of the gospel, there was no room for vacillation. Either you believed, or you didn't. The community viewed these Christians in the same way as the Jews of the synagogue. Martyn feels that some of this strong emotion may derive from a historical circumstance in which the crypto-Christians aided the synagogue leaders in expelling the Johannine Christians.

The second group would be the Christians who believed in Jesus; yet did not belong to the Johannine community. These included the apostolic churches. The community was not an island; they held much in common with the other Christian communities although their understanding of Jesus and church differed significantly.

The Johannine Community and the Apostolic Churches

The apostolic churches are the communities of Matthew, Mark and Luke. We also include the Pauline churches since many feel there is a strong link between the Lucan community and the Pauline churches. These communities held a "lower Christology" than the Johannine community. The apostolic communities saw Jesus as a fulfillment of Old Testament expectations. They applied to him many titles which expressed that expectation, e.g., messiah, Son of Man, Son of David, Suffering Servant, etc. These titles do not necessarily mean Jesus is a divine being. The title "Son of God" which one would think denotes a divine being does not. The title was used for the Kings in Israel (Psalm 2:7; and 2 Samuel 7:14). The Johannine community, on the other hand, sought to emphasize the divinity of Jesus. In the Gospel of John, the text specifically refers to Jesus' unity with the Father (John 5:18; 10:38; 17:11).

The Johannine community also differed with the apostolic churches in its understanding of church, what is known as "ecclesiology." The apostolic churches saw church as a hierarchical organization with strict order. We see this view in the pastoral epistles and in the discourses of the Gospel of Matthew (Matthew 18). The Johannine community saw church as a gathering of equals. The chief Johannine image for church was the vine and the branches (John 15). Each member of the church had equal access to Jesus the vine. There was a strong sense of equality among members of the community. The community saw itself led by the Spirit whom Jesus promised to send after his ascension. The sole arbiter of disputes became the Spirit (John 16:13). Also, the community lived according to a single ethical norm, "Love one another, as I have loved you" (John 13:34). The example Jesus set during his time on earth is to be the model for the conduct of the community. There is, therefore, no need for organization or hierarchy in the community.

JAMES P. McILHONE

The Johannine Community After the Written Gospel

When the persecution from the Jews quieted, the community faced a new crisis. This crisis stems from two groups *within* the community who are interpreting the gospel text from totally opposite points of view. Both claim that the Spirit is the source of their interpretation. This crisis caused a member of the community to write what has come to be known as the First Letter of John. In this letter, the separatist mentality of the gospel reasserts itself only this time the opposition is not the ''Jews'' but, rather, fellow Christians. The epistle shows that a division has taken place within the community. Some members have seceded (1 John 2:19).

From other parts of the epistle we can determine the reasons for their departure. Brown isolates four areas where problems exist between the community and the secessionists—Christology, ethics, eschatology, and the Spirit. The most significant of these is Christology. The secessionists try to stretch the high Christology of the gospel to its limits. The gospel, as Brown holds, identifies Jesus who ministered here on earth with the pre-existent Son of God. The problem for the author of the gospel was to prove the divinity of Jesus. No one had any problems with his humanity.

The author of the epistle had quite a different problem. Every one in the Johannine community accepted the divinity of Jesus. (That was the very point on which they had suffered so much.) Now, however, some in the community wish to deemphasize the humanity of Jesus the Son of God. They question whether the Son of God must live and die as Jesus did (1 John 4:2-3). It is possible that the secessionists were influenced by a group, prominent at the time, known as the Docetists. They denied the humanity of Jesus as mere appearance. The Son of God when he walked on earth only appeared to be human, it was a deception.

Since both interpretations derived from the same gospel, it became necessary to re-examine the gospel text. As a result, an editor reworked some of the more controversial units to emphasize that Jesus, the Son of God was a real human being. An example of this reworking is the death scene (John 19:34). The editor shows that when Jesus' side was pierced, blood and water flowed out. This proves that he was a real human being with real blood just like any other human being. This was real, not appearance.

In the area of ethics, the secessionists felt that their relationship with God made them sinless (1 John 1:8,10). As a result, there is little need for following commandments (1 John 2:4). That same relationship with God would naturally demand that they keep the commandments. The only commandment in the Gospel of John is the commandment to love one another. However, the author of the epistles feels hatred from the secessionists (1 John 4:19). And he is not without hatred for the secessionists. Just read the second letter where the author intimates that to greet a secessionist is tantamount to sharing in his evil (2 John 11). How can they be keeping the commandments?

The eschatological understanding of the secessionists is determined in part by their ethics. If they have not sinned, they have no need of judgement. They are in the light, they are united to Jesus, they are saved. They feel that salvation came into the world in the person of Jesus, and they participate in that salvation now. The author agrees but notes that union with Jesus is contingent on following the commandments, "having fellowship with one another," as he puts it (1 John 1:7). The author appeals to the gospel's ideal of future salvation. He agrees with the secessionists that "we are children of God." Yet he also informs them there is more to it than that (1 John 3:2).

The final area of dispute is the Spirit. The secessionists base their theology on the teaching of the Spirit. The gospel has said that the spirit will be their teacher when Jesus ascends. This leaves the author with little argument. He cannot use the position of the Spirit in the gospel to bolster his reasoning. Rather, he looks to the fruits of the Spirit which are not evident among the secessionists. They have broken off from the community denying the reality of Jesus in the flesh. Therefore, rather than trying to argue from the gospel about the Spirit, the author of the letters suggests that one test the Spirit (1 John 4:1).

The Final Test

The divisions in the epistles did not heal. After the epistles were written, the community continued as a loving community dominated by hatred. Soon, it became evident that something would have to be done if the community were to survive. The secessionists eventually were engulfed in the heretical gnostic movements of the day which were very close to their teachings. The group represented by the author of the epistles, on the other hand, realized that if it was to maintain its position it would have to join the apostolic churches. That group realized that a Spirit centered understanding of church did not provide protection against division. Therefore, it joined the hierarchically structured apostolic churches. In return for structure, it brought its higher christological understanding to those churches. It is an interesting anomaly that the Johannine Christology became the mainline understanding of Jesus; while the surviving Johannine Christians were forced to accept the ecclesiology of the greater church.

There is much that this story can tell us today. We find many groups who feel that they are spirit led. And there are groups who feel that the authority structure of the church today is somewhat oppressive. Each of these opinions is valid. Yet the history of the Johannine community tells us that neither is good of itself. Those who are spirit led need an authority structure for survival. While those who support a strong authority structure need the movement of the spirit in order to grow. Who said that the early church had it made?

Study Questions

1) Who is the beloved disciple according to the fourth Gospel? according to tradition?
2) How do Jewish expectations fit into the development of the Johannine Community?
3) What is the effect of the birkat-ha-minim on the development of the Johannine community?
4) Why does the Gospel of John seem so sectarian? How does its sectarianness help us understand why it is so popular among modern Christian groups?
5) What is the Johannine view of Church? How does it differ from the synoptic view, or the Pauline view?
6) What does the post-Gospel history of the Johannine community tell us about our church today?

Bibliography

Brown, Raymond E., *The Community of the Beloved Disciple The Life, Loves and Hates of an Individual Church in New Testament Times,* (New York: Paulist Press, 1979).

Kysar, Robert, *John's Story of Jesus*, (Philadelphia: Fortress Press, 1984).

Marsh, John, *St. John*, Pelican Gospel Commentaries, (Baltimore: Penguin Books, 1968).

Martyn, J. Louis, *The Gospel of John in Christian History*, (New York: Paulist Press, 1978).

Martyn, J. Louis, *History and Theology in the Fourth Gospel*, Revised and Enlarged Edition, (Nashville: Abingdon Press, 1968).

Chapter 15

The Book of Revelation
Should I Read it or Not?

One Christmas morning, I woke up and turned on the television looking for some Christmas carols. As I changed the channels, I hit upon a rather fiery preacher who was ripping down the Catholic Church. He was claiming that the Roman Catholic Church was the "woman seated on the beast" spoken of in the seventeenth chapter of the Book of Revelation. As I listened, I became more and more angry since this was not the way to begin Christmas morning.

A few weeks later, I was speaking to a group in a local parish. During the question period, several people began to ask about the book of Revelation. They were confused by the imagery and the numbers. They also had read interpretations which seemed to imply that the enemy in Revelation was the Catholic Church. When they asked their parish priest, they were told many hold that position. However, he could not explain the meaning of the text to them. Both of these incidents set me thinking that as Catholics, we need a deeper understanding of this final book of the Bible.

Historical Background of Revelation

It is generally agreed among scholars that Revelation was written toward the end of the first century C.E. The author identifies himself as "John, your brother, who shares with you in Jesus the tribulation and the kingdom and the patient endurance . . ." From this, many identify the author as John the Presbyter to distinguish him from the author of the fourth gospel. Since there is similarity in theme between Revelation and the fourth gospel, many feel that Revelation arises from a group that had some distant relationship with the Johannine community.

The book was probably composed sometime in the late 80s or early 90s of the Common Era. Since its literary style is apocalyptic, we can presume that it was written to provide consolation to a community experiencing persecution. Given the historical situa-

160

tion of the time, we can identify the source of the persecution as Rome with fair certainty.

When the early Christian community split with Judaism, they found themselves without the protection of the Roman Empire. It was Roman law that any secret society or religious group which originated after the foundation of the Empire (742 B.C.E.) was considered a "superstition." Such groups were not permitted to practice in the empire. Since Judaism had been founded long before the empire, Jews were free to practice their beliefs. As long as Christianity was under the aegis of Judaism, the Christians were also considered legal. Now that Christianity had split from Judaism, the Christians were considered a "superstition." Practice of their faith was a violation of Roman Law.

Toward the end of the reign of Emperor Nero unrest began to mount in the empire. In fact, many thought that Nero was assassinated. Three persons occupied the emperor's throne in the three-year period after the death of Nero. Each of them died by assassination. Finally, the general Vespasian was called back from Judea where he was trying to put an end to the revolt which the Zealots had incited. This revolt escalated into the Jewish War.

Vespasian returned to Rome and became emperor. His son Titus continued the war in Judea. During Vespasian's reign some stability returned to the empire. Although his reign was short, he was the first emperor to die a natural death since Claudius. His son, Titus succeeded him and continued the policy of stabilization. Upon Titus' death, Domitian, his son, assumed the position of emperor.

Vespasian and Titus brought some stability to Rome after the chaos of the late 60s. Still, there was urgent need for some principle of unity that would bring the empire together. The unity of the empire was secured by the army who protected the vast regions of Rome by force. Domitian realized that this could never bring lasting unity to his empire. He needed the loyalty of his subjects, a loyalty that arose from moral or religious conviction. As a result, he had himself proclaimed as god, *Dominus et Deus Noster*. He commanded that all loyal Romans, not exempted by law, should burn incense before his statue. The penalty for refusing to acknowledge the divinity of the emperor was a prohibition from carrying on commerce or business within the empire.

Most people in the empire did not find this a hardship. However, there were a few groups who found it unacceptable particularly the Jews and the Christians. When they protested the command, the Jews were exempted because of their position as a "legal religion" within the empire. The Christians, on the other hand, being a "superstition," were not exempted. Domitian wanted the Christians to conform to this command since he didn't trust them. Christians in the empire found themselves faced with a dilemma. They wanted to obey the civil mandate. Yet, obedience to it meant violating the covenant they had entered through belief in "Jesus as Lord."

Some within the church took the road of compromise. They thought this would be the greater good. They felt that placing incense before the emperor's statue was a civil act with no bearing on one's commitment to Christ. Thus, it would be legitimate to perform this one simple act in order to continue spreading the gospel. The Nicolaitans who appear in the second chapter of Revelation are a group who hold this view.

Others in the Christian community saw compromise as totally incompatible with belief in Jesus. Among these, the author of Revelation believed there was a necessity for the Christian community to take a stand. Those who believe in Jesus must remain strong in their faith. That would be a sign that the church is alive and active in the empire. Christians must refuse to follow the command to burn incense before the emperor's statue to speak forcibly the words, "The emperor is not god," "The emperor is not Lord," "Jesus is Lord." The author writes to encourage those who might compromise their faith in the face of Domitian's sanctions.

Literary Style

The literary style of Revelation is apocalyptic. This apocalyptic writing is similar to the Jewish apocalyptic of the Old Testament. The apocalyptic writings of the Old Testament placed the narrative in the past. Revelation, however, is a vision in the first century concerning contemporary first century events. This is crucial for a proper interpretation of the Book of Revelation. Many who do not accept the validity of the apocalyptic literary form prefer to view Revelation as prophecy which awaits fulfillment. They interpret the book to refer to situations of the twentieth, rather than the first century.

THE WORD MADE CLEAR

The author of Revelation draws on Jewish apocalyptic writings, particularly the Book of Daniel, and the visions of Zechariah from the Old Testament, and the visions of Enoch from extra-biblical Jewish literature. He reinterprets these to speak to the situation of his day. His use of familiar traditions makes it easier for his readers to grasp his message.

The Letters to the Churches

The book opens with a vision. This is followed by a series of seven letters to seven churches in Asia Minor. These letters have a common structure. They praise or admonish the receiving community for acceptance or rejection of the message of Jesus. Each letter ends with a promise of reward for perseverance. A careful analysis of the letters reveals much about the early Christian communities of Asia Minor in the final decades of the first century.

The Structure of the Apocalypse

The structure of the remainder of the book has been debated by scholars. Jan Lambrecht bases his structure on three series of seven events. These make up the main part of the text, the seven seals, the seven trumpets and the seven bowls. The author has chosen to include several visions which he intersperses with these. Many interpreters see the progression of the book as linear progression, that is the events follow each other in the order they are narrated. Lambrecht, on the other hand, narrates the events as three *concurrent* series. For Lambrecht, the history of the period is narrated in the seven seals; then in the seven trumpets, and finally a third time in the seven bowls.

The Vision of the Scroll

The vision of the scroll in chapters four and five provides the setting for the seven seals. This vision portrays one seated on a high and lofty throne. It draws upon similar visions in Isaiah, Ezekiel, and the first book of Enoch. The narrative in Revelation will return to this throne and the actions of the elders who worship the one seated on the throne many times.

The focus shifts to the scroll which the one on the throne holds in his right hand. There is a search for someone to open the seals of this scroll. No one is worthy to open them save the Lion of the tribe of Judah, the Root of David, who has conquered. We cannot help but be struck by the messianic character of these titles. However, the imagery shifts. A lamb stands next to the throne. This lamb is the one who conquered, the Root of Jesse. He alone is considered worthy to open the seals. The heavenly court acknowledges this.

The Seven Seals/Vision of the 144,000

The opening of the first six seals follows. As each seal is opened, trial and tribulation are set loose upon the earth. These trials echo visions of Zechariah. When the sixth seal is opened, there is another vision. This vision, the 144,000, has been misinterpreted by many. It begins when angels are sent to gather those who had been sealed as servants of God. The number of those sealed is 144,000 (12,000 from each of the tribes of Israel). Many interpret the number 144,000 to be only those who are saved. That is not the intent of the vision. The vision tells us there will be a large number, 144,000 if you wish, of the original people of God, that is, Israel who will be sealed as servants of God.

The vision continues showing a countless multitude from "every nation, from all tribes and people and tongues." These stand before the throne clothed in white robes with palm branches in their hands. Palm branches were a sign of victory. These later are identified as those who have survived the great tribulation. This is a reference to the persecutions that follow upon refuasl to acknowledge the emperor as God. This countless multitude has also achieved salvation. The vision presents two groups—a specified number from the original people of God, and a countless multitude from the new people of God.

The Seven Trumpets/Vision of Two Witnesses

The seventh seal acts as a link between the series of seals and the series of trumpets. When the seventh seal is broken, seven angels receive seven trumpets. As each trumpet sounds, affliction falls upon the earth. These afflictions resemble many trials from the Old Testament. Many are similar to the plagues which Moses inflicted upon the Egyptians.

After the sixth trumpet sounds, another vision is narrated. This vision calls to mind the inaugural vision of Ezekiel (Ezekiel 1-2). In that vision, he is told to take a scroll and eat it. It becomes sweet as honey in his mouth; yet turns bitter in his stomach. The symbolism is that the prophetic word of God will be easy for the prophet to hear; yet difficult to carry out. The prophetic message to John, seeing these visions, is that he must proclaim the uselessness of worshipping the emperor as a god. The truth is that the emperor is a mortal being who will someday die. Worship belongs only to the Lamb who has conquered death.

The vision continues introducing two witnesses. Their description recalls Zechariah's visions concerning Joshua the priest, and Zerubbabel, the heir apparent to the throne of Israel during the early post exilic period (Zechariah 4:3). When these witnesses finish their testimony, a beast from the bottomless pit rises and kills them. They lie dead for three days. After that they receive the breath of life from God. Then they ascend to heaven in a cloud. If we try to interpret these witnesses as two definite people, it becomes difficult to establish a definite identification. However, if we connect these witnesses to the messianic expectations of the day, we can understand the passage.

Among many groups, there was an expectation of two messiahs, a kingly messiah from the Davidic line, and a priestly messiah of the priestly descent. Some groups in the early Christian community saw Christ fulfilling both these messianic roles. We might therefore be able to understand the two witnesses as the messiah. Since the treatment of the two witnesses parallels the treatment of Christ, and Christ is the messiah, we could conclude that the two witnesses represent Christ. The seventh trumpet sounds announcing the eternal reign of the Lord who sits upon the throne and his Christ. Three visions follow which are inserted prior to the narration of the seven bowls.

The Woman Clothed With the Sun

The first vision reveals a woman clothed with the sun. She has the moon under her feet and a crown of stars on her head. The reader is reminded of the dreams of Joseph in Genesis here (Genesis 40-41). The woman is with child. When she delivers her male off-spring, a dragon with seven heads and ten horns (recall the beast of Daniel 7) appears. This beast intends to devour the child. How-ever, the child is caught up to the throne of God. The woman finds refuge in the desert. Many prefer to see allusions to Mary giving birth to Jesus in this vision. However, that does not explain the details of the vision fully. Another view supposes that the woman is Israel who gives birth to the messiah. Through the messiah, the early Christian community also becomes the woman's descen-dants. The dragon then becomes Rome. Rome is waiting to con-sume this child. Is this not what happened in the crucifixion? Rome put Jesus to death. Yet in the resurrection/ascension, he was raised and caught up to heaven.

After the child has been taken up, a new character appears, Michael. Michael is the prince who has charge of the people Israel in the book of Daniel. He is advocate for Israel against the rival angel of Persia (Daniel 10:13, 20). During a time of tribulation, he will lead his forces in the final battle with the forces of evil (Daniel 12:1). The war in heaven which now arises between Michael and the dragon recalls this battle. Contemporary rabbinic literature saw Michael as vindicator of Israel against Rome.

The outcome of the battle was Michael defeating the dragon and his angels. This recalls the taunt against the King of Babylon in Isaiah (Isaiah 14:12). The taunter speaks of the day star or son of the dawn as fallen from heaven. Is this not what Revelation tells us Michael does to the devil and his angels? When we exam-ine the Latin text of Isaiah, this becomes even clearer. Jerome chose to translate the Hebrew word for "daystar" as "Lucifer," the bearer of light.

The text of Revelation parallels this act of Michael in heaven to the action of Jesus in the cross and resurrection. Salvation comes when Michael casts out Satan; salvation comes when Jesus con-quers death. There is joy in heaven because the devil has been cast out; yet there is woe on earth for the devil now pursues those on the earth with his wrath. The dragon/devil hunts the woman who bore the child. She is able to find assistance, and the dragon is unable to destroy either the woman or her son.

Instead, the dragon wages war on the remaining descendants of the woman, the early Christian community after Christ's ascension. The author of Revelation identifies "the rest of her offspring" with "those who keep the commandments of God and bear witness to Jesus." (Revelation 12:17) This refers to the situation of the community of Revelation. Those who keep the commandments and bear witness to Jesus cannot burn incense to the statue of the emperor. Rome makes war on them. Therefore, we can see that the author of Revelation understood the actions of Rome against the community parallelling the actions of the beast against the woman's offspring.

The Vision of the Two Beasts

The second vision portrays two beasts. One rises from the sea, the other from the earth. This vision draws on material found in Daniel 7 and Daniel 8. It begins with a beast with ten horns and seven heads rising out of the sea. This reminds the reader of the beast in Daniel 7:7 with ten horns. Scholars have thought that the ten horns might refer to the emperors of the Flavian and Julian Dynasties. Most agree that the seven heads allude to the seven hills on which Rome sits. The beast utters blasphemous names which is reminiscent of the beast of Daniel 7:7 who spoke arrogantly. There is another allusion to the situation of Revelation. According to Jewish and Christian understanding, "setting oneself equal to God" is blasphemy. In reuniting the empire, Domitian set himself equal to God. The blasphemies uttered by the beast recall the blasphemous actions of Domitian in declaring himself divine.

The description of the beast shows that it is a combination of the four beasts Daniel saw in his vision (Daniel 7:1-8). It is given power by the dragon. Earlier power, honor, dominion and glory were given to the Lamb (Revelation 5:12-13). The author says that the power given to the beast through the dragon is really power that belongs to God. He has chosen to invest it in the Lamb. We see another reference to Domitian's claim to divinity.

The next part of this vision is difficult to understand. One of the seven heads had a mortal wound which had been healed. Scholars feel this refers to Nero. He was assassinated. Many presumed he arranged a plot, left Rome for the regions of Parthia, and would return with an army to recapture Rome.

When the mortal wound of the best was healed, "all the earth" worshipped the dragon and the beast. In fact, the song of praise for the beast (Revelation 13:4) is similar to the song which praises the Lamb (Revelation 5:9). The dragon blasphemes against God and his dwelling, while the beast wages war on the saints and conquers them. This is the persecution of the church by Rome.

Those who are outside the Christian covenant fall down and worship the beast. The author admonishes the readers to hear his message. This is not a story about the past. It speaks to the present. If the readers are followers of Christ, they will listen and not follow the beast. If captivity or the sword is the lot of a Christian, then that is to be their lot. The section ends with an apocalyptic exhortation. The saints are not to give in; rather, they must endure and be faithful.

Study Questions

1) What is the historical background of Revelation? How does this background help us to understand the book?
2) What is unique about the structure of the book of revelation?
3) What is the meaning of the vision of the 144,000 (Chapter 7)?
4) What is the meaning of the vision of the woman clothed with the sun (Chapter 12)? Who is this woman?
5) What do the visions of Revelation tell us concerning the first century church, concerning the church of today?

Bibliography

Collins, Adela Yarbro, *The Apocalypse,* The New Testament Message, Vol. 22, (Wilmington: Michael Glazier, 1979).

Collins, Adela Yarbro, *Crisis and Catharsis: The Power of the Apocalypse,* Philadelphia: Westminster Press, 1984).

Corsini, Eugenio, *The Apocalypse: The Perennial Revelation of Jesus Christ,* trans. and ed. by Francis J. Moloney, Good News Studies, Vol. 5, (Wilmington: Michael Glazier, 1983).

Harrington, Wilfrid, *Understanding the Apocalypse,* (Washington: Corpus Books, 1969).

Schüssler Fiorenza, Elizabeth, *Invitation to the Book of Revelation,* (Garden City: Doubleday & Co., 1981).

Chapter 16

The Book of Revelation:
The End of the Story

The vision of the two beasts continues when the second beast rises
from the earth. It has two horns like a lamb and speaks like the
dragon resembling the beast of Daniel 8. Later in Revelation, the
beast and the dragon will appear with a false prophet. Many conjecture that this second beast is that false prophet.

This second beast exercises authority similar to the first beast.
It is the duty of this beast to make the inhabitants of the earth worship the first beast. Their powers are definitely opposed to the
power of the Lamb. The second beast works great wonders to lead
the people astray. These wonders deceive those who dwell upon
the earth. They make an image of the first beast.

Nero's plot emerges once again. In 68 C.E., Nero tried to kill
himself with a sword. He was unsuccessful. Many believe Nero's
actions lie behind these allusions. Further, as we said in the
previous unit, Domitian, in his action toward the Christians, appears as Nero incarnated. The image of the first beast receives
the power to speak. (This probably was an ancient form of ven-
triloquism popular in many cults.) Whoever would not worship
the image of the beast was slain. Once again we see the situation
of the Christian community under Domitian.

Once citizens have offered incense as homage to the emperor,
they are marked. Without that mark, they are unable to engage
in any business. The mark of the beast allows those who bear it
to survive in the empire; those who do not will be killed. This
recalls the "seal" which the faithful received in Revelation 7:3.
It assured them eternal life; those who failed to receive it inherited
eternal damnation. The mark is the "number" of the beast. This
number refers to a man. It represents the sum of the numerical
equivalents of the letters in a particular man's name. There have
been theories through the centuries linking this number to almost
every evil person who has ever lived. The most likely candidate,
however, remains the emperor Nero or his reincarnation, Domitian. The letters of the Hebrew form of his name add up to 666.

The letters of the Latin form add up to 616. This number appears in several manuscripts.

The Apocalyptic Harvest

The final vision which interrupts the continuity of the trumpets and the bowls is the vision of the harvest. The 144,000 reappear with the Lamb on Mt. Zion. They have the name of the Lamb written on their foreheads. This contrasts them with those who have the mark of the beast on their foreheads. They sing a special song. Only those who are chaste, the first fruits of the Lamb, can learn it.

The scene switches, an angel flies in mid-heaven proclaiming the hour of judgment to those who dwell on the earth. All on earth must accept the gospel rejecting the beast, or accept the beast rejecting the Lamb. The narrative continues with two separate accounts of judgment—one against Babylon (Rome), the other against the remaining pagan nations.

A second angel announces the judgment against Babylon. Babylon is a code name for Rome. She makes the nations of the earth drink the "wine of her impure passion." This is a reference to the widespread immorality that characterized the Roman Empire.

A third angel announces that all those who worship the beast will be forced to drink of the wine of the "wrath of God." To choose the beast is to choose the wrath and anger of God. The author exhorts the community to keep the commandments of God and maintain faith in Jesus despite the cost.

Again the scene shifts. One "like a Son of Man" appears. This is similar to Daniel 7:13. The only difference is the crown suggesting royal dignity. This figure's arrival signals the beginning of the great harvest, the judgment on all the nations. The process of gathering and throwing grapes into a wine press to make wine becomes symbolic of this judgment. The grapes, those who did not remain faithful to the covenant, are thrown into the wine press of the wrath of God. A message of consolation to the suffering community is sent. Those who are not part of the community will suffer under the judgment of God.

THE WORD MADE CLEAR

The Seven Bowls

The third and final sequence of seven, the seven bowls, begins with an extended introductory vision. Those who have withstood the torments of the beast sing the song of the Lamb (Revelation 5:9). Then seven angels come forth from the heavenly temple. They receive seven bowls containing the wrath of God. These they will pour down on the earth. This introduction contains several references to the preceding three visions. Therefore, those visions do not interrupt; rather, they link the narrative of the seven trumpets and the narrative of the seven bowls.

The account of the seven bowls follows the pattern of the trumpets and seals. Several allusions to plague narratives in Exodus and other Old Testament passages characterize the narrative. When the sixth bowl is poured, the Euphrates River is dried up to prepare the way for the kings of the east. Rumors flooded the Roman Empire for decades that the Parthians, the empire to the east, would someday rise up and try to conquer Rome. Coupled with this, there was a belief that Nero had defected to Parthia to lead the Parthians in that attack. The accounts of the mysterious circumstances surrounding the "death" of Nero play an important role in the understanding of Revelation.

A further effect of the sixth bowl is a call to the kings of the world to gather in the place known as Armageddon for battle on the "day of the Lord." The name Armageddon, in Hebrew, means "field of Megiddo." There is a plain below Mt. Carmel near the town of Megiddo which is the only passage between the mountains in the area. As a result, this plain became a central travel and trade route. In fact, for centuries, whoever controlled this pass near Megiddo controlled most trade between Egypt and Mesopotamia. Consequently, the "field of Megiddo" was the scene of many battles and much bloodshed during Israel's history. Could there be a better place to situate the final battle?

The seventh bowl is the prelude to the judgment scene of Babylon. In the scenes that follow, the fall of Rome and the Roman Empire is predicted. The "great city" is Rome. The cities of the nations are the other cities of the empire. Using the symbol of the cup of wrath, the author tells the readers that Rome will be forced to pay for her actions. Such predictions are common in apocalyptic writing. Those who have suffered greatly will gain consolation when they realize that their persecutors will someday be brought down.

The Harlot Babylon

The vision of the harlot begins the judgment on Rome. This harlot stands in contrast to the woman clothed with the sun in Revelation 12. The woman clothed with the sun was Israel, the people of God who brought forth the messiah and the saints of the most high. This woman, a harlot, is seated upon "many waters." Jeremiah described the ancient city of Babylon as being by "many waters." In a prediction that Babylon has reached her end, Jeremiah declares she will soon be cut off (Jeremiah 51:13). Using that allusion, the author of Revelation transforms this into a prediction of the destruction of Rome (Babylon). The reason for Rome's downfall is the fact that she has forced many nations of the earth to accept her idolatrous ways.

The scene changes to the desert. Another woman seated on a scarlet beast appears. The beast has seven heads and ten horns resembling the beast of Revelation 13. This woman also represents Rome. As Rome sits on seven hills, so this woman sits on a beast with seven heads. She holds out a cup containing the many abominations and impurities of her fornication. Her name, "Babylon, the great" is emblazoned on her forehead. (There was a custom where Roman harlots showed their names on their foreheads.) The cup containing the blood of the saints and martyrs of Jesus has made this woman drunk. The abominations in the cup must be the actions of Rome against the Christians who rejected the cult of emperor worship.

To avoid misunderstanding, an angel explains the mystery of the woman and the beast. The beast was and is not and is to come. If the beast is Rome, we see Rome's destruction and future rise. Some conjecture yet another reference to the return of Nero. The events narrated in the remainder of Revelation probably lie at the root of this cryptic statement. The book will narrate the fall of Rome, its rise, and final condemnation by the Lamb (Revelation 19).

The angel continues explaining that the seven heads of the beast on which the woman sits are seven mountains (hills). The woman is Rome. The seven heads can refer to seven kings or emperors.

Five have passed, one reigns, and the final one is yet to come. If we look to Roman history for an interpretation, these were the five past rulers of the Julian Dynasty—Augustus, Tiberius, Caligula, Claudius, and Nero. The three short-lived emperors, Galba, Otho, and Vitellius, can be overlooked. The one who reigns becomes Vespasian. The one to come would then be Titus. The seventh king will reign for a short while. Titus reigned a mere two years; then, he died of natural causes.

As the angel's explanation continues, the beast is identified with an eighth king who is part of the seven. Continuing the line of emperors, the eighth would be Domitian. This identification of the beast matches the interpretation proposed in Revelation 13. The final part of the explanation shows the meaning of the ten horns. From Revelation 17:16, these horns cannot be Roman emperors who will follow Domitian. They will receive authority with the beast; yet they are against Rome. The harlot will be made desolate at their hands. They must represent nations outside Rome who will someday bring about the downfall of Rome. Again many see these as Parthian rulers who will overcome the Roman empire when Nero returns. (Note how the Nero expectations pervade the text.) Whatever the situation, these kings will initially wage war upon the Christian community (the Lamb). The Lamb will emerge victorious. The vision of the harlot becomes a prediction of the destruction of Rome.

The Fall of Babylon

What is predicted takes place in the next vision. Rome (Babylon) falls. Rome has brought wealth to many nations, yet she has also led many nations to follow her idolatrous ways. Therefore, she has fallen. An exhortation to Christians to flee Rome lest they become tainted by her evil ways follows. Rome is to suffer double the hardship that she has inflicted upon the church. Those who have grown rich through Rome stand weeping and lamenting as they witness the destruction. All the cargoes that moved in and out of the city will be no longer. All mourn the loss of the city except the "saints, apostles, and prophets," the early Christian community. In the fall of Rome, judgment has been passed vindicating the deaths of those who fell to Rome's violence.

In the final scene, an angel takes a millstone and hurls it into

173

the sea. As this millstone will disappear into the sea, the angel prophecies, so shall Rome disappear leaving nothing but desolation behind. This is a possible allusion to Jesus' words "And if anyone causes one of these little ones who believe in me to sin, it would be better for him to be thrown into the sea with a large millstone tied around his neck" (Mark 9:42). Rome was the cause of many little ones being led astray. Therefore, her end is symbolized as a millstone being thrown into the sea.

The Wedding Feast of the Lamb

The scene returns to heaven where there is great rejoicing. The Lamb has conquered. In contrast to the lamentations on earth over the destruction of Rome, hymns of joy are sung throughout the heavenly court. The messianic banquet, the sign of the inauguration of the final days, begins. The time of tribulation on earth has come to an end. Those who died because of their enduring faith in Jesus have been vindicated. As the scene ends, the seer is overcome by the message he receives. He believes the messenger is God himself. He bows down in worship. The messenger reminds him that he is an angel. Worship is restricted to God alone. The author subtly recalls a key theme of the book. Rome had demanded that everyone worship the emperor. The author here responds that worship is due God alone. Divine beings such as angels are not to be accorded worship, much less a human being like the emperor.

The Lamb's Victory Over the Beast

The final confrontation now takes place. Babylon, the earthly city of Rome, has been destroyed. The heavenly powers behind Rome (the beast and false prophet) and the community (the Lamb) must engage in battle. A white horse appears. Its rider whose name is "Word of God" wears a robe which has been dipped in blood. The armies of heaven, the heavenly host, follow behind him as he leads them to "tread upon the wine press of the fury of the wrath of God."

Another angel calls to the birds of heaven to prepare to feast on what remains after the battle. The beast and the kings of the earth have gathered to do battle. The battle is swift. The beast and the false prophet are seized and thrown into the lake of fire.

174

The kings of the earth are quickly dispatched. Their flesh is left for the birds of the air to devour. The message is clear. Those who have fallen prey to the machinations of Rome will eventually fall to the power of the Lamb. However, the end has not yet come.

The Millennium

The dragon, the one remaining power of evil, is seized. An angel binds him and throws him into the pit. It is sealed for one thousand years. All powers of evil have left the earth. There is no other reference in either the Old or New Testament to such a reign. Many early writers in the church were fascinated by this question. The idea that the world existed in several aeons of five-hundred to one-thousand years each was popular in ancient literature. The Persians viewed history as ten one-thousand-year periods. Many fathers of the church, particularly Lactantius, were influenced by such concepts. At the beginning of the Middle Ages, millennialism, as this belief came to be known, began to wane. It remained alive, however, among several sects peripheral to the church. Today, belief in the thousand-year reign remains central to many fundamentalist groups.

After the thousand years have ended, Satan will be released to gather his troops. He will make war on the saints in the "beloved city." This will prove unsuccessful. In the end, the devil will be thrown into the lake of fire to join the beast and the false prophet. At that point, all forces of evil will be subdued. Following the judgment on the dragon, the judgment of all who died takes place. Those who have been faithful receive eternal life. Those who have been unfaithful are condemned to the "second death." They are thrown into the lake of fire to join the dragon, the beast, and the false prophet. This becomes the final vindication of the saints of the most high.

The Vision of the New Jerusalem

The final vision of Revelation reveals a new heaven and a new earth. Descending from the sky is the new Jerusalem, God's dwelling among his people. The one who sits on the heavenly throne announces the real meaning of the book. The visions that have preceded—the harlot, the fall of Babylon, the feast of the lamb, the millennium and the judgment—show what will happen in the end. Those who are faithful in the present trials will inherit the joy and peace of the New Jerusalem. The agents of trial and tribulation will inherit the everlasting torment of the lake of fire. This should provide encouragement for those who are wavering in their faith. They are to be patient, endure, and they will conquer.

A description of the New Jerusalem follows. The city has twelve gates each decorated with magnificent jewels. These gates bear the names of the twelve tribes of Israel. The city sits upon a foundation of twelve pillars which bear the names of the twelve apostles. The new Jerusalem has no temple. In the old Jerusalem, the temple was the dwelling place of God among his people. God is no longer confined within the walls of a building. The presence of God is in the community itself.

The book ends with a promise of the imminent return of the savior. Since the Lord is coming soon, the usual apocalyptic command to seal the words is omitted. The final lines of the book continue this. The Lord says he is coming soon, and the community responds with the plaintive plea. "Come Lord, Jesus."

Conclusions

Despite many attempts to interpret this book as contemporary prophecy, it should be clear that any interpretation must take into consideration the original situation of the author and the readers. The book was written for Christians who were suffering persecution at the hands of the Roman Emperor Domitian. They faced a choice of either giving up their faith and saving their lives, or holding fast to their faith and losing their lives. The book was written to encourage them to hold firmly to their faith. The encouragement comes from a series of visions which show the readers that there is more to life than what they are experiencing. There is a future in which the tables will be turned. The persecutors will be persecuted and their victims will be vindicated.

Once that is understood, it is possible for later generations to take that message and apply it to their situation. We, in twentieth-century America, are not experiencing circumstances where adherence to our faith might be life threatening. Yet, at times we find it easier to hide our faith because of ridicule, or verbal harassment. The message of Revelation to us becomes "hold strong to the faith." Through the centuries, the victory of God has repeatedly been shown. Patiently enduring difficulties, we will also share the victory celebration of the Lamb.

Study Questions

1) Idolatry in the form of emperor worship was the problem of first century Christians. What are the forms of idolatry today? How does the book of Revelation speak to them?
2) What is the significance of 'Armageddon?'
3) What is the function of the harlot introduced in Revelation 17?
4) How does the fall of Babylon correlate to the Wedding Feast of the Lamb?
5) Follow the images of the beast, the dragon and the false prophet through the book of Revelation. What does the use of these images tell you concerning the meaning of the book?
6) What does Revelation say concerning the 1000 years reign, the millennium?
7) What is peculiar about the New Jerusalem? Why?

Bibliography

Stringfellow, William, *An Ethic for Christians and Other Aliens in a Strange Land,* (Waco, Texas: Word Books, 1973).

Chapter 17

The Kingdom of God Is Like . . .
The Parables of Jesus

In the novel, *The Heart is a Lonely Hunter,* there is a scene where a young teenage girl is listening to one of her favorite records with a friend, Mr. Singer, who is deaf and dumb. As she listens, she tries to explain to Mr. Singer what music sounds like.

Standing directly in front of him so he can read her lips, she gestures with her hands to get her ideas across. After much gesturing, she gives up realizing that describing sound to a person who is deaf is like describing color to a person who is blind.

Jesus encounters this problem when he attempts to teach people about the Kingdom of God. The people of Jesus' day had their own ideas about the Kingdom of God. The idea that Jesus presented to them was beyond their experience. However, Jesus did not give up as the teenage girl in the novel. He used his audience's experiences as the basis for his explanation of the Kingdom of God. In other words, he employed "parables" in his teaching.

Parables: What Are They?

The word, "parable," is derived from two Greek words, *para* meaning "beside," and *ballō* meaning "to throw." In its root derivation, the word means something that is "thrown beside." We might ask, "What is thrown or set beside what?" When Jesus taught using parables, he illustrated ideas about the Kingdom of God by examples drawn from the everyday experience of his hearers. He would begin, "The Kingdom of God is like . . . a fig tree, a pearl, a sower, a mustard seed, a king who goes on a journey, etc." In the words of one scholar, "The parables are the recounting of a common incident from daily life in concise, figurative form to illustrate a spiritual truth." Put very simply, the parables take the familiar and use it to explain the unfamiliar. The areas that Jesus chose to draw images for use in parables were nature (the mustard seed), agriculture (the sower), shepherding (the lost sheep), fishing (the net), or banking (the talents).

THE WORD MADE CLEAR

Jesus was not the first to use parables as a teaching device. We find several parables in the Old Testament. The earliest form of parable in the Old Testament derives from the *mashal,* a word meaning "make up or repeat a saying or proverb." The oldest form of *mashal* is the proverb. A classic example of this literary form is the Book of Proverbs.

Through the influence of Eastern thought, the *mashal* acquired many of the characteristics of the "riddle," *hidah.* Sirach calls "riddles" obscure sayings of the sages (Sirach 39:3). These short sayings soon developed into full stories of comparison. To illustrate recall the "parable of the trees" told by Jotham in the book of Judges (Jdg 9:7-15) which was discussed in Chapter 6. The purpose of this parable is to show the futility of making Abimelech, son of Gideon, king over the tribes of Israel.

The prophet Nathan uses a parable in 2 Samuel 12:1-6 to illustrate David's injustice in his treatment of Uriah the Hittite after taking his wife, Bathsheba. A rich man owned many flocks and herds, while a poor man had only one ewe lamb. When the rich man invited guests, he killed the poor man's ewe lamb to serve to his guests. David becomes outraged at this act. The rich man should have known better. Nathan points out that David's action with Bathsheba is similar. Through Nathan's illustration, David gets the message.

The literary form, parable, is not unique to the Old Testament and Jewish culture. In Greek literature, "parable" is a rhetorical device for comparison, also known as "similitude." Aristotle in his *Rhetoric* describes parables as taking their material for comparison from observation in real life and not from imaginary life as the fable does. In his teaching, Jesus employs all these forms to illustrate his points.

Types of Parables

I. *The Proverb.*—The proverbs used by Jesus are short sayings of comparison. They are the simplest form drawing from ordinary experience to illustrate how life should be lived. The Sermon on the Mount in Matthew provides an example of Jesus' use of proverbs, "You are the light of the world. A city set on a hill cannot be hidden" (Matthew 5:14b).

179

II. *Parables which reflect data about ourselves.*—Jesus also uses stories to narrate familiar experiences to reflect the deeper spiritual values of the Kingdom of God. An example would be the parable of the Good Samaritan. Jesus takes the experience of a fellow human being in need and shows that help knows no boundaries.

Often this parable is read apart from its context. To understand it properly, it is necessary to examine its context. A lawyer comes to Jesus with a question. Luke tells us that the lawyer intends to "test Jesus." His question, "What must I do to inherit eternal life?," is answered, according to Jesus, in the law. The lawyer demonstrates his knowledge of the law citing two central passages from the law concerning love of God and neighbor (Deut. 6:4-5; Lev 19:18). Jesus affirms the lawyer's response telling him to observe those commandments and he will have eternal life.

At first sight, this dialogue between Jesus and the lawyer might seem unrelated to the parable which follows. The lawyer is not satisfied with the answer. Leviticus 19:18 which he has cited concerning love of neighbor implies that "neighbor" means only one's fellow countrymen. The lawyer wants to be sure this interpretation of the law is correct.

Therefore, in order to *justify* himself, he poses a second question, "Who is my neighbor?" Jesus answers telling the parable of the Good Samaritan. The man who has fallen among robbers is near death. Two fellow citizens, a priest and a Levite, who are traveling on the same road pass by him. That doesn't seem too neighborly, does it? The man looked as though he were dead. Their action was simply observance of the law about touching corpses. To insure a proper observance of the law, rabbis taught that one should presume the widest possible infraction of the law and avoid that. This man looked dead, therefore, they presumed that he was. If they touched a corpse, they would become unclean, and could not perform their duties. It was better to continue walking and not get involved.

Another traveler on the road sees the wounded man, cares for him, binds his wounds, and gives him food. Then he brings the wounded man to an inn where he can be provided for until he is able to continue his journey. The parable contrasts the priest and the Levite with the man who helped. This contrast becomes more remarkable since the person who provided help is identified as a Samaritan. Throughout the history of Israel, Jews and Samaritans

180

viewed each other as enemies. So a Samaritan stopping to help a Jew is astonishing. When Jesus asks the lawyer who was "neighbor" to the man in need, we can be sure that he nearly choked on the words, "the one who showed mercy to him." He never says, "the Samaritan." The conclusion to the parable certainly forces the lawyer to reflect on who he considers "neighbor." When we read the parable in its context, the answer to the lawyer's question concerning eternal life demands that he be a neighbor to those who are in need no matter who they are. The parable demands that we evaluate who our neighbor is.

III. *Parables which reveal something about God.* Parables can also give us a better idea of what God is really like. This type of parable, Mark Link notes, does not "mirror" our actions. Rather, it provides a "window" through which we can glimpse the reality of God. An example of this type of parable would be the prodigal son. The point of this parable is the love of God the Father for his people.

The prodigal son is one of the most vivid, story-like parables in the gospels. To understand this parable, we must look at the context of the parable in the gospel. The parable is the third of three parables about the lost and the found—the lost sheep, the lost coin, and the lost "prodigal" son. These parables are an answer to a comment from the Pharisees and scribes concerning Jesus' presence with tax collectors and sinners. As we saw in the parable of the Good Samaritan, the context of a parable is a prime indicator for how we should interpret a parable.

The structure of this parable consists of four scenes. After introducing the major characters, a father and his two sons, the first scene begins when the younger son requests his portion of his father's property. This request must have been devastating to the father. Such a request implied a wish that the father be dead. Yet the father complies with his son's request, giving him his just portion of the inheritance. Jewish law provides that an estate be divided among the sons. The eldest receives a double portion. In this case, the elder son would receive two-thirds while the younger would receive one-third.

In the second scene, the younger son is in a distant land. After he recklessly squandered his inheritance, he is reduced to feeding swine. Coming to his senses, he decides to return home. Thinking that he will no longer be welcomed as a son, he resolves to ask for a job as a hired hand. All the way home, he rehearses his speech to his father. The third scene is his arrival at home. His father greets him joyfully, kissing him, arraying him in a bright robe, giving him a ring and offering sandals for his feet. To his surprise, his father treats him as a son. The fatted calf is killed and the feast begins.

The final scene between the father and his elder son follows. The older son is jealous. He feels he has been cheated. Hid father never provided any party for him. He has faithfully served his father; his brother has not. This final scene contains the message of the parable. If we look at the words of the father to his older son recalling the question that introduced the parable, we see that the message is clear. The tax collectors and sinners are like the younger son. The Pharisees and the scribes are like the older son. Jesus is like the father. In the parable, the father showers his love on whomever he wishes. The joy and happiness that the father shows at the return of his lost son does not in any way detract from the love he has for his older son. The problem is that the older son is blinded to that love since he has viewed himself as a hired hand, and never has allowed himself to experience his father's love. At the end, he remains unwilling to accept the fact of his father's love. The Pharisees feel that they have a corner on the Father's love; they are unwilling to admit that the Father can accept tax collectors and sinners. Like the older son in the parable, they are unable to experience the true love of the Father.

Interpreting Parables

There are nearly forty-five parables in the gospels. They include several aspects of life. In order to interpret these parables properly, we must, as we have seen, read the parables carefully in context, and place ourselves in the situation of the people who heard them. We can then apply a few principles to help us comprehend the message of the parables.

1. *Look for the primary intent of the parable.* A way we can find the primary purpose of a parable is to see how it ends. Recall how the message of the parables we have examined appears in the final lines. However, there are some parables where the primary

message does not appear in the ending. The parable of the sower is an example (Mark 4:3-9). In that parable, Jesus likens the process of the Kingdom of God to the process of sowing seed. The message is that all the seed that is sown will not bear fruit; yet the seed that is fruitful will produce a large harvest.

2. *Interpret any subordinate details of the parable in light of the main intent.* Again, using the parable of the sower, we note that seed falls on different types of land. The seed that fell on the side of the road was eaten quickly, it never could bear fruit. The seed that fell on rocky ground did sprout but, having little root, it soon died. The seed that fell among thorns also sprouted, but was soon was choked by the thorns. The seed on good ground bore fruit thirty, sixty, and a hundredfold. Interpreting these subordinate details in light of our primary purpose, we see that the seed fell on various types of ground with various results. Therefore, the proclamation will come to many different types of people in different ways, yet all will be part of the kingdom of God.

3. *Not all details have a spiritual meaning.* We must refrain from the habit of finding meaning in every detail of a parable. There is a tendency to allegorize the parables among many scholars. A parable illustrates a single point. In the parable of the sower, there are four types of soil. The point of the parable concerns a process involving all four types. We do not need to know what kind of seed is being sown or the significance of each of the types of soil to interpret the parable.

4. *The context of the parable is significant in interpretation.* The importance of this principle is clear from the discussion of the parables of the prodigal son and the Good Samaritan. The context of the parable of the sower is a discourse which is composed of several parables which Jesus delivers while sitting in a boat. The context of a parable can be determined by asking a few simple questions:

a) What is the occasion of the parable?
b) To whom was the parable addressed?
c) What was the effect of the parable on the listeners?

Let us take another parable as an example of these contextual questions. In the Gospel of Mark, after Jesus has entered the city of Jerusalem, he is teaching. Part of that teaching is a parable addressed to the chief priests, scribes and elders (Mark 11:27; 12:1). The parable tells of a vineyard which is leased to tenant farmers. On several occasions when the owner sends for his portion of the fruit of the vineyard, his servants are killed. Finally, he sends his son. The tenants see this as their final chance. They kill him thinking that the vineyard will now become theirs. The parable ends when the owner takes the vineyard from the tenants and gives it to others.

This parable is part of Jesus' Jerusalem ministry. It immediately follows his action in the temple. There is considerable opposition between Jesus and official Judaism. The parable is addressed to the leaders of the Jews, chief priests, scribes and elders who are questioning Jesus' authority. Those who listen to the parable try to arrest Jesus. Mark makes the reader aware that the Jewish authorities knew that the parable was told against them.

The meaning of the parable of the wicked tenants becomes clear when we apply these contextual questions. The chief priests and other Jewish leaders have had the vineyard entrusted to them by the Father. He has sent prophets to them on several occasions. They have failed to listen to them; they have even killed them. Now he has sent his only Son; they are about to kill him. They are not worthy of the vineyard and it will be given to others.

5. *The cultural background of the parable must be recognized.* Special attention should be given to the cultural background of the parables. If one tries to interpret the parable of the sower using modern farming methods, there will be several problems. To understand the parable correctly, the interpreter must first examine farming methods in the first century. The sower carried a bag of seed out to the field. He threw the seed across the field so it landed everywhere. Again, in the parable of the Good Samaritan, a knowledge of Jewish law and legal practice is necessary to realize that the priest and Levite are not wrong in their actions. They are simply following what the law prescribes.

6. *Doctrines are not established by parables; parables are illustrations of doctrine.* Parables are not definitive teaching. They are a means of illustrating a particular point which is taught. Parables are illustrations intended to give a clear picture to the listeners. They are intended to make the assimilation and under-

standing of truth easier. Jesus used parables to challenge his listeners to listen and understand that they might remember his message easier.

Narrative Analysis and the Parables

John Dominic Crossan in his book, *In Parables,* presents a new way of looking at the parables. He sees the future orientation of the parables counterpoised to the eternal presence of God. Using the parable of the hidden treasure as a paradigm, he shows that the verbs in that parable provide a pattern for understanding all the parables.

The man who finds the pearl lived his life planning for the present and the future. Suddenly, he discovers this pearl which upsets all of his plans. Crossan terms this the *advent* of the treasure. This treasure causes a total *reversal* of his life. He sells all that he has to purchase the pearl. The treasure now becomes the center of his existence. All that he does, his *action,* centers around the treasure.

Crossan notes that Jesus, in the parables, opposed the view of time as man's future. He proposes, rather, the notion of time as God's present. It is not an eternity to be hoped for in the future but, rather, a reality whose advent is already within us. The parables thus proclaim the temporality of the kingdom in three simultaneous modes, advent, reversal, and action. He then proceeds to examine individual parables in each of these categories. In the parables of advent, we find the parable of the mustard seed. These are parables which see the kingdom as hidden. However, when they are understood in human life, they lead to surprise and mystery.

Parables of reversal such as Lazarus and the rich man overturn the smug quiet world of people who live in security. The reversal is complete, whole and total. In the parable of the Pharisee and the publican, the Pharisee who thinks he has it made appears in second place to the poor publican who prays honestly.

The parables of action show people who have become active through the inbreaking of the kingdom. This inbreaking demands a response which is complete and final. In this category we have the parable of the wicked tenants, the parable about the watchful servants, and the parable of the talents. Whoever carefully keeps what is entrusted is censured in favor of one who is willing to risk. The gifts given by the inbreaking of the kingdom must not be put away, they must be used to further the development of the kingdom.

Study Questions

1) Give some examples of common experiences you have used in your life to explain some deeper concepts.
2) How does the parable of the Good Samaritan 'shock' one into seeing its point?
3) How does the distinction 'window' parable and 'mirror' parable help to illustrate what the parables are?
4) Take a few of your favorite parables and use the method described in this chapter to interpret them.
5) What is meant by 'allegorizing a parable?' How is that different from interpreting the parable as we have described?
6) How does Crossan's distinction of parables of advent, reversal and action shed light on the interpretation of the parables?

Bibliography

Boucher, Madeleine, I., *The Parables,* The New Testament Message, Vol. 7, (Wilmington: Michael Glazier, 1981).

Crossan, John Dominic, *The Dark Interval: Towards a Theology of Story,* (Niles: Argus Communications, 1975).

Crossan, John Dominic, *In Parables: The Challenge of the Historical Jesus,* (San Francisco: Harper and Row, 1973).

Dodd, Charles H., *The Parables of the Kingdom,* (New York: Charles Scribners Sons, 1961).

Donahue, John R., *The Gospel in Parable: Metaphor, Narrative and Theology in the Synoptic Gospels,* (Philadelphia: Fortress Press, 1988).

Scott, Bernard Brandon, *Hear Then the Parable: A Commentary on the Parables of Jesus,* (Minneapolis: Fortress Press, 1989).

Thomas, Clemens, and Wyschogrod, Michael (eds), *Parable and Story in Judaism and Christianity,* (New York: Paulist Press, 1989.

Chapter 18

The Reign of God
Will Come Upon You

The opening words of Jesus in the Gospel of Mark proclaim, "The time is fulfilled, and the kingdom of God is at hand . . ." Jesus' mission was to announce to the people of Israel that the time of salvation was upon them. In particular, that salvation was to be understood as the long awaited coming of God's kingdom. Our task in this unit will be to discover what Jesus' hearers understood when they heard him proclaim this message, and to understand what Jesus himself meant by the "Kingdom of God." To accomplish this we shall look first at how the Kingdom of God was understood in the Old Testament and early Jewish literature. Then we shall turn to Jesus' understanding of the Kingdom of God.

The Kingdom of God in the Old Testament

During the patriarchal, exodus and conquest periods of Israel's history, the Israelites were a wandering nomadic people who were in bondage under the Egyptians and later regained their freedom in the Exodus. This wandering people did not conceive their God, Yahweh, as king. Yahweh was the father of the tribe or the people. As Sigmund Mowinckel put it, God was "often identified with the tribal progenitor." It was this idea that grounded most of early Israel's concept of God.

God As Active in Israel's History

The great moments of Israel's early history were interpreted in sacred writings as times when the saving presence of Israel's God was most keenly felt. The dominant moment of Yahweh's saving presence for Israel was the Exodus. As we saw in Chapter 5, this event marked the beginning of Israel as a nation. It is appropriate that when Israel recounted these events, they narrated them in language drawn from the creation myths. Pharaoh and his host are the primeval monsters who are swallowed up by the sea. The sea which the Israelites crossed was seen as the primeval sea from which land emerged at creation. Just as the chaos of the primeval sea was ordered in creation allowing the dry land to emerge, so also the new nation Israel emerged from the chaos of the Reed Sea.

The early writers of Israel took the experience of the Exodus and interpreted it in terms of creation. They saw a parallel between God's saving acts in the Exodus and his saving acts in creation. The poetry of the prophet Deutero- Isaiah best expresses this understanding:

> Awake, awake, put on strength,
> O arm of the Lord;
> awake as in days of old,
> the generations of long ago.
> Was it not thou that didst cut Rahab in pieces,
> that didst pierce the dragon?
> Was it not thou that didst dry up the sea,
> the waters of great deep;
> that didst make the depths of the sea a way
> for the redeemed to pass over?
>
> (Isaiah 51:9-10)

The chief saving acts of God became part of the earliest creeds of Israel. An example can be found in Deuteronomy 26:5b-9. These creeds were recounted when Israel celebrated the great festivals at the central sanctuary. Eventually these acts of God formed the basis of the narratives of Israel's history which were brought together to form the Torah.

The Myth of God as King

The nations surrounding Israel, particularly the Canaanites who inhabited the promised land when Israel returned, were established peoples. They had settled agricultural centers and great urban centers. The government they established was monarchy. It was not unusual for them to view their deity as king. The Canaanites, according to Mowinckel, adopted this idea from the great kingdoms of Babylon and Egypt. From earliest Sumer, Babylonian reflections on the origin of the world were expressed in mythic form. Creation was an act of God overcoming and slaying the primeval monsters. This is the thrust of the Babylonian myth of Marduk and Tiamat, or the Canaanite myth of Baal and Mot. In Marduk's act of slaying Tiamat, he begins his rule over the world as king. In that myth, the god's kingly reign is interpreted as his creation of the world.

In these cultures, the earthly king represented the deity, the great heavenly king. Just as the deity fought the archetypal battle with the forces of evil in creation, each year the earthly king, in these cultures, re-enacts the mythic battle during the early spring to insure the fertility of the crops. Winter made the threat of permanent infertility a real possibility. In spring, as the earth sprouted anew, a great festival re-enacted the victory of deity over the forces of evil, a victory which ended in creation, and which each year insured renewed fertility. Each year as this cultic festival of the New Year was celebrated, the people experienced god as king touching their lives at the very core of their existence.

Israel's Encounter with Canaanite Religion

When Israel conquered the land of Canaan and established the tribal confederation, there was adaptation of Canaanite customs and myths. In particular, the Canaanite myth of God as king was adapted in Israelite understanding to the myth that Israel's God, Yahweh, was king. Israel's God became the creator God who destroyed the powers of evil in creation.

When the confederacy proved to be a weak governmental structure, and the people cried out for a king like the other nations, one of the prime objections was that Yahweh was Israel's king. Nevertheless, when the people persisted, the monarchy was established. (Chapter 6 discussed the origin and development of the monarchy.) This monarchy was unique, yet it also had many characteristics of surrounding cultures. The king in Israel remained Yahweh, the God who had acted decisively in Israel's history. The earthly king was his representative. This was declared in the coronation ritual when the earthly king was declared Son of God. His rule was intimately connected to the kingly rule of Yahweh over Israel.

The coronation ritual of the Israelite king drew heavily upon the enthronement ritual of the Canaanite king in the New Year's festival. The emphasis on renewing creation which was found in the myth of God as king became prominent. Thus, in the enthronement ritual, the uniquely Israelite myth of Yahweh acting decisively on behalf of his people at key moments in history was linked to the myth of God as king who acted in creation and acts again and again in renewing the earth. This link is seen in the hymns which accompanied the coronation ritual, the enthronement psalms. Psalm 145 extols Israel's God and King (Psalm 145:1):

> They shall speak of the glory of the kingdom
> and tell of thy power,
> to make known to the sons of men thy
> mighty deeds
> and the glorious splendors of thy kingdom.
> (Psalm 145:11-12)

In these verses, the reader finds reference to the Kingdom of God. The parallel structure of these verses shows that to speak of the glory of the Kingdom of God is equivalent to telling of his power (might). The structure also shows that declaring the mighty deeds of God is equivalent to telling the splendors of the Kingdom of God. Therefore, to speak about the Kingdom of God is the same as speaking of God's mighty power, his kingly activity, or the very deeds he does in which he is shown to be king.

In the Kingdom of God, therefore, the myth of God as King is linked to the myth of God as active in history. The deeds which Yahweh does to show himself as king are creation, election (choosing Abraham and his descendants), and liberation (the Exodus, wandering, and conquest). Kingdom of God evokes a new myth for Israel, the myth of God who created the world and who remains active in the world on behalf of his people. When one speaks of the Kingdom of God, the myth of Israel's creative and active God is effective because it provides an interpretation of the real life experience of Israel.

The Kingdom of God: Myth and Symbol

We have used the term "myth" in the above discussion without any explanation. Myth is a complex of narratives which are regarded as demonstrations of the inner meaning of the universe and of human life. This is an adaptation of the definition of myth given by Phillip Wheelwright. In this context, myths of God's creative activity, and God's salvific actions in history demonstrate Israel's understanding of life in the world. In both cases, Israel is seen under control of God who acts as king. The core understanding of myth is evoked by means of symbol. Norman Perrin noted, symbol is effective because of its power to evoke myth. Symbol is, therefore, dependent upon myth. Conversely, myth is powerful because it makes sense of the life of people in the world. Myth provides people with an understanding of the nature of life in the world. It is precisely this understanding that is celebrated each time the people of Israel come together to celebrate their great festivals.

After the Monarchy

As long as there was a monarchy, the myth of Yahweh as king active on behalf of his people was effective. The Kingdom of God symbol had meaning evoking that myth. However, the monarchy came to an abrupt end with the Babylonian crisis. When God's people found themselves exiled in Babylon, the myth was reinterpreted to introduce a hope that God would act on behalf of his people to deliver them once again as he had from Egypt. That deliverance came about at the hands of Cyrus the Persian. In the post-exilic period, Yahweh once again was seen as King.

The monarchy was, however, never re-established; the Jews were dominated by the Persians for nearly two centuries. When Alexander the Great conquered Persia, they fell under the domination of the Greeks, and later the Romans. What was the fate of the Kingdom of God symbol and the myth that it evoked during these trying times? The symbol came to express the hopes of God's people. They felt that Yahweh was still active on their behalf, and someday the Kingdom of God would appear.

During the crisis precipitated by Antiochus Epiphanes IV the hopes expressed in the Kingdom of God symbol changed dramatically. One text from that period shows the shift:

Then his (God's) kingdom will appear
throughout his whole creation.
Then the devil will have an end.
Yea, sorrow will be led away with him.

For the Heavenly One will arise from his
kingly throne.
Yea, he will go forth from his holy habitation with
indignations and wrath on behalf of his sons.

> For God the Most High will surge forth,
> the Eternal One alone.
> In full view he will come to work vengeance
> on the nations (Gentiles).
> Yea, all their idols will he destroy.
> > (Assumption of Moses 10:1,3,7)

The language employed here is cosmic. The kingdom will appear and Satan shall be no more. God will rise from his throne and work vengeance upon the Gentiles destroying their idols. This wrath will be visited upon the Gentiles on behalf of God's sons. The Kingdom of God symbol still evokes the myth of God's activity on behalf of his people. However, now that activity becomes destruction and vengeance, not deliverance as it had been at the time of the Exodus and Exile. The Roman period did not see any change in understanding. Kingdom of God, in the Roman period, remained apocalyptic. God's decisive intervention was seen as a final destruction of all oppressors and a victory for God's people. Kingdom of God evoked a myth of God as king active in destroying the current oppressive order and establishing a new order of freedom. This destruction would take the form of a war against Rome.

Kingdom in Prayer

Destruction of oppressors was not the only understanding evoked by the Kingdom of God symbol at the approach of the Common Era. The prayer Kaddish which concluded the synagogue service of Jesus' day petitioned the coming of the kingdom:

> Exalted and hallowed by the great name
> in the world which he created according
> to his will.
> May he let his kingdom rule
> in your lifetime and in your days and
> in the lifetime
> of the whole house of Israel, speedily
> and soon.
> And to this, say: Amen.

This prayer was prayed in common by Jews in the synagogue. Some may have seen it as expressing the violent destruction of the oppressor; yet others may have seen it as a cry for the revelation of God's glory. As Norman Perrin notes, the Kingdom of God symbol was understood in several different ways by the people of the first century. It is, in his terminology, a "tensive-symbol." A tensive symbol has a one-to-many relationship with that which it symbolizes. It is not a "steno-symbol" which has a one-to-one relationship with that which it symbolizes. The tensive-symbol has a set of meanings which will never be adequately expressed by any one referent. The Kingdom of God symbol had many referents in the minds of the people of the first century. When Jesus used the symbol, it was heard with many understandings, not one concrete conceptual referent. To these, we must now turn.

The Kingdom of God in the Teaching of Jesus

Scholarly discussion concerning Jesus' understanding of the Kingdom of God has not confirmed Perrin's conclusion that the Kingdom of God is a symbol. Before Perrin, all scholarly discussion treated Kingdom of God as a concept having a single referent. A concept always has the same meaning. Scholars who discussed Jesus' concept of the Kingdom of God accepted the fact that when he used the term, he always meant the same thing.

Perrin, on the other hand, views Kingdom of God as a symbol which has many referents. As Kingdom of God conjured up different images in people of the first century when they heard it, it also produced many images when used by Jesus.

Scholarly Discussion

Johannes Weiss—The first scholarly discussion of Jesus' concept of Kingdom of God was the work of Johannes Weiss. He saw the kingdom as an "overpowering divine storm which will erupt into history to destroy and renew." That kingdom was in the future. Jesus preached to prepare people for this overpowering irruption. For Weiss, the kingdom was imminent and Jesus' teaching was meant to prepare people for its arrival.

Albert Schweitzer—Schweitzer, following Weiss, saw the kingdom in the future. Jesus proclaimed a way of life to be lived between that proclamation and the actual arrival of the kingdom.

For both Weiss and Schweitzer, Jesus' concept of the Kingdom of God had apocalyptic overtones. It was future. It was to bring about destruction and renewal. This apocalyptic notion of kingdom dominated scholarship for nearly twenty-five years.

C.H. Dodd—The British scholar Charles Horton Dodd introduced a radical shift in understanding Kingdom of God. For Dodd, the kingdom was present. In the preaching of Jesus, the Kingdom of God had actually come. It was not dependent upon the response of the people. The kingdom had arrived. This is Dodd's "realized eschatology." Dodd used the present aspect of the kingdom as a cornerstone for his understanding of the parables of Jesus. Since the kingdom is present, one should be willing to take risks to possess it (Parable of the Tower or Counting the Cost). The kingdom shows concern for the lost (The Parables of the Lost and the Found). Dodd felt the parables which refer to a future coming of the kingdom were a warning to people to recognize the presence of the kingdom in their midst. The way in which they responded to the kingdom in the present would determine their faithfulness or unfaithfulness in the future.

Joachim Jeremias—Jeremias nuanced the shift made by Dodd. He accepted Dodd's understanding of the kingdom as present (realized eschatology). However, he added a future dimension. For Jeremias, the kingdom was in a process of realization. There was a tension between the kingdom as proclaimed in the present, and the full realization of the kingdom which was to be achieved in the future. This is the tension between the "already" and the "not yet." The kingdom is already present, but it is not yet complete.

Norman Perrin—From the time of Jeremias, most scholars advanced variations on the theme of Dodd and Jeremias. Norman Perrin, however, shifted the discussion in the current period. His analysis of Kingdom of God posed the question whether it is correct to discuss the kingdom in such terms as present or future. These terms assume that Jesus' use of Kingdom of God was conceptual. Perrin, as we have seen, has chosen to see Jesus' use of Kingdom of God as symbolic. Kingdom is a symbol which evokes the myth of God active in history on behalf of his people. We now turn to Jesus' use of the Kingdom of God symbol presented in the gospels to see what referents the symbol might have evoked.

THE WORD MADE CLEAR

Jesus and the Kingdom of God Symbol

The best approach to Jesus' use of the Kingdom of God symbol is to examine the sayings where the symbol appears. The largest group of sayings which use the Kingdom of God symbol are the parables discussed in Chapter 17. As we saw in that chapter, the parables provide a multifaceted view of the Kingdom of God by applying many ordinary experiences from the lives of people. The picture of kingdom that the parables present is not the radical apocalyptic vision that dominated understandings of the symbol in the first century.

On the contrary, the parables present the kingdom as something beyond all price. One will sell all to gain it. The kingdom is something which contains both good and bad co-existing together until the end. The kingdom is not something which will grow and expand of itself without active participation. The kingdom is something which begins small, but will grow into something quite large. The kingdom demands that people not be caught off guard. It will arrive unexpectedly and they must be ready. The kingdom is characterized by mercy rather than justice.

Proverbial Sayings in the Kingdom

A number of Jesus' sayings containing the Kingdom of God symbol are proverbs. They are short meaningful statements which appeal to the practical experience of the hearer. Mark introduced a proverb on the kingdom when the disciples attempt to prohibit people from bringing their children to Jesus. Jesus responds, "Whoever does not accept the Kingdom of God like a little child will not enter it" (10:15). This use of the Kingdom of God symbol emphasizes dependence on God. The focus in this saying is on response to the kingdom. The proper response to the kingdom is that of a child who is totally dependent on parents. This use of the Kingdom of God symbol and others like it in the gospels becomes, as Perrin puts it, a metaphor of the hearer's response to the kingdom. The person who does not accept the kingdom as a little child becomes a metaphor of one response to the kingdom. This metaphor challenges the hearers to re-evaluate their attitude toward the kingdom.

In the following unit, a discussion on wealth and riches, Jesus introduces two more proverbial sayings. The first "How hard it is for a rich man to enter the Kingdom of God," (Mark 10:23, 4) challenges the hearer. The Kingdom of God symbol evoking the myth of God's active presence challenges current attitudes. The decisive action of God announced in the Kingdom of God demands that people rethink their attitudes toward wealth and riches.

The second proverbial saying reinforces the first, "It is easier for a camel to pass through the eye of a needle than for a rich man to enter the Kingdom of God" (Mark 10:25). On the surface, this saying stresses the incompatibility of riches and the kingdom. Centuries of interpretations of "a camel passing through the eye of a needle" show the difficulty which this incompatibility has produced. The proverb declares that one who is rich cannot experience God's saving action.

Seeing the astonishment of the disciples at this incompatibility, Jesus utters a further proverb, "For men it is impossible, but not for God; everything is possible for God" (Mark 10:27). A rich person who surrenders to God has the possibility of experiencing the decisive saving action of God. This final proverb shows that the incompatibility is not between riches and the kingdom, rather it is between riches and the ability to trust God. The Kingdom of God symbol in these proverbial sayings evokes the myth of God's activity in order to challenge the hearer to trust God.

Conclusion

The Kingdom of God symbol evokes the myth of God decisively acting on behalf of his people. Prior to the ministry of Jesus, this decisive action was envisioned as a final inbreaking which would destroy the present order and establish his people as free once again. Jesus did not employ the symbol in this way. On the basis of several of Jesus' sayings, the early church did expect an imminent end of the present order. However, when it failed to materialize, that expectation was reinterpreted.

The Kingdom of God symbol continued to evoke the myth of God decisively acting in the lives of his people. However, that decisive action was no longer seen as a destruction of the present order, but the action of God in Jesus through the cross and resurrection. As we saw in our discussion of Pauline theology, the saving actions of Jesus became the central theme of early theological reflection. In that decisive saving action, the kingdom dawned. When gospel writers use the Kingdom of God symbol, the myth of God's kingship manifest in his decisive salvific actions in Jesus is evoked. Those who hear the proclamation of this Good News are challenged to evaluate their way of life in light of that myth, and need to respond. Through the Kingdom of God symbol Jesus and the gospel writers address their hearers with the realities of God's saving actions on behalf of his people in the past, and the promise of his continued saving actions in the present.

This reality is multifaceted. It is apprehended in different ways by different people. This is the wonder of the Kingdom of God symbol. The myth of God as king acting decisively on behalf of his people is played out on one level in the historical development of that people, yet it is also played out in the individual lives of that people. God acts in our lives as a people and in our lives as individuals. When we pray, "thy kingdom come" in the Lord's Prayer, we seek that continued action on our behalf. When we follow that petition with, "thy will be done," we acknowledge that decisive action makes demands on our lives. The Kingdom of God symbol demands that we acknowledge God as active, and challenges us to respond through allowing that action to affect and change our lives radically.

Study Questions

1) What is the connection between kingship and creation? What is the role of myth in this?
2) How does the notion that "Yahweh is king" influence the monarchy in Israel?
3) What do we mean by the term 'Myth?' How is myth related to symbol?'
4) What is meant by a 'tensive' symbol? How does this differ from a 'steno' symbol?
5) In Israel's understanding of the Kingdom of God, what does it mean to say that the myth of God as King is linked to the myth of God as active in history.
6) What does Dodd mean when he uses the term "realized eschatology" in regard to the Kingdom of God? How does Jeremias nuance this?

JAMES P. McILHONE

7) How do the parables of Jesus present the Kingdom of God? Is this a valid understanding in everyday life?
8) How is the kingdom of God symbol active challenging us in the Lord's prayer?

Bibliography

Chilton, Bruce, and McDonald, J.I.H., *Jesus and the Ethics of the Kingdom,* (Grand Rapids: Wm. B. Eerdmans, 1987).

Perrin, Norman, *Jesus and the Language of the Kingdom: Symbol and Metaphor in New Testament Interpretation,* (Philadelphia: Fortress Press, 1976).

Perrin, Norman, *Rediscovering the Teaching of Jesus,* (San Francisco: Harper and Row, 1976).

Willis, Wendell, ed., *The Kingdom of God in 20th Century Intrepretation,* (Peabody: Hendrickson, 1987).

Chapter 19

Who Do You Say that I Am?
What is Jesus Called in the New
Testament?

"Who do people say that I am?" This is the question Jesus poses
to his disciples after they had witnessed him preaching, teaching
and performing miracles for quite some time. The disciples'
response echoed the typical expectations of the day. Some thought
he was John the Baptist come back to life. After John had been
beheaded by Herod, many felt that he would return. Since Jesus'
preaching was similar to John's, it was felt he might be John returned. Others thought he might be Elijah. Since the prophecy of
Malachi (Malachi 4:3), there was an expectation that Elijah, who
had been taken up into heaven, would return to prepare the way
for the messiah. Others claimed that he was Moses or one of the
prophets. This alludes to a statement of Moses at the end of his
life that God would send a prophet like him (Moses) who would
interpret the law for the people (Deuteronomy 18:15).

Jesus follows with a climactic question to the disciples, "Who
do you say that I am?" Peter, the spokesman for the disciples,
responds, "You are the Christ, *the son of the Living God.*" (Matt
16:16). Peter declares that Jesus is the one Israel had been expecting. Yet, Peter's understanding of Jesus expressed by this title
did not encompass the complete identity of Jesus. For several centuries after Jesus' death and resurrection, the early church struggled
to answer that question adequately. Today scholars still debate the
identity and nature of Jesus and the role he played in salvation
history. A branch of theology known as Christology systematically
studies these questions.

In this unit, we shall look briefly at how the New Testament
sheds light on some of the more significant issues of Christology.
After a brief examination of the quest for the historical Jesus, we
shall examine how the early church saw Jesus' work (functional
Christology) and how it saw who Jesus was (ontological Christology).

199

JAMES P. McILHONE

The Historical Jesus

Scholars of the Enlightenment (1648-1789) subjected everything to careful scientific scrutiny to determine its "truth." As a result, several scholars in the eighteenth century questioned the historocity of the biblical accounts of Jesus. As we saw in the discussion of the infancy narratives (Chapter 11), a historical kernel was joined to early church theological reflection to produce the gospel narratives. These eighteenth-century scholars attempted to separate the historical kernel from church reflection. That task came to be known as "The Quest for the Historical Jesus."

Applying the methods of historical criticism developed during and after the Enlightenment, scholars sought to strip away from the gospel narratives anything which could be traced to the early church. What remained after such careful analysis would be the material pertaining to the "historical Jesus." Given this process, it is clear that the historical Jesus is not the real living person, but rather is the result of applying historical critical methods to biblical texts. The real living Jesus was much more than can be ascertained by critical methodology.

When the results of scholars' quests for the historical Jesus are analyzed, it is evident that their research contains several subjective elements. Essentially each scholar produces a portrait of the historical Jesus which reflects his own ideas and biases. George Tyrell sums this up when speaking of Adolph von Harnack. He says, "The Christ that Harnack sees, looking back through nineteen centuries of Catholic darkness, is only the reflection of a liberal Protestant face, seen at the bottom of a deep well." The danger of embarking on the quest for the historical Jesus is that one will make him whatever one wants him to be.

Why is it so difficult to discover the historical Jesus? The only data we possess are the gospels. These were written down several years after Jesus walked the earth. They are written in light of the resurrection and the Ascension. As a result, they do not neutrally portray what Jesus was like before his passion, death and resurrection. All events of his ministry are narrated in light of the understanding of Jesus which comes as a result of his passion, death and resurrection. As the church preached more and more, the historical events became intertwined with their theological faith reflection. That Jesus whom the early church preached was more like the "Christ of faith" than the historical Jesus or the Jesus of history. In this century, the German scholar Martin Kähler carefully distinguished the historical Jesus (Jesus as reconstructed via scientific methodology) from the Christ of faith (Jesus as object of Christian faith and worship).

By 1930, scholars abandoned the quest for the historical Jesus, because they felt it was an impossible task. The historical kernel of the gospels was so deeply intertwined with the faith reflection of the early church that its recovery was next to impossible. By the middle of the twentieth century, the quest for the historical Jesus re-emerged. A student of Rudolf Bultmann, Ernst Käsemann saw the necessity of connecting the historical Jesus with the Christ of faith. If there were no such connection, Käsemann contends, Christianity would be nothing more than mythical stories without basis in history. If the early community was not interested in the historical Jesus, why preserve four gospels? Käsemann contended that even though the gospels are the result of later theological reflection, it is necessary that the object of the gospels, the Christ of faith, have some identity with an actual historical being, Jesus, who walked on earth.

Käsemann's questions led several scholars to rethink their positions. His teacher, Bultmann, had said that in the early church, the Jesus who preached (the historical Jesus) became the Jesus who was preached (the Christ of faith). The apostles did not merely repeat the words of Jesus as they preached, rather, they preached their experience of Jesus. They preached how Jesus affected their lives. Underlying this is the fact that the Jesus event affects believers here and now in all ages. Therefore, to speak only of the historical Jesus is to lock Jesus into a past event. The words and deeds of the historical Jesus are just that, historical.

The events which happened once in history must be transformed into a "once and for all." In other words, they must have an effect on our present lives. Hence, the early church preached Christ, not his message. The Christ which the early church preached, and who is still preached today, is present in the historical Jesus. To spin one's wheels searching for the historical Jesus can be a copout. The message of the gospels is a living message which challenges us here and now to respond. It is a present reality. One can hide behind the guise of searching for the historical Jesus of the past because it enables one to avoid responding to the message preached by the gospels in the present.

JAMES P. McILHONE

Functional vs. Ontological Christology

There is yet another danger in looking at the New Testament data on Christ; the danger of reading later statements back into the New Testament. The earliest reflection on Christ and his role in salvation history presents what God was doing with and through Christ. In other words, the church reflected on the "function" of Christ in God's plan. Such reflection is called "functional Christology." These reflections do not speak of who Jesus was. As a result, there are no formal statements of Jesus being human and divine in the New Testament. These are the products of later reflection. The New Testament speaks of Jesus' *role* in salvation, of his mission. It does not treat his nature and being. This latter is known as "ontological Christology."

It is true that the data of the New Testament raise questions concerning the nature of Jesus. The Prologue of John states that "the Word (which is 'with God' and 'is God') became flesh." But it does not state how. It does not give an explanation of how the Word, which was one with him yet distinct from him, became united in human flesh in the person of Jesus. It merely makes statements concerning the function of "the Word made flesh"—to allow humanity to see the glory of God, a major theme of the fourth gospel. The functional Christology of the New Testament will naturally raise ontological questions. It is these ontological questions which the early church addressed in formulating the doctrines of Nicaea and Chalcedon.

We must always be aware of those developments as we read the New Testament. There is nothing in the New Testament which would contradict those doctrines. Yet, despite the fact that we are reading with the enhanced knowledge provided by those doctrines, we cannot read the New Testament texts as though they were as conversant with those doctrines as we are. To do so would be a grave injustice to the authors and a distortion of their meaning.

New Testament Understandings of Jesus

We move now to a discussion of the various ways Jesus was presented in the New Testament to discover the early Christian community's growing understanding of Jesus. Raymond E. Brown has noted in several places that such a survey uncovers a rather

202

peculiar phenomenon. Using the term "Christological moments," Brown discusses "scenes in the life of Jesus which became the vehicle for *giving expression* to post-resurrectional Christology" (New Jerome Bible Commentary 81:12). In other words, a Christological moment was an event in Jesus' life which triggered an awareness in the reflection of the early church that Jesus was the Christ.

The earliest layers of New Testament tradition shift the Christological moment beyond the life of Jesus into the future, placing it at the *parousia* (the second coming). The next traditions move the Christological moment back to the resurrection. As the writings move further and further from the time of Christ's life, the Christological moment moves further and further back through the ministry, to the baptism, to the boyhood, to conception. The latest New Testament writings place the Christological moment long before the birth of Jesus, depicting him as the pre-existent logos become incarnate. A deeper look into each of these will make this movement clearer.

Parousia Christology

The predominant expectation of the early church after the Ascension was the imminent return of Jesus. As we saw in the last chapter, the petition of the Lord's Prayer, "Thy kingdom come," embodies that expectation. Another significant expression of that expectation is a prayer that arose among the early Aramaic-speaking Christians, *Maranatha,* which means "Come, Lord Jesus."

Underlying this prayer was a belief that when he came he would be appointed messiah. In this understanding, the Christological moment was seen in the future, at the return of Jesus, the *parousia.* Such an understanding probably flowed from the fact that Jesus did not fulfill the traditional Jewish messianic expectation during his lifetime. He did not set up a Davidic monarchy in Jerusalem. Nor did he bring victory, peace and prosperity to Israel. It was thought these tasks would be accomplished when he came again.

Exaltation Christology

As the imminent return of Jesus was delayed and Christianity moved from Palestine into Hellenistic (Greek-speaking) Judaism, a major shift occurred. In the speeches of Acts, Jesus is not the one who will return as messiah, rather, he is "Lord" and "Christ" (Acts 2:36). This designation originated in the resurrection and exaltation of Jesus to the right hand of the Father. The emphasis on what God would accomplish in the future when Jesus returned shifted to an emphasis on what God had already accomplished in Jesus.

In the experience of the resurrection, the disciples came to a fuller understanding of Jesus. This understanding was expressed in terms like "God made him Lord and Messiah," or "He was begotten as Son," or "He was exalted and given a name above all other names." The Christological moment becomes the resurrection. In this understanding, the Jewish expectation of messiah was not fulfilled; it was transferred to heaven where the exalted messiah reigns. This understanding is typical of the Pauline School (1 Corinthians 15:12-19; Philippians 2:6-11). We also find it in Acts 13:33 which cites the messianic Psalm 2:7 as fulfilled in the resurrection of Jesus. Psalm 2 was interpreted by the early church in conjunction with 2 Samuel 7:14. The union of the two texts announced that the Davidic monarch would be both "Christ" and "son of God." The citation in Acts affirms that in the resurrection Jesus became both messiah (Christ) and son of God.

Baptism Christology

The earliest written account of the words and deeds of Jesus, the Gospel of Mark, shifts the Christological moment back even further to the baptism. In the Markan account of the baptism, the voice from heaven declares, "You are my son, my beloved one, in you I am well pleased" (Mark 1:11). A careful analysis of this declaration shows that it is a union of three Old Testament allusions. The first, "You are my son," is from Psalm 2:7, the same text used earlier to confirm a resurrection Christology. Now it is used in a baptismal Christology. Jesus is declared "son of God" in the moment of his baptism.

The voice continues, "My beloved one." This is an allusion to Genesis 22:3, where God tells Abraham to take Isaac, his beloved son. That allusion draws a parallel between Jesus and Isaac. For the first-century Jewish Christians, the Isaac traditions saw Isaac offered by his father in expiation for sins. By alluding to the Isaac traditions in this declaration, Jesus is portrayed as one offered by his father for the expiation of sins. Linking this to the citation from Psalm 2:7, Jesus becomes the messianic son of God who will be an expiation for sins.

The declaration concludes: "My chosen one, in whom my soul delights," an allusion to Isaiah 42:1, which is the first servant canticle. In Chapter 8, we mentioned that these canticles portray a servant who vicariously suffers for the people. The tradition of the suffering servant provided an Old Testament model for explaining the experience of Jesus who innocently suffers. When this passage is linked to the others, the full impact of the declaration becomes evident. Jesus is the messianic son of God who will become an expiation for sins through innocent suffering. The early church has advanced in its understanding of Jesus. He is messiah, but his messiahship must be understood in conjunction with the suffering servant and the expiatory sacrificial traditions surrounding Isaac. There is a danger of misinterpretation in this understanding. When the voice declares, "You are my son," it could be perceived as God adopting a human being, Jesus, as his son. That misinterpretation became the heresy of adoptionism.

Conception Christology

The Gospels of Matthew and Luke begin with an infancy narrative. As we pointed out in our discussion of these narratives (Chapter 11), their purpose was to narrate the infancy of Jesus so that his origin, identity and mission would be clear to readers. Those narratives, in effect, moved the Christological moment back still further to the conception. In both narratives, Jesus was conceived without a human father, something which was unheard of in Jewish circles yet was prominent in Hellenistic circles.

Matthew and Luke independently describe the virginal conception yet do not agree in many other details of their narrative. Raymond Brown has pointed out that this may indicate that the idea of virginal conception of Jesus was already well known in the Christian community before the gospels were written down. Matthew and Luke may have found it necessary to emphasize this idea in their narratives to correct the adoptionist misconception that Jesus was a human being adopted by the Father at baptism.

JAMES P. McILHONE

Pre-Existence Christology

In the fourth gospel, the Christological moment is pushed back to the beginning of time. The shift became necessary as the early preachers moved into the Gentile world. The Christological moment in the preaching of the Palestinian and Hellenistic Jews was tied closely to Jewish tradition and messianic expectations. This tradition and these expectations had little meaning to Gentiles. When the message was preached to Gentiles, it became necessary to move the Christological moment beyond the confines of Judaism to embrace both Jew and Gentile.

Drawing heavily upon the Hellenistic Jewish Wisdom tradition which was also understandable in terms of Greek philosophy, Jesus was depicted in Wisdom (Proverbs 8:22; Sirach 24:9) terms as the "image (*eikon*) of the invisible God" and the "firstborn of all creation in whom all things were created" (Colossians 1:15-16). The most definite expression of the notion is found in the great hymn in the prologue to the Gospel of John which states that the Word (*logos*) which became flesh (1:14) existed before creation (1:1-2).

The Titles of Jesus in New Testament Christology

One way scholars have come to understand the role of Jesus was analysis of the titles used to address and refer to him. Many of these titles originated in the life of Jesus (Messiah, Son of Man, Savior and Prophet). However, several are the result of reflection by the early Christian community on their experience of salvation in Christ (Lord, Servant, Son of God, High Priest, Word).

Since we touched on the significance of the titles messiah (Christ), Son of God and Lord in Chapter 13 on Pauline theology, we shall concentrate our attention on the remaining titles in the New Testament.

Son of Man

The title "son of man" has a double origin in the Old Testament. The term son of man comes from the Hebrew *ben 'adam* or the Aramaic, *bar 'anash*. These terms could normally be translated "human being." In the prophecy of Ezekial, the Lord

206

addresses the prophet with the title son of man. The purpose is to contrast the mortal humanity of the prophet who is God's messenger with the immortal divinity of the one who is giving the message. The Psalms and the Book of Job use the phrase, son of man, in a similar manner (Psalms 8:4; 80:17; Job 25:6).

In the Book of Daniel, the title son of man appears in a different sense. Daniel 7:13 speaks of one "like a son of man" who is approaching the throne of the ancient days. The meaning is one like a human being. However, the style of writing is apocalyptic. Humans represent divine beings. The son of man, following the interpretation given in Daniel, is a superhuman divine being who represents the nation, Israel (Dan 7:17-18,27). In later Jewish literature, this title came to be applied to the judge who would appear at the end of time.

In the gospels, Jesus uses only this title to refer to himself. The use of son of man in the gospels can be classified in three categories. The first group is sayings which are equivalent to Jesus speaking in the first person. These are the earthly son of man sayings. A second group consists of the suffering son of man sayings where Jesus explicitly speaks of his passion. The final group would be the eschatological son of man sayings where the influence of the Danielic son of man is most prominent. It is possible that the first two uses derive from Jesus himself, while the final use is a product of the early church.

Prophet

This expectation, based on Deuteronomy 18:15, developed into the expectation that a prophet would once and for all declare God's word. Among some, particularly the Samaritans, it developed as an expectation of a new Moses. That was joined to the expectation of Malachi 4:3 that Elijah would precede the messiah. This designation of Jesus as the one who fulfilled the role of eschatological prophet remained alive largely among Jewish Christians.

Servant

The title "servant of God" originates in the servant canticles of Second Isaiah. The final canticle depicts this servant as one who vicariously suffers for the people. When the early church began to reflect on the sufferings of Jesus and sought justification in the Jewish scriptures for that suffering, they immediately turned to that canticle which stressed the atoning value of suffering. This atoning value struck the early preachers as being a clear and concise explanation of the mission of Jesus both in the present and throughout the history of God's people. Jesus suffered and died to atone for the wrongs of God's people once and for all. In that he fulfills the role of the servant as portrayed by Isaiah.

High Priest

In Jewish-Christian circles, later reflection on the role of Christ envisioned Jesus as the eternal high priest. The result of that reflection is Hebrews. The major Old Testament use of this title is the high priest of the temple of Jerusalem who offered sacrifice and acted on behalf of the people especially on the day of atonement. There is a further allusion suggested by the title high priest. In the fourteenth chapter of the Book of Genesis, an amazing character appears, the priest-king Melchizedek. He blesses Abraham, and he vanishes from the narrative.

He reappears in Psalm 110:4. This psalm was used at the royal coronation. That verse declares that the king being enthroned is a priest in the line of the priestking Melchizedek. This psalm provides the possibility for a link between priesthood and messiahship. That link is the center on which the argument concerning Jesus and Davidic descent turns in Mark 12:35-37.

In Hebrews, the high priest according to the order of Melchizedek has an eternal priesthood and he enters once and for all to perform the once and final sacrifice. The repeated sacrifices of the high priests in the temple are no longer necessary. Jesus is that eternal high priest who has acted definitively.

Word

The title "Word" or "*logos*" has a long history both in Judaism and Hellenism. In the Jewish understanding dabar Yahweh (the word of Yahweh) was the means the Lord used in creation. The word of Yahweh is always active. It accomplishes the task for which it was sent forth. As Isaiah says, "My word will not return to me empty" (Isaiah 55:11).

When Hellenistic philosophy, particularly the writings of the Stoics and Philo, began to influence Judaism, the Hellenistic concept of *logos* was joined to the Hebraic concept. For the Stoics, the *logos* was the cosmic law which rules the universe while, at the same time, being present to the individual intellect. Plato sees the *logos* related to the *real* being.

Philo of Alexandria, at the time of Jesus, saw *logos* as a personified intermediary being. Philo's notion is closer to the conception of *logos* which we find in the Gospel of John. There *logos* was present with the creator at creation and then entered into the human world becoming flesh. Such incarnational theology was a radical step which would be unheard of for the Stoics, Philo or Plato.

Conclusion

Through this survey of the quest for the historical Jesus and the varied understandings of Jesus present in the early church, we can see that even though Jesus is the central figure of our faith, there has been much debate over who he actually was, what he actually said, and how he affected those he encountered. Absolute hard answers to these questions will probably never be found. The multiplicity and plurality of portraits of Jesus have provided through the centuries a multi-faceted picture of Jesus. However, that fact makes it even more certain that the central significance of Jesus can be grasped only through the eyes of faith.

Study Questions

1) Who do you say that Jesus is? What does belief in Jesus mean in the twentieth century?
2) How does the "historical Jesus" differ from the "real living Jesus?" Which is more believable? Which do we know more about?
3) What do we mean by the distinction, the "historical Jesus" and the "Christ of Faith?"
4) What is the drawback of the quest for the "historical Jesus?"

5) What is the danger of reading the New Testament texts in light of later doctrine?
6) What do we mean by the term "christological moment?" How do the christological moments of the New Testament help us understand early thinking of Christ?
7) Which of the early New Testament Christologies seems to predominate today? Why?
8) What does the use of Titles tell us about the early Church's understanding of Jesus? Which titles speak to contemporary society?

Bibliography

Cullmann, Oscar, *The Christology of the New Testament,* trans. by Shirley C. Guthrie and Charles A.M. Hall, (Philadelphia: Westminster Press, 1959).

de Jonge, Marinus, *Christology in Context: The Earliest Christian Response to Jesus,* (Philadelphia: Westminster Press, 1988).

Dunn, James D.G., *Christology in the Making: A New Testament Inquiry into the Origins of the Doctrine of the Incarnation,* (Philadelphia: Westminster Press, 1980).

Dunn, James D.G., *The Evidence for Jesus,* (Philadelphia: Westminster press, 1985).

Fuller, Reginald, *The Foundations of New Testament Christology,* (New York: Charles Scribners' Sons, 1965).

Fuller, Reginald, and Perkins, Pheme *Who is this Christ: Gospel Christology and Contemporary Faith,* (Philadelphia: Fortress Press, 1983).

Richard, Earl, *Jesus: One and Many, the Christological Concept of New Testament Authors,* (Wilmington: Michael Glazier, 1988).

Chapter 20

How Should I Understand
Jesus' Resurrection?

Several years ago a newspaper reported that the tomb of comedian Charlie Chaplin had been found empty. The immediate assumption was that the cemetery had been vandalized. Someone had tampered with the grave and carried off his body. The thought of any other explanation for that empty tomb never crossed anyone's mind.

This incident of grave tampering serves to illustrate the principle that an empty tomb is not a sign of resurrection. This final chapter will be an investigation of the biblical evidence for the resurrection of Jesus to determine how the early church understood that event. After looking at the earliest testimony of 1 Corinthians 15:3-8, we shall turn to the gospels to examine the appearance narratives, and the narratives of the empty tomb. We shall conclude with some observations about the resurrection based on this biblical evidence.

Biblical Evidence for the Resurrection

The earliest New Testament material on the resurrection derives from early Christian preaching. In this preaching, two Greek verbs are used, *egeirein* and *anistanai. Egeirein,* which describes raising from the dead, appears only in the New Testament. Secular Greek literature uses the verb, *anistanai* to describe raising from the dead. Paul's letters and Acts state, "God raised Jesus from the dead." In other places, the simple phrase, "The Lord was raised," appears. (Raymond Brown has shown that this phraseology does not in any way detract from or deny the divine status of Jesus.)

Very early formulas appeared which coupled the resurrection with the passion and death. The antithetical formula repeated throughout the early speeches of Acts is a good example. "By the deliberate plan of God he was given into your power and you killed him. . . . But God raised him to life again." (Acts 2:23).

JAMES P. McILHONE

1 Corinthians 15:3-8

In answering the Corinthians' question about resurrection, Paul presents a tradition he had received. Paul's language suggests that this is an ancient formula. The structure consists of four clauses introduced by the conjunction "that": (a) Christ died; (b) He was buried; (c) He was raised; (d) He appeared. The first and the third clauses are expanded by qualifying prepositional phrases. This formula is a miniature form of the structure which will appear in the resurrection narratives in the gospels. Many have seen this four part structure as verifying that the Jesus who was raised and appeared is the Jesus who died and was buried.

Paul continues presenting a series of witnesses who "saw" the risen Lord, ending with himself. It is significant that although he has seen the risen Lord, he provides no description of him here. Later in the chapter, he draws parallels between Jesus' resurrection and the resurrection of the individual Christian. Therefore, we can presume that what he says there can also apply to the resurrection of Jesus.

He begins with the question, "Into what kind of body are the dead raised?" (1 Corinthians 15:35). His answer is that such questioning is foolish. Using an example, he says a seed which is sown will not produce life unless it dies. The seed is not the same as what shoots forth when it is full grown. It is merely grain. Similarly, in the resurrection, what is sown in the earth is perishable, dishonorable, weak and physical. What is raised is imperishable, glorious, powerful and spiritual.

He concludes stating that "flesh and blood," the body, as we know it cannot possess the kingdom (1 Corinthians 15:50). But all "flesh and blood" beings will die, and we shall be changed and rise imperishable and immortal. For Paul, resurrection implies the body will be changed. Those who are buried are those who will be raised. Applying this to Christ's resurrection, his body was changed; yet it was still his body. The Jesus who was buried is the Jesus who was raised.

The Gospel Traditions

Most scholars today accept that the resurrection traditions in the gospels emphasize two related themes, the empty tomb and the appearances of the risen Jesus. We shall briefly look at each of these beginning with the appearances.

The Appearance Traditions

Mark, the earliest gospel, does not record any appearances (unless we include the Longer Ending which is accepted by most scholars today as a later addition composed of appearance traditions from Matthew, Luke and John). There is only a command to the women to announce to the disciples that the risen Jesus precedes them to Galilee (Mark 16:7). The implication is that he will appear to them in Galilee.

Matthew follows the Markan tradition where the messengers in the tomb tell the women the risen Jesus will appear to the disciples in Galilee (Matthew 28:7). But Matthew continues adding an appearance to the women as they are on their way back (Matthew 28:9-10). They take hold of Jesus' feet and worship him. Jesus concludes repeating the message to go to Galilee. The gospel concludes with an additional appearance of Jesus to the disciples on a mountain in Galilee where he gives them the commission to go forth and preach the word (Matthew 28:18-20).

Luke departs radically from the Markan tradition, incorporating three separate appearances in the Jerusalem area. The command to the women in Mark becomes a recollection that, in Galilee, Jesus told them he had to suffer. The first appearance is to two disciples traveling away from Jerusalem to the village of Emmaus (Luke 24:13-35). Jesus appears as a follow traveler whom they are unable to recognize. At Emmaus, he stays with them and breaks bread. At that moment, they recognize him and he vanishes (Luke 24:31). One must realize that this narrative employs several Lukan techniques, e.g., keeping Jesus' identity from the disciples until the moment of revelation. Thus, it is problematic to use the details of this narrative to provide an analysis of the nature of Jesus' body.

When the two disciples return from Emmaus, the second appearance is mentioned. They announce that Jesus has been raised and has appeared to Simon (Luke 24:34). They continue explaining their own experience on the road. In the third and final appearance to the disciples, Luke takes care to let the reader know that it is Jesus who appears, but he is changed. He can appear and disappear at will. Again, Luke does not dwell on how that can happen. In this appearance the risen Jesus commissions the disciples to preach and be witnesses (Luke 24:47-48). The gospel ends with Jesus ascending to heaven (Luke 24:50-53).

The Johannine tradition is similar to Luke. The geographical location of the appearances is Jerusalem. The risen Jesus appears to Mary Magdalene at the tomb (John 20:14-18). She is unable to recognize him until he calls her by name. An appearance to the disciples (minus Thomas) follows (20:19-22). They are commissioned to continue Jesus' mission. The final appearance in John takes place one week later when Thomas is present (20:26-29). These appearance narratives affirm that the risen Jesus is the Jesus who walked the earth, yet he has been changed. The final chapter of John (which most scholars believe is an addition to the original text) narrates an appearance of the risen Jesus to the disciples at the Sea of Tiberias in Galilee.

Placing these narratives side by side, several inconsistencies emerge. However, each narrative tries to show that, in the resurrection experience, something has happened to Jesus. The risen Jesus is changed. These inconsistencies stem from the difficulty of speaking of resurrection in terms of space and time. Hence, one tradition may portray Jesus appearing and not being recognized while another tradition will portray the risen Jesus passing through walls and locked doors to appear and be recognized. The reactions to these appearances may help us understand their purpose. The disciples from Emmaus announced, "The Lord is risen." The disciples tell Thomas, "We have seen the Lord." Thomas proclaims, "My Lord and My God." Mary Magdalene says, "They have taken away my Lord." Jesus is no longer called "Jesus," but "Lord." The title Lord shows that, in the experience of the resurrection, Jesus has been brought into Lordship. Raymond Brown sums up the purpose of the appearance narratives when he says, "the appearances entail a sight that involves revelation, a sight that goes beyond ordinary experience." That revelation is the revelation of Jesus as Lord.

The Empty Tomb Traditions

Each of the passion narratives concludes with the burial of Jesus' body which the women see. This provides a connection to the narratives of the empty tomb. A close examination of the Gospel of

Mark shows that there are discrepancies between the account of the burial and the account of the empty tomb. The names of the women who observe the burial (Mark 15:47) are different from the names of the women who return to the tomb on the first day of the week (Mark 16:1). This raises the question: "Did the empty tomb tradition have a different origin from the passion narrative?" The answer of many scholars is "Yes!"

The tomb tradition in Mark shows women early on the first day of the week approaching the tomb to anoint Jesus' body. The hastiness of the burial prevented any chance of anointing the body on Friday. Upon arrival, they discover that the stone which sealed the tomb had been rolled back, and a youth was sitting inside. He announces that Jesus has been raised. The women flee.

Matthew follows the Markan structure with a few changes (Matthew 28:1-7). The women approach the tomb at daybreak. They come to see the tomb, not to anoint the body. As they approach the tomb, an apocalyptic opening takes place—an earthquake, an angel rolling the stone and sitting on it. The angel tells the women that Jesus has been raised. They leave in fear, but tell the disciples.

Luke also incorporates some changes into the Markan structure (Luke 24:1-11). The women approach at early dawn. They bring the oils which they prepared after the crucifixion (Luke 23:56). Arriving at the tomb, they discover the stone rolled back and two men standing inside who announce the resurrection to them. The women then leave and tell the eleven, but they do not believe (Luke 24:11).

The Johannine narrative centers on Mary Magdalene. Mary comes to the tomb while it is dark (John 20:1-2; 11-17). The stone has been moved away. Mary peers into the tomb and sees two angels who question why she has been weeping. She responds that the Lord has been taken and she does not know where. Without going into detail, most scholars hold that a second tradition centering on Peter and the beloved disciple has been joined to this one. In that tradition, Mary goes immediately to Peter and the beloved disciple to tell them about the tomb. They run to the tomb, enter, and see the burial cloths lying there (John 20:3-10). The beloved disciple believes and they return home.

Each of the four empty tomb narratives highlights an angelic appearance. It has been suggested that angels appear to interpret divine mysteries in Jewish literature. The mystery which the angels reveal here is that Jesus has been raised. Therefore, one can say that the narratives of the empty tomb become another way in which the experience of the resurrection of Jesus was interpreted through the addition of the angelic interpreters. Given this conclusion, it would then be logical to make the empty tomb narratives the link between the Passion narratives and the appearance narratives. The Passion narratives, the appearance narratives and the empty tomb narratives would then have been written to explain the full meaning of the experience of Jesus being raised from the dead.

From this study of the New Testament evidence on the resurrection, we can see that the early church believed that Jesus conquered death. In that conquest, he was changed. His conquest of death and the corresponding change was interpreted through the Jewish notion of resurrection of the dead. Also, except for Paul's statements in 1 Corinthians 15, the early preachers and writers never chose to investigate the nature of resurrection. They only affirm it through its effects—the appearances and the empty tomb.

Jewish Notions of Life After Death

The question has been raised: Why resurrection when Judaism had other understandings of life after death? An examination of the Old Testament understanding of life after death will answer that question. In addition to resurrection, the Old Testament uses the notions translation into heaven and immortality of the soul to explain life after death.

Translation Into the Heavens—In early prophetic literature, Elijah is assumed into heaven carried by a whirlwind (1 Kings 2:9-12). There is no reference to his death in this account. It presumes he continues living eternally. That presumption is further verified in the expectation that Elijah would return before the coming of the Messiah found in Malachi 4:5-6. A similar translation into the heavens is the fate of one of Israel's earliest ancestors, Enoch (Genesis 5:22).

Immortality of the Soul—The writings of the Platonic school interpreted life after death as immortality of the soul. The body, being a prison in which the soul existed, was not necessary after death. The soul continued immortal. This notion entered into Jewish thought in later Alexandrian wisdom literature. Wisdom 3:1-8 tells the fate of the just who have suffered persecution. In the eyes of the foolish, they seem to be dead. But they have a sure hope of immortality (Wisdom 3:4). They are, through persecution, found worthy of being called God's possession. Those who have not survived the persecution will meet with punishment (Wisdom 3:10).

Resurrection of the Body—The resurrection of the body first appeared in Jewish thought as a response to the martyrdom of faithful Jews under Antiochus Epiphanes IV during the Maccabean revolt. In earlier periods of Israel's history, war, attack and bondage were punishments from God for violating the covenant. During the later monarchy, the prophets constantly called the people back to faithfulness to the covenant to avoid invasion from foreign powers. The destruction of Jerusalem was interpreted as a failure to heed the covenant.

As we saw in the discussion of apocalyptic literature, Antiochus' persecution was different. He martyred the people of Israel because they obeyed their law and kept the covenant. This led apocalyptic writers to speak of vindication in another life. There would be life after death. The faithful martyrs may have died, but they would rise again to new life.

Two significant points should be noted about the Old Testament notion of resurrection of the body. First, the exact nature of that resurrection, or the exact nature of the resurrected body, is nowhere described. The best description is Daniel 12:1-3, where it is described as those sleeping in the dust of the earth awaking. Second, this resurrection is different from resuscitation—bringing one back to this life—as described in the cycles of Elijah (1 Kings 17:17-24) and Elisha (2 Kings 4:31-37). In both these narratives, there is a resuscitation of a corpse. There is no hint of life after death; they will die again. In the resurrection from the dead in Daniel they will not die again.

How does all this apply to Jesus? Looking at the volume of literature that has been written on the resurrection, one realizes there are many opinions as to what happened. We shall begin with the pronouncements of the church.

JAMES P. McILHONE

Church Pronouncements

Each of the early church creeds is clear concerning belief in the resurrection of Jesus. Each states: "He (*Jesus*) rose (*from the dead*) on the third day." The first official doctrinal statement on the resurrection occurs in the creed of the eleventh council of Toledo (675). It states, "*He* suffered real death of the flesh on the cross, and on the third day, brought back to life by his own power, he rose from the tomb. . . ."

More recently, the Pontifical Biblical Commission issued a study on Christology (April, 1983) which states: "By its very nature, *the resurrection* cannot be proved in an empirical way. For by it Jesus is introduced into 'the world to come.' This can, indeed, be deduced as a reality from the appearances of Christ in glory to certain preordained witnesses, and is corroborated by the fact that Jesus' tomb was found open and empty. . . . In this matter there is also needed 'the decision of faith' or, better, 'an open heart,' so that the mind may be moved to assent."

We must note that, as in the biblical evidence, each of these statements makes an affirmation about the reality of the resurrection, but says nothing about the nature of the resurrection.

Theological Opinions

The opinions of theologians on the resurrection vary greatly. On one side, there are those who feel that resurrection is an antiquated concept that does not make sense in the modern scientific world. However, that is the image employed in the New Testament. To avoid that fact places one on the very shaky ground of saying that the resurrection is a symbolic event which never really happened.

There are scholars who claim that resurrection language limits the phenomenon that occurred. Confusing resurrection and resuscitation, some will explain the resurrection as the resuscitation of the corpse of Jesus which lay in the tomb. The empty tomb thus becomes a confirmation of the reality of the resurrection. This understanding is common among fundamentalists who base their faith on the empty tomb. We must remember that our faith is based on Jesus, not on a tomb. Further, the evidence which was presented above does not confirm that understanding. The risen body of Jesus is glorified, transcending the limitations of space and time. This glorification is what God chose to do in Jesus. As Raymond Brown notes: "We cannot impose on the picture what we think God should have done."

Realizing that other notions were available from the Old Testament to explain life after death, some scholars investigated the New Testament to see if resurrection was the only way Jesus' conquest of death was explained. They saw the "exaltation" language of the hymn in Philippians 2 as a possibility. This hymn speaks of Jesus' exaltation, not his resurrection. Exaltation may be seen as a different facet of the resurrection; however, any conclusion concerning exaltation language must consider that most early preachers and writers chose to interpret the event of Jesus' victory over death in resurrection language.

Another group of scholars understands the resurrection as primitive and mythical. They hold that Jesus' body did decompose in Palestine. They do not deny that Jesus conquered death. Nevertheless, they feel that resurrection is not the best way to describe that victory. Such a view seems very much out of line with both the New Testament evidence and the church teaching. The general understanding among scholars today is that the resurrection is an event which is beyond time and space. But scholarly opinion varies. In the midst of all this variety, the positions of three Catholic scholars should be noted.

Raymond Brown—In the resurrection, Jesus moves from the historical realm of time and space to the realm of the eternal. Adjectives such as "meta-historical" or "eschatological" are used to describe it. This means the resurrection is beyond the confines of what we call "historical." Brown's position has been misinterpreted by many who feel he is saying that the resurrection is not historical. They see Brown holding that the resurrection never occurred, whereas he really understands the resurrection as beyond history.

Wolfhart Pannenburg—Wolfhart Pannenburg, a German theologian, clearly says that something beyond the disciples' understanding happened in the resurrection. That event is unique in all biblical experience. Therefore, the disciples chose to interpret it using the "metaphorical expression of apocalyptic expectation," resurrection of the dead. Pannenburg concludes, "the resurrection of Jesus is a historical event,'' where he sees historical as meaning, ''an event that really happened at that time.'' If the event of raising Christ takes him beyond history, he is still able to affect people who are within the bounds of history. Therefore, our limited historical understanding does not permit us to appreciate the nature of the resurrection. Therefore, using language of ''speaking,'' ''hearing,'' or ''seeing,'' we can only approximate the reality of the resurrection.

Edward Schillebeeckx—In his great work *Jesus,* Edward Schillebeeckx presents the thesis that between the flight of the apostles and the proclamation of Jesus as the risen Lord, there was an experience of conversion. He then investigates whether the apostles' experience of the risen Lord can be explained by the movement from experience of conversion to experience of mission. Since, as we have shown, the resurrection is beyond human experience, it is meta-historical, and meta-empirical, it cannot be narrated. Yet Schillebeeckx holds that the resurrection presupposes experiences which can be interpreted as saving acts of God in Christ. For Schillebeeckx, the resurrection is an experience which of itself is unexplainable.

For Schillebeeckx, the disciples have an experience of forgiveness and mercy from Jesus. They had fallen short in the task of discipleship. Now, through Jesus, they experience the unconditional mercy and forgiveness of God. The experience is one of conversion. This experience involves a relationship with the one whom they had let down, Jesus of Nazareth, and the one through whom they experience forgiveness, and to whom they return, Jesus the Christ. The one to whom they return is identified with the one they had let down. Yet their relationship with the one to whom they return is completely new.

For Schillebeeckx the experiential event that resurrection presupposes is this experience of conversion. Schillebeeckx realizes that the evidence we possess in the New Testament assumes that the disciples have regrouped after Jesus' death. Something had to trigger that regrouping. Why should they gather around a dead Jesus? There had to be some experience which put Jesus' life together for the disciples, an experience which showed them the significance of Jesus' life. The disciples' recognition of Jesus in the fulfillment of his life Schillebeeckx calls the Easter experience. Peter was the first to experience it and his experience became the basis for the gathering of the twelve.

Conclusion

This examination of the resurrection in biblical theology has shown that there are many different ways that event has been understood. Yet in the last analysis, the biblical evidence does not urge us to question how or why. The biblical question is: "What did God do for Jesus?" As Brown says, "Only because God has done this for His Son are new possibilities opened for His many children who have come to believe in what He has done."

Study Questions

1) What is the first reaction on encountering an empty tomb?
2) How does the profession of faith in I Corinthians 15:3-8 explain the earliest belief in the resurrection?
3) Do the Gospels give us any information regarding the nature of the resurrection? What is significant about this?
4) What is the purpose of the 'appearance narratives?' How do they complement the narratives concerning the 'empty tomb?'
5) What are the various Jewish understandings of life after death? Is resurrection the best way to express what happened to Jesus?
6) What is the difference between 'resurrection' and 'resuscitation?'
7) What is the official teaching of the Church on the resurrection?
8) What does contemporary theology say concerning the resurrection?

Bibliography

Brown, Raymond E., *The Virginal Conception and Bodily Resurrection of Jesus,* (New York: Paulist Press, 1973).

Fuller, Reginald, *The Formation of the Resurrection Narratives,* (Philadelphia: Fortress Press, 1980).

Hendrickx, Herman, *Resurrection Narratives,* (London: Geofrey Chapman, 1984).

JAMES P. McILHONE

Perkins, Pheme, *Resurrection: New Testament Witness and Contemporary Reflection*, (Garden City: Doubleday and Co., 1984).

Perrin, Norman, *The Resurrection according to Matthew, Mark, and Luke*, (Philadelphia: Fortress Press, 1977).